Just One of the Guys?

Just One of the Guys?

Transgender Men and the Persistence of Gender Inequality

KRISTEN SCHILT

THE UNIVERSITY OF CHICAGO PRESS   CHICAGO AND LONDON

KRISTEN SCHILT is assistant professor of sociology at the University of Chicago.

The University of Chicago Press, Chicago
The University of Chicago Press, Ltd., London
© 2010 by The University of Chicago
All rights reserved. Published 2010.
Printed in the United States of America

20 19 18 17 16 15 14 13 12 11 10   1 2 3 4

ISBN-13: 978-0-226-73805-5 (cloth)
ISBN-13: 978-0-226-73807-9 (paper)
ISBN-10: 0-226-73805-1 (cloth)
ISBN-10: 0-226-73807-8 (paper)

Library of Congress Cataloging-in-Publication Data

Schilt, Kristen.
   Just one of the guys? transgender men and the persistence of gender inequality / Kristen Schilt.
      p.   cm.
   Includes bibliographical references and index.
   ISBN-13: 978-0-226-73805-5 (alk. paper)
   ISBN-13: 978-0-226-73807-9 (pbk. : alk. paper)
   ISBN-10: 0-226-73805-1 (alk. paper)
   ISBN-10: 0-226-73807-8 (pbk. : alk. paper)   1. Transgender people—Employment.
2. Sex discrimination in employment.   I. Title.
   HD6285.S35 2010
   331.5—dc22

2010014183

Contents

Tables

Acknowledgments

This book would not be possible without the contributions of my respondents and support from several organizations that allowed me to publicize and/or conduct research at their meetings. In order to maintain personal confidentiality, and anonymity in the locations of this research, I cannot thank them by name. But I am grateful for their participation in this project as well as many people's willingness to provide feedback on my research findings. I also must thank all the funding agencies that made this research possible: the University of California Institute for Labor and Employment, the UCLA Department of Sociology, the UCLA Center for Women's Studies, and the Rice University Department of Sociology.

For their guidance and insight on the dissertation from which this book originated, I thank Ruth Milkman, Gail Kligman, Abigail Saguy, and Christine Littleton. Christine Williams also provided invaluable feedback at every stage of this project. The Sociology of Gender Working Group at UCLA was a valuable resource—particularly Rene Almeling and Stephanie Limoncelli. The Sociology Department at Rice University aided me tremendously during my postdoctoral research. I particularly would like to thank Elizabeth Long, Bridget Gorman, Jenifer Bratter, Michael Lindsay, and Melanie Heath. My colleagues at the University of Chicago in Sociology and in Gender Studies also have provided critical feedback, which has helped tremendously to shape this book. I have benefited as well from the help and support of a small network of sociologists working in the area of transgender studies: Elroi Windsor, Eve Shapiro, Tey Meadow, Laurel Westbrook, Cati Connell, Raine Dozier, and Henry Rubin. I also want to thank Mary Blair-Loy and all the anonymous reviewers who gave me critical feedback on the manuscript. Their comments improved this book immeasurably. Finally, this book would not have been possible without the care and handling provided by Doug Mitchell, Tim McGovern, Carol Saller, and Rob Hunt at the University of Chicago Press. Susan Cohan also did a rigorous and thoughtful copyedit of the manuscript, which I greatly appreciate.

My friends and family have been an invaluable source of support during this project. Keith Murphy has acted as a sounding board for my theoretical and empirical ideas from the onset of my project. Paige Schilt and Katy Koonce read a great deal of my work and provided feedback. Becky Cortez was a wonderful roommate in the final throes of my dissertation writing. Stacey Landino allowed me to read the entire manuscript out loud to him, for which I am eternally grateful. Both of my parents also provided emotional, and at times financial, support for this research.

An earlier version of chapter 3 that includes only my California data appeared originally in *Gender & Society* 20, no. 4 (2006). A small portion of data from chapter 5 appeared in *Gender, Work and Organization* 14, no. 6 (2007), and *Gender & Society* 23, no. 4 (2009). I thank Christine Williams, Dana Britton, Beth Schneider, Jane Ward, Betsy Lucal, and all the anonymous reviewers for their comments on these articles. I additionally presented several chapters of this book at meetings of the American Sociological Association. I have benefited greatly from all these presentations.

Introduction

In a 2005 speech about the predominance of men in math and science, then Harvard president Larry Summers offered several hypotheses to account for the persistence of a gender gap in these fields. He noted that society must perpetuate this gap, as "somehow little girls are socialized toward nursing and little boys are socialized into building bridges" (2005, 3). Yet, for him, the main culprit was innate gender differences. Summers described giving his daughters toy trucks in an effort to break down gender stereotypes. When they began to separate the trucks into "daddy trucks" and "baby trucks," he realized how hard it was to overcome biological instincts. These differences, he continued, create the gender gap in the math and science fields. Seeing that engineering or science demands eighty to one hundred hours a week, many women opt for less demanding careers that will more easily accommodate their child-rearing plans. And because more men fall into the high end of math and science aptitude tests, they are more likely than women to choose math and science careers. He considered that discrimination could contribute to women's scarcity but dismissed it as a major factor.

Summers's comments evoked many responses. Feminist groups demanded his resignation. Some Harvard alumni withdrew their contributions, shocked by what they considered an embarrassing stain on the university's image. Women professors in the fields of math and science characterized Summers's explanation as oversimplified. MIT professor Nancy Hopkins called his speech "destructive," adding, "It is one thing for an ordinary person to shoot his mouth off like that, but quite another for a top educational leader" (Ramachandran 2005, 1). Other professors and cultural critics rushed to his defense. Rush Limbaugh, the conservative radio talk show host, claimed that "feminazis" were pillorying Summers for speaking an unpopular truth. Richard Freeman, the economist who had invited Summers to give the lecture, responded to the criticism by saying people were being "sensitive," adding, "It does not seem insane to me to think that men and women have biological differences" (Goldenberg 2005, 1).

One response that garnered a great deal of media attention came from Stanford professor Ben Barres, who argued that Summers too easily dismissed how gender stereotypes inhibit women's success in the fields of math and science. As a counterpoint, he offered his own experiences as someone who had lived both as a man and as a woman. Barbara Barres struggled to have her intellectual abilities taken seriously as one of few women in undergraduate and graduate science courses. Yet, when Barbara became Ben, his intellectual capabilities and research suddenly gained more value. Illustrating this change, he wrote, "Shortly after I changed sex, a faculty member was heard to say 'Ben Barres gave a great seminar today, but then his work is much better than his sister's'" (Barres 2006, 134). For Barres, these experiences suggested that he was evaluated as a better scientist when he looked like a man.

Barres and Summers illuminate conflicting perspectives on the persistence of gender inequality. Summers's comments represent cultural schemas about innate differences between men and women. Cultural schemas are cognitive maps used to make sense of the world that can be applied in a variety of contexts and social interactions (Blair-Loy 2003; Sewell 1992; Valian 1998). These "natural differences" schemas attribute divergent and often unequal outcomes for men and women to innate distinctions in cognitive and physical abilities, reproductive roles, and emotional landscapes. Such schemas readily explain why there is a high concentration of men in math and science, and high-level professional and managerial jobs, and why women continue to be the primary caretakers of children. The varied reactions to Summers's invocation of natural differences as an explanatory framework for the gender gap in math and science shows that these schemas are not seamless. Yet that he saw these views as unproblematic for the president of an Ivy League university to espouse publicly highlights their continued cultural legitimacy.

Barres's experiences exemplify a counterargument to natural differences schemas, what can be termed social constructionist explanations of gender inequality (see Bem 1993; R. Connell 1995; Lorber 1994, 2005; Risman 1998; West and Zimmerman 1987). Social constructionists acknowledge that there are biological differences between men and women. However, these differences are not vast enough to account for their differential treatment (Bem 1993; R. Connell 1995). Just because women bear children, in other words, does not mean they have to be primary caretakers. And while people make individual choices about work and family, these choices are constrained by social structures. From this perspective, gender inequality is maintained and reproduced in part by these natural differences schemas, which are embedded in institutional structures and reproduced in interactions. Yet the social processes that support this reproduction are difficult to disrupt because they are so naturalized. Current gender relations gain further justification from historical weight. Seeing gender disparities as "how men and women are and always have been" provides little incentive for change, as differences that are rooted in tradition and biology seem daunting, if not impossible, to transform.

In this book, I show how the workplace experiences of transgender men ("transmen") such as Ben Barres—individuals assigned female at birth who transition to become men—can illuminate the ways in which natural differences schemas justify gender inequality. Having worked on both sides of the gender binary, transmen have a unique body of experiences to compare and contrast, which can give them an "outsider-within" (Collins 1986) perspective on gendered workplace practices. Not all transmen are treated like "one of the guys" at work. In contrast, some transmen experience ostracizing reactions from employers and coworkers, particularly in retail occupations. Yet other transmen report more recognition and respect as men than when they worked as women—particularly white professionals who can physically "pass" as men. These contrasting experiences show that gender boundaries can be policed (employers can encourage transmen to continue working as women and/or push them out of the workplace), or they can be flexible (employers and coworkers can do interactional work to incorporate transmen as men at work). Yet, in both these situations, notions about men and women's inevitable differences remain unchanged. On a structural level, incorporating transmen as one of the guys does the same work as pushing them out of the workplace—maintaining the gender status quo. These two different modes of understanding—individual experience and structural inequality—can be difficult to synthesize, particularly as individual transmen's accounts about the workplace can be compelling and personally specific. I attempt to make such a synthesis in this book, honoring individual experience while illustrating what these experiences can tell us about the persistence of workplace gender inequality. Understanding the social processes that support and maintain structural inequality is a necessary step toward disrupting the seeming naturalness of an unequal gender system that disadvantages transgender and nontransgender people alike.

Men are from Mars, Women are from Venus: The Notion of Gender Difference

Sex and gender are central organizing categories of daily life. Checking the "Male" or "Female" box for jobs, credit cards, and loans is a typical part of an application process. An "M" or "F" is listed on official documents, such as passports, birth certificates, and driver's licenses, providing people with a binding legal gender. Biological processes are commonly understood to dictate this division into men and women. Men have XY chromosomes, testosterone, and the ability to produce sperm. Women, in contrast, have XX chromosomes, estrogen, and the ability to carry babies—biological ideal types that science textbooks position as consistent across history and culture and stable across a person's lifetime. Counterexamples do exist. Research on intersex people demonstrates that chromosomes do not always fall neatly into female and male categories (Fausto-Sterling 2000; Kessler 1998; Preves 2003). Many transgender people also live their lives in a gender that differs from how they were assigned at birth. These examples typically are dismissed, however, as medical anomalies or fringe lifestyle choices.

Under a binary system, men and women have different, though complementary, interests, abilities, and emotional landscapes. Popular culture abounds with examples of these differences. Expressions like "male bonding" and "girls' night out" assume that men and women feel a special kinship with others of their gender. Yet while men and women may be from different planets, as John Gray's (1992) successful self-help empire with which I titled this section implies, their differences bring them together. The logic that opposites attract supports heteronormativity— cultural, legal, and institutional practices that maintain that only sexual attraction between different genders is acceptable and normative (Kitzinger 2005; Lancaster 2003; MacKinnon 1982; Phelan 2001; G. Rubin 1984). These views on gender and heterosexuality gain credence from Christian religions that position them as God-given, and from psychological and medical sciences that locate them as deriving from biological distinctions in reproductive roles, hormones, brain development, and genetic predispositions (Lancaster 2003).

Commonsense knowledge about these natural differences is used to explain patterns of differential outcomes between men and women, such as the long-standing gender gap in workplace outcomes. Sociological research reveals a complex relationship between the gender of an employee and that employee's opportunities for advancement in both authority and pay. While white-collar men and women with equal qualifications can begin their careers in similar positions in the workplace, men tend to advance faster, creating a gendered promotion gap (Padavic and Reskin 2002; Roth 2006; Valian 1998). While jobs stereotyped as feminine are devalued (Petrie and Roman 2004), white men still outpace women in advancement to positions of authority within so-called women's professions, such as nursing and teaching (Simpson 2004; C. L. Williams 1995). Similar inequalities exist among blue-collar professions, as women often are denied sufficient training for advancement in manual trades, passed over for promotion, or subjected to sexual, racial, and gender harassment (Byrd 1999; Miller 1997; Paap 2006; Yoder and Aniakudo 1997). Women also suffer from a motherhood penalty at work (Correll, Bernard, and Paik 2007) while men can be advantaged by fatherhood (Glauber 2008).

Although gender scholars have amassed a great deal of empirical evidence on the ways in which interactional, structural, and cultural discrimination maintains workplace gender differences, two counterexplanations—both evident in Larry Summers's speech—repeatedly surface: human capital and gender socialization. Human capital theory posits that labor markets are neutral environments that reward workers for their skills, experience, and productivity. Yet there are patterns of gender difference in workplace investment. Women are more likely to take time off from work for childrearing and family obligations than men. They end up with less educational investment and work experience, leading to less economic reward than their male counterparts. Gender socialization theory locates the etiology of these gender differences in occupational choices within society. As children, girls and boys are taught at home, at school, with their peers, what behaviors and expectations are appropriate and inappropriate for their gender. These gender lessons have implications for adult employment trajectories. As women are socialized to put family obligations first, women workers choose part-time jobs that allow more flexibility for family schedules but bring in less money. Men, on the other hand, seek higher-paying jobs with more authority to reinforce their desire to be the primary earner—a staple of masculine socialization. In both explanations, workplace gendered disparities are a result of differences in personal choices shaped by a combination of individual psychology, society, and biology. Yet neither explanation can account for why women and men with comparable prestigious degrees and work experience still end up in different places, with women trailing behind men in advancement (Valian 1998; C. L. Williams 1995). They also neglect structural aspects of the workplace that support gender inequality, such as the lack of workplace childcare services, as well as gendered assumptions about what workers are best suited for what types of jobs (Padavic and Reskin 2002; Valian 1998; C. L. Williams 1995).

Symbolic interactionist theories of gender are a useful tool for analyzing the persistence of workplace gender inequality. This body of theory highlights how masculinity and femininity are not natural offshoots of maleness and femaleness, respectively, but rather social constructs achieved interactionally (Garfinkel 1967; Goffman 1977; Kessler and McKenna 1978; West and Zimmerman 1987, 2009). While men and women may make different choices about work, they make these choices within a system that holds everyone accountable to normative gender expectations (R. Connell 1995; Fenstermaker and West 2002; Ridgeway and Correll 2004; West and Zimmerman 1987). These cultural schemas about gender shape social structures (Ridgeway and Correll 2004; Sewell 1992) as deeply held ideas about how men and women *are* and what they *should* do, and are embedded in social institutions and reproduced in social interactions. These schemas constitute and are constituted by the current gender order—the patterns of power relations between men and women that shape and define expectations about what is gender-appropriate in arenas such as romantic partner selection, occupational choice, and parental roles (R. Connell 1987; Heath 2009; Lorber 1994; Risman 1998; West and Zimmerman 1987). While expectations for masculinity and femininity vary across history and cultures (R. Connell 1995; C. L. Williams 1995), the characteristics associated with men always carry the greater rewards (Acker 1990; Bem 1993; R. Connell 1995; Schippers 2007)—illuminating the power differential behind seemingly innocuous arguments about difference.

A social order that perpetuates gender inequality persists because the reiteration of the naturalness of this way of organizing the world makes change seem impossible. Structural and legislative interventions appear as artificial attempts to change relations that derive from nature and tradition. As white men's open hostility toward workplace affirmative action programs shows (Paap 2006; Rhode 1997), change is also difficult because it requires a redistribution of privilege. Historically and today men gain a "patriarchal dividend" in the form of honor, prestige, and material reward from the subordination of women (R. Connell 1995, 82). The amount of this dividend varies. White, heterosexual, middle-class masculinity (often termed "hegemonic masculinity") commands higher returns than racialized, gay, or working-class masculinities (often termed "subordinate masculinities") (R. Connell 1992, 1995; Nixon 2009; Wingfield 2009). The potential benefits of authority, respect, and economic gains give men an incentive to resist change (R. Connell 1995; Goode 1992). Further, many women do not experience these gender relations as unequal but rather as offshoots of natural abilities and interests (Hochschild 1990; Rhode 1997). This normalization of inequality persists because change demands a reallocation of resources and a major transformation of deeply held beliefs about the place of men and women in society.

From Gender Difference to Gender Inequality

To understand this stasis in the face of enormous social change, I conceive of gender as both ubiquitous and dynamic—a structural and interactional process that shapes and is shaped by social life but also encompasses new expectations, possibilities, and constraints. This understanding of gender takes "into account the constraining impact of entrenched ideas and practices on human agency but also acknowledges that the system is continually construed in everyday life and that, under certain conditions, individuals resist the pressures to conform to the needs of the system" (Essed 1991, 38). This type of analysis presents an empirical challenge, however. The working of social structures can be difficult for researchers to observe directly. Critiques of symbolic interactionist approaches to gender charge that face-to-face interactions are used as a stand-in for structure, and that top-down constraints on social life are downplayed (see Andersen 2005; Collins 1995; Winant 1995). Yet, while "institutional structures influence the nature, content, and meaning of whatever face to face interactions occur within them" (Dalton and Fenstermaker 2002, 169), an overly structural approach to gender can make social change seem impossible—a source of some consternation for organization theorists who want to simultaneously account for the stability of institutions and the reality of social change. Structural change does not happen without social actors engaged in face-to-face interactions, illustrating that to understand the persistence of gender inequality requires an analysis of the interplay between structural, cultural, and interactional processes. But "how culture works" (Schudson 1989) can be tricky to document empirically. While individuals have "cultural toolkits" (Swidler 1986) or "cultural repertoires" (Lamont 1992), they do not always operate on the level of practical consciousness (Bourdieu 1977; Giddens 1984).

I argue in this book that the experiences of transgender people in the workplace can provide theoretical and empirical leverage on how unequal gender relations are maintained in the face of challenges to natural differences schemas that legitimate inequality. Transgender people may be statistically rare.[1] Their workplace experiences, however, can make a major contribution to analyses of the social processes that uphold inequality. Crossing seemingly natural gender boundaries can create a "fish out of water" (Dozier 2005, 297) perspective, similar to being a racial minority in a predominantly white space (Collins 1986; Yoder and Aniakudo 1997) or a biracial person carving out identity space in the borders between white and black (Rockquemore and Brunsma 2008). Highlighting transgender people's unique perspective on gender is not a new idea. Harold Garfinkel (1967) used his interviews with Agnes, a transgender woman, to construct his social rules of gender. Candace West and Don Zimmerman's "doing gender" theory (1987) builds on this work by showing how gender is an active, interactionally achieved social process. Judith Butler (1989, 1993) similarly relies on examples of drag shows and analyses of films featuring transgender people to build the theory of gender "performativity," a humanities-based cousin to "doing gender." Yet the leverage gender crossing gives to these analyses remains theoretical.

This book gives empirical weight to interactionist theories about the social construction of gender difference (Garfinkel 1967; Kessler and McKenna 1978; West and Zimmerman 1987). I go further by illustrating how transmen's unique perspective provides insight into not just the cultural workings of *gender difference* but also the social maintenance of *gender inequality.* Transmen can become insiders in men's spaces at work, as continued use of testosterone can give them an appearance indistinguishable from any other man. However, their previous experience working as women can create an internalized sense of being a gender outsider. This "outsider-within" perspective allows transmen to see "the contradictions between the dominant group's actions and ideologies" (Collins 1990, 12). In other words, some transmen can see the advantages associated with being men at work while still maintaining a critical view on how this advantage operates, and how it disadvantages women.

I also examine how people who are not transgender—whom Garfinkel terms "gender normals" (1967), in a tongue-in-cheek reference to natural differences schemas—make sense of transmen at work. Within sociology, the typical model for understanding the interactional achievement of gender is asking transgender people (the margins) to illuminate the workings of everybody else (the center). This model assumes that people who gender-cross can clearly articulate the cultural and social processes involved in gaining a new gender identity—processes that "gender normals" cannot articulate because they experience them as natural and unproblematic. However, as I show in this book, people who feel they are "born in the *right* bodies" still do a great deal of interactional work to maintain a reality in which a male/female binary occurs naturally. Coworkers and employers who witness transmen's gender transitions adopt strategies that allow them to ignore the potential challenge this transition presents to commonsense ideas about gender. Incorporating transmen as one of the guys at work simultaneously repairs any breach to natural differences schemas and maintains the belief that workplace gender hierarchies derive from nature, not culture.

This dual analysis reveals how gender inequality is produced in face-to-face interactions (West and Zimmerman 1987) and maintained within workplace structures that assign tasks, authority, and reward by gender (Acker 1990; Britton 2003; C. L. Williams 1995). Cultural schemas integrate these analytic levels, as beliefs about natural differences between men and women are embedded in structures and played out in interactions. Conceptualizing gender as a system of boundaries that are fluid and changeable at the same time that they display enormous stability is a useful way to analyze the intersecting processes that maintain gender inequality. Gender boundaries "mark the social territories of gender relations, signaling who ought to be admitted or excluded" (Gerson and Peiss 1985, 319), and determine who has access to what resources.

This conceptualization of gender allows for the exploration of how gender relations shift as well as how they maintain themselves in the face of overt challenges (ibid.). While documenting how social movements and individual actors resist oppressive elements of gender is an important research goal (Deutsch 2007), sociologists must not "fall back on our belief in transformative social change" (Fenstermaker, West, and Zimmerman 2002, 33). A major contribution of this book is to show how potential challenges to unequal relations between men and women can be absorbed by institutions and social actors in a way that minimizes change; structural gender inequality continues as business as usual even as some people see a change—positive or negative—in their individual lives. This analysis of change and stasis is vital to understanding why gender inequality continues in the face of enormous legislative and demographic change in the workplace.

Transmen at Work: Project Design and Overview

In crafting this project, I purposefully put my analytic focus on the experiences of transmen—people assigned female at birth who transition later in life to live as men. With a few exceptions (see Cromwell 1999; Devor 1997; Dozier 2005; H. Rubin 2003), the lives of transmen have received little attention in the social sciences compared to the abundance of research on transwomen. While transmen and transwomen often are lumped together under the rubric of "transgender," their experiences do not always mirror each other (Griggs 1998; Perkins 1983; Schilt and Wiswall 2008). Transmen are in the unique position of moving into a gender category that theoretically carries more social, cultural, and economic advantages, a type of "status-boosting" transition understudied in sociology. Additionally, with the use of testosterone, transmen can develop an appearance indistinguishable from nontransgender men. Looking like men affords them great leeway in making decisions about publicly identifying as transgender—a leeway many transwomen do not have, as estrogen cannot change body cues read as male, such as big hands, Adam's apples, and height over six feet tall. I bring in comparative data on the workplace experiences of transwomen in the last chapter of the book to illustrate the differences between the experiences of transmen and transwomen—and to highlight how these differences reflect broader patterns of gender inequality.

I selected the workplace as an arena of study for several reasons. First, research on transgender people typically focuses on the personal experience of transitioning. While important for understanding identity transformation processes, this narrow focus neglects to examine how transgender people live their everyday lives in locations such as the workplace. Second, workplaces are not neutral institutions; rather, there is a long history of gender disparities in men's and women's outcomes. I theorized that becoming a man at work could throw the social processes that create gender difference and gender inequality into high relief. As transmen are entering a gender category that theoretically carries more advantages, I hypothesized that such a move, if done openly, could bring out boundary guarding from people who might contest any potential reallocation of advantage. Third, as some transmen work as men with people who are unaware of their transitions, I anticipated that their workplace experiences could provide unique insight into how gender inequality is maintained organizationally and interactionally. To examine these hypotheses, I focused on three central research questions: (1) Does occupational context aid or hinder the ability of transmen to become men at work? (2) How do employers and coworkers interact, knowingly or unknowingly, with transmen? (3) Are transmen able to access the benefits of being men at work (namely, occupational prestige, respect, and authority)?

Between 2004 and 2008, I conducted interviews with transmen about their workplace experiences. As I was interested in how transmen negotiated *working* as men and/or as transmen, I limited the criteria of inclusion to people who had transitioned and remained in the same job, who had found new jobs where they were known only as men, or who had found new jobs where they were known as transgender. Transmen did not have to be currently working to be included in the study. But I did require that they have once attempted to be hired as men or have once told potential or current employers that they preferred male pronouns and identified as men or transmen—regardless of whether they were successfully hired or retained. I conducted these interviews in two regions of the United States: California and Texas. California is stereotyped as politically liberal and Texas as politically conservative. While this is a gross generalization, California has a state law protecting gender identity expression in the workplace—a law that offers some employment protections to transgender workers. Texas, in contrast, had no such law at the time I did this research. Major urban areas in Califor-

nia also have a wide variety of resources for transgender people, rang-
ing from free medical services to support and social groups. Texas has
fewer established resources and a much less visible transgender community even in major urban areas. Within this regional comparison, I interviewed transmen from a range of occupations—high-level professional
occupations, such as lawyers; blue-collar trade occupations, such as construction; "women's professions," such as elementary education; and retail and service jobs, such as food service. Transmen ranged from being
employed in entry-level jobs to running their own companies with a staff
of subordinates.

The fifty-four transmen I interviewed were predominantly white
(about 80 percent) and ranged in age from eighteen to sixty-four (see
the methodological appendix for more details on demographics and
data collection). I conducted life histories with an emphasis on employment experience. Analyzing these interviews, I compared two workplace
strategies: (1) acknowledging one's gender transition at work either in a
job one held as a woman previously or in a new job; (2) getting a new
job as a man (that is, where one's gender transition is not known to employers and coworkers). I refer to transmen who adopt this first strategy as "open transmen" and transmen who adopt the second strategy as
"stealth transmen." As "stealth" and "open" are strategies rather than
fixed identities, the same person could have experience with both workplace strategies across his employment trajectory.

Workplace experiences are interactional events. As there are many
barriers to studying transgender workplace experiences ethnographi-
cally—barriers I detail in the methodological appendix—I sought other
forms of data that could provide a broader perspective on my interview
data. I interviewed fourteen coworkers of eight open transmen. I also
was a participant observer in the Southern California transgender community for two years, and in central Texas for two years, attending social groups, conferences, and educational panels. Through this research,
I stayed in touch with many of the men I interviewed, following their
workplace trajectories. Between 2003 and 2007, I attended ten conferences in different regions of the country that focused on transgender
issues. At these conferences, I compared the experiences of transmen
across the country with the experiences of the men I interviewed. I also
noted differences between the workplace experiences of transmen and
transwomen. To further examine these observed patterns, I gathered
questionnaire data about workplace experiences from transmen and

transwomen conference attendees. To get a historical perspective, I also conducted a content analysis of newspaper stories and legal cases about transgender workers, spanning the years from 1971 to 2008.

The workplace experiences in this book come from this triangulation of multiple sources of data. As none of these data are derived from a random sample of transgender men, I do not intend these data to be generalized to all transmen or to all transgender people. My data show a range of experiences from which I draw conclusions about the conditions and social processes that underlie these varied experiences. Some transmen do find employer support for their open transitions, or secure employment as one of the guys. Yet these experiences typically occur for a certain group of transmen—those who are white, educated, and physically "passable" as men. As I suggest in this book, transmen are more likely to experience some forms of employment discrimination if they do not get support from employers, if they are visibly gender-variant, if they are racial minorities, and if they work in entry-level retail jobs. Additionally, transgender people who live in states and cities without protections for gender expression and identity work in precarious environments—any support they receive is always at the whim of their employer. At the end of the book, I offer suggestions about how to improve workplace conditions for transgender workers. I also focus on illuminating the social processes that underlie the naturalization of gender difference and gender inequality at work. As these processes shape institutional practices and workplace outcomes for all workers, I see this focus as an important step toward addressing gender-based employment discrimination.

A Note on Terminology

Terminology about individuals who may use surgeries and/or hormones to bring their bodies in line with a gender identity that differs from the sex they were assigned at birth changes rapidly. Historically, such individuals have been referred to as *transsexuals*—a term developed within the psychological community in the 1940s (Meyerowitz 2002). In popular culture, these same individuals often were termed "sex changes." With the rise of gender activism in the 1990s, *transgender* developed as an umbrella term for a wide variety of "differently gendered" identities (MacKenzie 1994; Valentine 2007). In the early 2000s, individuals blending elements of masculinity and femininity—with or without physical body modifications—began to use the term *genderqueer* (Nestle, Howell, and Wilchins 2002) to challenge male/female binarism. I give these definitions with caution, as they are always works in progress and are always contested. Distinctions among these identity categories are also academic. By this I mean that someone who "technically" fits the definition of transgender may identify as genderqueer, transsexual, all of these identities together, or some other identity entirely. I use the term *transsexual* when I am referencing the 1960s through the 1980s. Otherwise, I use *transgender*. To reference people who are not transgender, I use the term *cisgender*.[2] *Cisgender* replaces terms such as *bio-man* and *genetic girl*, which reify the primacy of biology for determining gender (E. Green 2006).

The uses of terms such as *sex* and *gender* are changing as rapidly as identity terms. In gender studies, sex and gender have long been separated, with "sex" being biological distinctions between males and females and "gender" being the cultural meanings of masculinity and femininity overlaid onto those differences (see Delphy 1993). Yet sociology of gender is increasingly recognizing that notions of an innate sex binary are also a cultural construct (J. Butler 1993; Dozier 2005; Laqueur 1990; Nye 2005). In this book, I use *gender* to refer to natural differences schemas that incorporate both biological and cultural ideals about how men and women are and should be. These schemas are structural—they shape patterns of social life through institutions such as schools, the media, and the workplace—and interactionally produced (Ridgeway and Smith-Lovin 1999). Further, most people see gender as an important feature of their identity. In describing this sense of gender as an identity, I make a distinction between social and personal identity. Personal identity encompasses "meanings attributed to the self by the actor . . . brought into play or asserted during the course of interaction" (Snow and Anderson 1987, 1347). Social identity, in contrast, is how actors are viewed by others in social situations. These identities may line up (an individual may personally feel like a man and be seen by others as a man), or they may conflict (an individual may feel like a woman but be socially gendered as a man on the basis of appearance).

Female-to-male (FTM) is a term often used interchangeably with *transgender men*. Yet some people experience themselves as *male-to-men* (MTM)—a term that highlights a consistency in personal identity across the physical transition process. Other transgender men modify their bodies with surgeries and hormones but do not personally identify

as male or as men. To incorporate this diversity of personal gender identities, I refer to transgender men who physically bring their bodies and
appearances in line with expectations for males as "transitioning into social maleness." For clarity in writing, I adopt the general term *transmen*
when referring to people who make this transition into social maleness
and *transwomen* for people who transition into social femaleness. When
I refer to transmen as once "living as women," I am referencing their
previous social gender, not making the claim that they once personally
identified as female or as women. As most of the transmen in this study
share the experience of having been raised as girls—even when some of
them personally saw themselves as male—I refer to them as "female-
socialized."

Transgender people who do not disclose their transitions to new
friends or coworkers often are referred to as "passing" (Garber 1997;
Goffman 1963b). I use the term *physically passing* in discussions of
transmen's concerns about looking like men at the onset of their transition. However, as *passing* suggests acting rather than embodying, I adopt
the term many transgender people I encountered in my fieldwork used,
going stealth, to discuss transmen who choose not to disclose their gender transitions at work. *Stealth* might seem like a strange choice of word,
as its definition includes "furtive," "sly," and "underhanded." However,
its meaning also encompasses "covert" and "clandestine," synonyms that
are in closer keeping with a view that transitions are part of a private
history that may be disclosed in some circumstances and not in others.
Stealth also avoids the assumption of fraud or deceit implied by *passing*.

Plan of the Book

In chapter 1, I provide a historical overview of the shifting cultural understanding of transgender people. These cultural explanations attempt
to account for the existence of transgender people within a system in
which gender identity and genitalia are assumed to line up naturally into
a binary of male and female. I merge life histories I collected with sociological research and newspaper accounts about transgender people to
show these shifting cultural frames—mental pathology, gender diversity
and fluidity, and, more recently, benign biological diversity. The most recent frame, biological diversity, provides a compelling justification for
tolerance of transgender lives: gender-variant people are born this way

rather than making an active choice. It does not, however, challenge deeply held beliefs about the naturalness—for most people—of the male/female binary. This binary continues to be institutionalized in governmental and legal practices, which means that transgender people must bring their legal gender in line with their new social gender to avoid not just societal stigma but potential consequences in employment, housing, and finances.

Chapter 2 examines the interactional processes that underlie achieving social maleness. At the beginning of their physical transitions, many transmen grapple with simultaneously inhabiting social space as men while maintaining, to varying degrees, an internal repertoire of female-socialized behaviors. In this process, they can develop a double consciousness on gender, as they work to synthesize a female history and a male social identity—two identities that natural differences schemas position as innately opposing. The interactional negotiations involved in achieving this social maleness illuminate the cultural processes that underlie natural differences schemas as well as the hierarchical power dynamics behind seemingly innocuous notions of gender difference.

The next three chapters focus on transmen's discussions of their experiences becoming men at work. Within the gendered organization of the workplace, men are not assumed to be simply *different from* women but actually *better than* women. Chapter 3 demonstrates the outcomes of these cultural assumptions, drawing on transmen's outsider-within perspective on workplace gender inequality. Two-thirds of transmen in both states reported changes in their treatment at work after they began working as men. Showing the importance of an intersectional analysis, transmen who were white, tall, and passable as men reported more gains at work than transmen who were men of color, short, or not passable as men. These experiences suggest that workplace gender inequality is not continually reproduced only because women make different educational and occupational choices than men; rather, coworkers and employers rely on natural differences schemas—schemas that privilege hegemonic expectations of masculinity—to evaluate men's and women's achievements and skills.

Chapters 4 and 5 unpack the interactional and institutional mechanisms behind these workplace experiences, examining stealth and open transmen, respectively. Stealth transmen have the experience of watching supposedly natural gender differences be socially created in workplace

structures and interactions. Many of them are hired for jobs that employers tell them are unsuitable for women. Women exclude them from "girl
talk," while men engage with them about cars, sports, and sex. Rather
than being benign differences in conversational topics, these gender divisions can provide stealth transmen with more authority and economic
opportunities in the workplace than women. That stealth transmen are
given more authority, structurally and interactionally, shows how the invocation of cultural schemas about inevitable gender differences covers
up the active processes that create and maintain gender inequality.

Chapter 5 examines reactions to open workplace transitions. Some
employers reject the transition, thereby neutralizing challenges to the
male/female binary. Others anchor transmen to a female legal gender,
policing the male/female binary. Some workplaces treat transmen as
"token trannies." In still other cases, employers and coworkers reshape
gender boundaries, incorporating transmen as one of the guys at work.
In these cases, employers give top-down dictates directing coworkers to
change names and pronouns, and give transmen access to men's restrooms and lockers. Heterosexual men include transmen in "guy talk"
and engage them in exaggerated displays of masculinity. Women ask
them to do heavy lifting. These incorporation responses contradict theoretical notions of how people respond to breaches to deeply held cultural schemas. However, on a structural level, incorporating transmen as one of the guys does the same work as pushing them out of the
workplace—maintaining the gender status quo. What these incorporation
responses do show is that gender boundaries can shift for individuals—
former women can be accepted as men—without making workplace gender trouble and without causing a change to business as usual.

Chapter 6 returns to the larger societal context, with a comparison
between the workplace experiences of transmen and transwomen. Drawing on questionnaire data, content analysis, and participant observation,
I show that transmen and transwomen can have different workplace experiences even though they share an identity assumed to carry a social
stigma. While transmen in this study could be incorporated as one of the
guys at work, transwomen who attempt to stay in jobs they held as men
can be met with extreme harassment and, in some cases, face termination. It is the logic of the workplace as a gendered organization that encourages everyone to adapt to masculine expectations and devalue femininity that allows for these different workplace reactions. Analyzed

through the understanding of the cultural logics of the workplace gender system, the marginalization of transwomen at work and the incorporation of transmen can be seen as the result of the same structural and interactional mechanisms that maintain workplace gender inequality more broadly.

CHAPTER ONE

Framing Transgender Difference

Pathology, Diversity, Biology

In 1976, Steve Dain, a high school physical education teacher in Emeryville, California, filed a discrimination suit against the Emery Unified School District. Dain alleged that he had been wrongfully suspended from his teaching position after undergoing a "sex change" to become a man. His employers countered that his suspension was justified, as his continued presence on campus posed psychological harm to students and disrupted campus life. Reviewing the case, Alameda County judge Robert Barber ruled that Dain must be reinstated with back pay. Dain's victory was short-lived. The day after the court ruling, he was again fired by the superintendent of the Emeryville School District, who claimed Dain's actions constituted "immoral conduct" and signaled his "evident unfitness for service" (*New York Times* 1976, 26).

Thirty years later, Dain might have been met with a different reaction. In 2001, newspapers across the country carried stories with titles similar to this one from the *Philadelphia Daily News*: "San Francisco Will Pay for Workers' Sex Changes" (2001, 14). That San Francisco, long famed as a liberal bastion for "alternative lifestyles," would make this decision may be unsurprising. But, by 2007, many major U.S. corporations had followed the city's lead. Discussing Eastman Kodak's choice to cover gender transitions, spokesman David Kaffnoff noted, "We took a look at it, and the cost was negligible, so we said it was the right thing to do" (Buchanan 2007, B4). Even more staid Wall Street companies have

followed suit. In 2008, the accounting firm Goldman Sachs began cover-
ing hormone treatments and some types of surgeries for transgender employees. A spokesperson for the company noted that this coverage was
necessary to be competitive in attracting a diverse workforce (Chang
2008). These policy changes do not guarantee transgender people will
not face employment discrimination; they do, however, signal that the
concept of "transgender" has become facially included in discussions
about workplace diversity in professional settings in the 2000s.

Changes in the cultural framing of transgender people accompanied this new awareness of "transgender" as a diversity issue. Journal-
ists, psychiatrists, and academics have made sense of transgender people
in a variety of ways—sexual perverts, mental patients, cultural dupes of
a patriarchal gender order. In the 1990s, transgender activists offered a
counterframe that emphasized gender *diversity* rather than gender *perversity*. This perspective championed the notion of gender as a continuum or a constellation with many different, yet equally valid, possible
configurations. This gender diversity frame has gained salience in the
popular press. Yet the concept of diversity has come to be more firmly
anchored in biological understandings of sex rather than in poststructuralist deconstruction of binaries and categories. In this new frame, transgender people are nonpathological variations in the normal development
of males and females. This understanding provides a compelling justification for transgender rights—gender-variant people are born this way—
without challenging many people's deeply held beliefs about the naturalness and normalcy, for most people, of a male/female binary.

Pathologizing Transsexuals: The Gender Clinic Era (1960s–1980s)

Reflecting on his childhood, Chris (b. early 1960s) recounts always thinking of himself as just like any other little boy.[1] Yet the onset of menstruation brought with it the realization that he was going to grow up to be
a woman. He experienced a deep disconnection between his social gender as a teenage girl and his personal sense of himself as innately male.
He describes this internal maleness as unable to be masked by dresses
and makeup. He walked and talked like a boy, had an interest in boys'
activities, was sexually attracted to girls. While he briefly called himself
a lesbian, he felt that his attraction to women was heterosexual, not ho-

mosexual. He did not relate to women on the basis of similarity—shared bodies, emotional landscapes, interests—but on the basis of difference. Like many people, Chris believed in a male/female binary. His dilemma was being on the wrong side of that binary. His inner turmoil caused a "mental meltdown." "Basically, I told my parents, I need to be a guy. I got really defensive, and I told them, 'I'm gonna give you four months [to help me] or I'm gonna [kill myself].'" Alarmed, Chris's parents turned to their family doctor for help. Acknowledging that Chris needed a specialist, he recommended Stanford.

In the 1970s, Stanford University was *the* place to go for people on the West Coast who felt that their internal gender identity did not line up with their bodies. The Stanford Gender Dysphoria Clinic, opened in 1969 by Dr. Donald Laub, a plastic surgeon, and Dr. Norman Fisk, a psychiatrist, was one of several gender clinics—university-affiliated research institutions that provided psychiatric testing to potential transsexual clients—across the country. Johns Hopkins had a similar clinic under the guidance of Dr. John Money. Other clinics emerged at the University of California at Los Angeles, the University of Minnesota, and Northwestern. By the end of the 1970s, more than one thousand sex reassignment surgeries had been performed in the United States, and there were gender clinics in fifteen to twenty major U.S. cities (Meyerowitz 2002).

For psychologists and surgeons working in the clinics, transsexuality was a statistically rare, severe mental pathology that manifested as a deep fissure between mind and anatomical sex—a condition they termed "gender dysphoria." While being masculine or feminine was assumed by most people at the time to be an offshoot of chromosomal maleness or femaleness, respectively, doctors who worked with transsexual and intersex clients argued that biological sex must be separated from gender (Fausto-Sterling 2000; Meyerowitz 2002). In psychological circles, *sex* came to refer to the physical attributes of males and females that were anatomically determined. *Gender* became the psychological or internal process of feeling like a man or a woman, and the behaviors and attitudes that accompanied those feelings. In this understanding, there was a clear binary—people were either biologically male or biologically female. The transsexual dilemma was being anatomically of one sex but having the gender identity of the other.

This medical model clashed with views on transsexuality in the general public. The radical social movements of the times, such as the feminist movement (Echols 1989) and the budding gay and lesbian movement (Faderman and Timmons 2006; Raeburn 2004), challenged many ideas about men's and women's roles in society. Yet even many radical feminists endorsed the idea that sex categories—male and female— were biologically determined and therefore fixed (see Raymond 1979). "Sex changes" violated these deeply held beliefs. Reacting to this violation, most of the newspaper stories about transsexuality in the 1970s and 1980s were sensationalistic, such as "Stole for Operation to Make Him a Woman but Going to Prison a Man" (Finke 1980). Stories about transsexuals also ended up in "Quirks in the News," illustrating the equation of transsexuals with the bizarre. This news coverage reinforced a particular model of posttransition life for transsexuals—what I call the "deep stealth model"—as it emphasized the consequences that could result from being known as a transsexual. To be deep stealth, the only pathway viewed as psychologically healthy by therapists and doctors (Bolin 1988; Stone 1991), transsexuals had to start new lives with coworkers, friends, and romantic partners who did not know about their pasts.

Medical professionals working with transsexuals navigated a fine line between treating a legitimate mental illness and endorsing what many saw as an abomination of nature. The appropriate treatment for gender dysphoria was a topic of wide debate. Robert Stoller (1968), the head of the UCLA gender clinic, argued for making the mind fit the body through the use of psychotherapy—giving primacy to biological sex. Harry Benjamin (1966), an endocrinologist, argued in contrast that psychotherapy was useless for people who were truly gender dysphoric. His solution for these extreme cases was to make the body fit the mind through hormone treatment and surgeries—giving primacy to internal gender identity. Benjamin's treatment model eventually won out. Yet, because its effectiveness was unknown in the 1970s, psychiatrists and surgeons associated with gender clinics were anxious about how they were viewed by their peers (Meyerowitz 2002). Showing this anxiety, Donald Laub and Norman Fisk began a paper to the American Association of Plastic Surgeons as follows:

> To change a person's God-given anatomical sex is a repugnant concept. Morally and instinctively, it is difficult enough for a surgeon to perform an amputation of an arm and a leg; it is even more so to consider genital amputation and castration. How then does a surgeon ever approach the problem of gender dysphoria—the patient who has an unalterable disgust for his genital anatomy. . . . a patient who has demonstrated repeated failures in his orig-

inal gender, a patient for whom psychiatry claims no ability to achieve any success . . . and a patient whose determined quest for rehabilitation via surgery is almost a psychopathic drive? (1974, 388)

With this opener, they maintain the normalcy and naturalness of a male/female binary while simultaneously making a case for surgical sex changes as "rehabilitation" for people who are almost "psychopathic."

The association of gender clinics with elite academic institutions such as Stanford lent them some legitimacy. To further institutionalize the enterprise, doctors such as Laub formed the Harry Benjamin International Gender Dysphoria Association in 1980, now called the World Professional Association for Transgender Health (WPATH), to create a set of standards of care for transsexuals. The guidelines, which are relatively similar today, stipulated that potential clients must undergo therapy for a minimum of three months, though the time limit was at the discretion of the therapist. In these sessions, therapists assessed whether their client met the diagnostic criteria for gender dysphoria, now "Gender Identity Disorder" (American Psychiatric Association 2001) in the *Diagnostic and Statistical Manual IV* (DSM). If diagnosed, clients could get access to hormone treatment—estrogen for transwomen and testosterone for transmen. They then had to pass the "real-life" test, living in their destination gender for one year, to be given access to surgeries, such as genital surgery, breast enhancement (for transwomen), and chest reconstructive surgery (for transmen).

In practice, cultural expectations about masculinity and femininity determined access to gender clinics much more so than any diagnostic criteria. Interviewed about how he determined which clients were *real* transsexuals and which were merely self-hating homosexuals, one physician at Johns Hopkins noted that he bullied feminine men to see their reactions. He found this tactic effective, as "the girls [that is, transwomen] cry, the gays get aggressive" (Billings and Urban 1982, 275). Physical appearance was also important. Clients who convincingly looked like the "opposite sex" without hormones generally had truncated intake sessions (Billings and Urban 1982). Chris's experience shows an example of this. At eighteen, he looked like any other teenage boy. Describing his first trip to Stanford, he says, "I met [with] Norman Fisk for about forty-five minutes. He reviewed me. Then I saw Dr. Laub. I was with my [parents]. . . . I had to answer a few questions, and then a few months later I got my first shot [of testosterone]." He adds, "I think I somehow slipped through the cracks or something because I didn't do any therapy." Showing a very different experience, a transman I met at a conference told me about being rejected by Stanford in the 1980s. Having a slight build and delicate features, he did not make it past the first intake session because the doctor said he could too easily imagine him as an attractive, feminine woman.

Meeting expectations for behavior and appearance opened the gender clinic door for transsexuals, but it did not guarantee access to surgeries and hormones. Presenting any information that did not fit the *DSM* diagnostic criteria could be a problem, as Louis Sullivan discovered (J. Green 2004). When he announced that he had always felt like a *gay* man in a woman's body, he was rejected for genital surgery by Stanford (Meyerowitz 2002). Sullivan was seen as suffering from a pathology deeper than gender dysphoria: the desire to be homosexual. Sullivan's experiences show that these criteria were, for many psychiatrists, the only legitimate pathway to transsexuality: childhood cross-dressing and cross-gender behavior, a disgust for one's genitalia that created an inability to form heterosexual relationships, and a sense of despair at being trapped in the wrong body. Wayne (b. early 1960s), who went to Stanford for the first time in the late 1970s, says, "You had to be a certain kind of person [in the intake session]. This was long before anyone conceptualized that transguys could ever be attracted to men. If you had ever been pregnant or had a child, they would not even evaluate you." He adds, "It fostered a situation where we would just lie. How do you want me to be? What do you want me to say? I will say it." Showing the irony of the situation, when I asked where he had learned what he was expected to say, he answered, "It was actually in the information that [Stanford] mailed to you! It essentially said, don't bother if you don't meet [these] criteria."

Like Chris, Wayne always thought of himself as male despite the insistence of his parents and peers that he was a girl. In adolescence, he took notice of transsexuals he saw on talk shows. While these appearances gave him hope that he could find a solution to the internal dilemma between what he termed his "mind and body," all of the resources were on the East Coast—a world away for a preteen growing up in suburban California. In the 1970s, however, Jude Patton, one of the first transmen to go public as an activist, appeared on *Donahue*. "It said he was in [California]. And I thought, wow! As soon as I am sixteen, I am going to go see this guy. When I could drive." Through correspondence with Jude,

Wayne learned about West Coast resources. At the age of eighteen, he traveled to Stanford against his family's wishes. Though his life history fit the criteria, he was rejected. "They took a lot of money from me for the evaluation, but they said that because I didn't have any family support, I was too young. In those days, you had to be twenty-one to vote, and there was a feeling that until you were twenty-one, you were not really an adult."

Such rejections were common. Between 1969 and 1973, 769 potential clients contacted Stanford. The clinic immediately rejected 398 as "nontranssexuals." Of the remaining 371 who were evaluated, only 74 were recommended for surgery (Laub and Fisk 1974). Wayne's lack of parental support put him into group B—clients for whom surgery was probably warranted but who needed some type of rehabilitation to reach group A (clients recommended for surgery). Rehabilitation suggestions show clinicians' preconceived notions about gender: transwomen could undergo feminine grooming courses, and transmen could work with a body builder (ibid.). Or people could begin transsexual group therapy, where they were certain to learn the criteria doctors were expecting. Wayne did consider contacting another clinic. "There was no way I could imagine going that distance. The other places were Texas, Oklahoma, Canada, New York. I couldn't imagine doing that at that age." He returned to Stanford at twenty-one and made it into group A. Like Chris, he began testosterone injections, from which he developed facial hair and a lower voice. He also had a hysterectomy, which limited the amount of estrogen his body produced, and underwent a double mastectomy. With flat chests, facial hair, and low voices, transmen like Chris and Wayne could easily adhere to the dominant stealth model—cutting off any contact with other transsexuals and working and living among people who had always known them as men.

Roger (b. early 1960s) also found out about gender clinics through a visible transman, Mario Martino, author of one of the first transgender autobiographies, *Emergence* (1977). Martino provided some contact information for East Coast transgender resources, through which Roger learned about what was available on the West Coast. Growing up in the South, in contrast, Jason (b. mid-1950s) did not learn about the existence of transsexuals until the late 1980s, when he moved to a gay enclave in an urban center of Texas. Growing up in Europe, Paul (b. early 1960s) also found little information about transsexuality. In adolescence, he came across a news report about a girl who had spontaneously transformed into a boy—a type of sensationalistic story that often made the news in the 1960s (Meyerowitz 2002). "And so I thought, well no matter what this is, I'll find out when I am eighteen. You're an adult, you can do that." At eighteen, he contacted a local doctor to ask about the possibility of undergoing such a change. The encounter had disastrous results. "He actually chased me out of his office. . . . It shattered my whole [out]look. All these years I looked forward and thought, 'Now I can do this.' And it turned out I couldn't do it at all." He did not start his physical transition until he encountered a visible transgender community in California thirty years later.

In the 1960s and 1970s, most of the public information about transsexuals, such as talk shows, autobiographies, novels, and films, focused on transwomen, as the implied surgical removal of the penis made for sensationalistic news (Meyerowitz 2002). The coverage of the employment case of Steve Dain, the activism of Jude Patton, the autobiography of Mario Martinez, paled in comparison to the news coverage of Christine Jorgensen, the ex-GI turned blond bombshell who became the first public transsexual in the 1950s (ibid.). Nathan (b. early 1940s) remembers seeing Jorgensen on television: "That was the first I heard about it [transsexuality]. . . . I thought, 'Wouldn't that be wonderful?' But . . . I couldn't find anything at that time for female to males." Joseph (b. early 1940s) says, "I couldn't find anything about gender dysphoria when I was in high school. I sort of figured that I was gay. They didn't have gay and lesbian when I was in high school. Everything was just gay." All of the information he could find about homosexuality suggested he would be choosing a hard life. "Female gay people were painted as . . . alcoholics who hung out in pool halls. I thought, 'I am not going to go that route.' So I just buried it [gender dysphoria] at the time." The strong social pressures in place in the late 1950s pushed him to cultivate a heterosexual façade to fit in with his peers. He married a man in his late teens and had two children. Then, in 1970, he and a friend went to the drive-in to see the sensationalistic film *The Christine Jorgensen Story*. "That film just blew me away. . . . It hit me right square between the eyes. But, at the same time, it was like, oh, well, sure, that's fine for guys, but girls can't do that. . . . I had to bury it [my gender dysphoria and attraction to women] again."

Major gay enclaves existed at the time in New York, Los Angeles, and San Francisco (Chauncey 1994; Faderman and Timmons 2006; Stryker and Van Buskirk 1996), while smaller networks emerged across the country. After divorcing his husband and coming out as a lesbian—an action that resulted in the loss of his children—Joseph became part of a small gay community in the Northwest. He says, "There was not L, G, B, T, or anything back then. I just got involved in the gay community." He did not encounter transsexuals until the late 1980s, when he moved to a large urban center in California. Nathan, too, became involved in a gay community after moving away from his Midwest hometown. Describing his personal sense of gender identity, he says, "I have always [identified as male]. I don't know if I can say I outwardly thought about it [my gender] in those terms, but I have always been in that [male] role since I was twelve." However, while he felt like a heterosexual man inside, lesbian enclaves were the only place to go in the fifties and sixties if he wanted to wear men's clothing and date women. "I didn't feel I fitted in there, but that was the closest I could identify with. . . . There was something missing there, too. I always felt like I was living in disguise." Having spent the majority of his life in the South, Nathan did not learn about the existence of transmen until he was in his sixties—at which point he began to physically transition.

Lesbian communities were not always welcoming places. Eric (b. mid-1950s) dated feminine lesbians in what were termed "butch-femme" relationships. However, in the 1970s, many lesbians aligned with feminist equality movements (Echols 1989), an alignment that brought a push toward androgyny in an effort to resist the "compulsive heterosexuality" (Rich 1980) that was part and parcel of a patriarchal society. The masculine appearance and behaviors of butches became characterized as an "old gay" model that signaled an investment in women's oppression (Minter 2006; H. Rubin 2003; Stein 1993, 1997). Describing this, Eric says, "As the [lesbian] scene changed, the real[ly] feminine lesbians—the lipstick lesbians—changed. A lot of us [butch] dykes were kind of derided, like we think we have to be a man. But it wasn't like that. They didn't understand [us]." For Eric, he was not trying to emulate men; rather, he felt that his masculine appearance and behavior sprang naturally from his internal sense of maleness. Feeling shamed, he began using drugs and alcohol in what he describes as a way to keep the conflict between his mind and body buried for over forty years.

Most of the men who came of age in and/or transitioned in the gender clinic era make sense of their gender in a similar way—what I term "essentialist" understandings.[2] They see a clear male/female binary. Their dilemma is being on the wrong side of that binary. While many of them had social identities as lesbians for a period of time, they felt internally that they were heterosexual men who related to women on the basis of difference, not similarity. Seth (b. mid-1950s), in contrast, presents a different personal identity, which I term a "transformable" understanding of gender. For him, his sense of internal gender identity, and his resulting idealized body image, shifted across his life course. "Growing up, I never thought I was a boy or wanted to be a boy. . . . My idealized anatomy as a young child was hermaphroditic to some degree. Typical female genital structure but no breasts and fairly lean and muscular." He notes, "I was always skeptical of femininity and masculinity, I was so non-essentialist." However, as he learned more about transmen in his forties, he began to feel that taking testosterone would enhance his comfort in his body. The decision to go forward with testosterone in the 2000s ultimately came from his past. "Back in the seventies, there was this old lesbian saying, 'Don't die not knowing.' So it was kind of that. I thought, 'I will go do this.'" The saying he references was a radical lesbian slogan aimed at heterosexual women: Don't die without knowing what it is like to be in a lesbian relationship. For Seth, the underlying meaning of this slogan, the leeway to make life decisions that might violate normative expectations, became a justification for physically transitioning—a life choice that many seventies lesbians (and many nineties lesbians, for that matter) did not support.

Queering the Binary: The Rise of Transgender Activism (the 1990s)

At the age of three, Sam (b. early 1970s) remembers telling his mother that he would grow up to be a man, marry a woman, and have children. Feeling male but being treated as a little girl, he experienced a conflict between his "soul and body." Even without surgeries and hormones—options for transmen he did not know existed until he was in his twenties—he looked so much like a boy, he enrolled himself in high school as male until his mother found out. Describing how he lived as a boy in adolescence despite his family's opposition, he says, "I didn't make a decision so much as it was who I was." After high school, he married his girlfriend—who was unaware at the time that he had been assigned female at birth—after altering his birth certificate with an eraser. "Back in the day, the kind of birth certificates they gave you, they were

erase-off." Removing a letter from the end of his given name masculinized it. He erased the *F* and typed in an *M*.

In the early 1990s, a relative of Sam's saw a Texas-based therapist on
television talking about transsexuality. Identifying this term with Sam,
she made an appointment for him. According to Sam:

> I spent forty-five minutes with [this doctor]. That is the most I have ever spent
> with a therapist in my life. She asked me how I feel about myself, and I told
> her, "I am a guy. I don't care what you think. I don't care what anyone else
> thinks." When we finished, . . . she said, "I have never met any man in my life
> who is as sure that he is a man as you are."

Sam left her office with a prescription for testosterone and the number
of a local endocrinologist. He remembers the endocrinologist fondly,
saying, "He really wanted to help. Unfortunately, he didn't know what
he was doing." After a few months on testosterone, Sam still had not developed much facial hair. In an attempt to hasten the development, the
doctor continued to increase his dosage. When Sam moved to California
and entered the care of a new endocrinologist, he discovered his dosage
was three times the recommended amount. Sam learned to his surprise
that as a Latino, he might not develop much facial hair, no matter how
much testosterone he took.

Sam's story illustrates the end of the gender clinic era. While a small
group of medical and psychological gatekeepers regulated access to gender transitions in the 1970s and 1980s, by the 1990s, more therapists, surgeons, and endocrinologists were willing to take on transsexual clients.
This change came from a convergence of multiple political and social developments. Some clinics closed of their own accord over internal debates about the effectiveness of surgical cures for transsexuals. Others
were victims of massive funding cuts to health programs in the Reagan
years of the 1980s (Meyerowitz 2002). The clinics that stayed open oper-
ated in a new political terrain. Under the guidance of psychologists Robert Stoller and Richard Green, the UCLA gender clinic specialized in
treating gender dysphoric children (Burke 1996). When Green began his
work with what he termed "sissy boys" (1987), homosexuality was still
a mental illness listed in the *DSM*. Trying to cure it (or its close cousin
transsexuality) in children was an accepted medical intervention. In the
1970s, however, gay and lesbian activists successfully lobbied the American Psychiatric Association to remove homosexuality as a disorder

(Faderman and Timmons 2006; Kirk and Kutchins 1992). While Green's work once received major federal grants, the changing political landscape questioned its legitimacy (Burke 1996).

Ideas about transsexuality also underwent a shift, as gender and sexual activism brought new focus on how women and men were held accountable for violating culturally constructed norms of masculinity and femininity—a focus that challenged norms that many people believed derived from biology and/or God. While some radical feminists in the 1970s had argued that women had an innate, feminine essence (Daly 1978; Echols 1989; Rich 1977), other branches of feminist theory separated gender (the cultural expectations of and characteristics associated with women and men) and sex (the biological differences between males and females that result from hormones and chromosomes) (Chodorow 1978; Hartmann 1979; Mitchell 1966; Oakley 1972). This separation deviated from the psychological split between biological sex and internal gender, as feminist theorists emphasized the role of socialization in creating gender identity (Chodorow 1971; Mitchell 1966; Lorber 1994; Thorne 1990). From this social constructionist perspective, masculinity and femininity were culturally created ideas that varied across historical time periods, political regimes, and cultures (G. Rubin 1975; Scott 1988)—a theoretical idea that opened up possibilities for transformation within oppressive expectations of femininity.

For many theorists, transsexuals presented an easy example of this sex/gender distinction: they could change *gender* but were forever wedded to the reality of biological *sex* (Bem 1993; Lorber 1994). This view of transsexuals had its roots in a short book, *The Transsexual Empire* (Raymond 1979). To emphasize the binding reality of sex, the author, Janice Raymond, referred to transmen as "female–to–constructed males," arguing: "Can we call a person transsexed, biologically speaking, whose anatomical structure and hormonal balance have changed but who is still genetically XY or XX? If we don't recognize chromosomal sex as determinative . . . what are we really talking about when we say female or male?" (1979, 11). Echoing Raymond almost twenty years later, sociologist Judith Lorber posited, "Transsexuals do not change their sex completely. Their chromosomes remain the same, and no man-to-woman transsexual has a uterus implant, nor do women-to-men transsexuals produce sperm. They change gender" (1994, 84). For Lorber, transsexuals move from the cultural identities of "men and women" rather than from the biological realities of "male and female." While one of the goals

of second-wave feminism was to problematize the conflation of women
with sexual reproduction (see Chodorow 1978; Mitchell 1966), this definition of transsexuals returned to defining "females" by their reproductive abilities.

Using transsexuals as an example of the reality of sex and the con-
structedness of gender formed the basis for what I term a "sociocultural"
frame of transsexuality. Unlike the mental illness frame that dominated
the gender clinic era, this new frame emphasized a sick society, not a
sick individual. Sandra Bem sums up this position, arguing: "Transsexualism would be much better conceptualized as a social pathology than
as an individual pathology . . . as the underside of the same process of
gender polarization that also produces highly conventional males and
females" (1993, 111). If normative and hierarchical expectations of gender were deconstructed, transsexuals—the cultural dupes of a patriarchal gender system—would no longer have to exist. Similar to feminist
critiques of cosmetic surgery (see Davis 1995), this frame positions transsexuals' body modifications as self-hating acts driven by misplaced adherence to oppressive gender ideology. Showing how debates come full
circle, some gender scholars argued for a return to psychotherapy treatments for transsexuals that encouraged making the mind fit the body
(see Lienert 1998).

This sociocultural frame had a great deal of influence in some lesbian
communities that were undergoing major changes from the androgyny-
focused 1970s. Lesbian separatism had largely died out, as women's businesses and organizations struggled to stay afloat in the 1980s, and the
ravages of AIDS brought lesbians closer to gay men (Faderman and
Timmons 2006; Stein 1997). Younger generations of lesbians reclaimed
sexual practices deemed patriarchal by seventies lesbian feminists, such
as femme/butch relationships and prowomen pornography (Burana,
Roxxie, and Due 1994; Nestle 1992; Stein 1993, 1997). Reopening space
for butches meant that some transmen who would go on to transition in
the 1990s were previously integrated into lesbian networks (Califia 2002;
H. Rubin 2003). About his lesbian past, Henry (b. early 1970s) says, "I
loved being a dyke! I found a really great place in my community. It was
really warm and welcoming and a great home. Most [trans]guys I know,
they are like, oh, I never really felt like a lesbian. They never felt right.
They were in that community, but they never really fit in. I loved it!" Winston (b. early 1960s), who tried to be a heterosexual woman in his teens,
said of finding a lesbian community, "When I was with a woman sexu-

ally, I finally found a way to identify. Finally! . . . I am woman, hear me
roar! I was like 'Patriarchy? Fuck that bullshit!'" Trevor (b. late 1960s),
Douglas (b. mid-1960s), Brian (b. late 1960s), and Thomas (b. early
1960s) also describe similar positive experiences in lesbian communities,
seeing "lesbian" as an identity that was right for them at the time.

While butch made a comeback in some lesbian spaces in the 1990s,
transsexuals—men or women—often were not welcome (Califia 1997;
Gamson 1996; Valerio 2006). In 1991, the National Lesbian Conference
excluded transwomen by banning "non-genetic women" from attending
(G. Rubin 1992). In the same year, a transwoman was expelled from the
Michigan Womyn's festival, a long-standing lesbian feminist concert and
camping event, which then adopted an entrance policy of "womyn-born
womyn" only (ibid.)—a policy that was still intact at the end of the 2000s.
This animosity toward transsexuals from gays and lesbians was not new
(Califia 2002; Meyerowitz 2002; Minter 2006; Perkins 1983; Stryker
2008). Dating back to Christine Jorgensen's highly publicized transition
in the 1950s, gay activists in the homophile movement worried that "sex
changes" would be viewed as a normalized, heterosexual solution to homosexuality (Meyerowitz 2002). With the increasing visibility of transmen and transwomen in the 1990s (H. Rubin 2003), many lesbian communities drew tighter boundaries between insiders (here female-born
lesbians) and outsiders (here all transgender people). Transwomen were
discredited as "men in dresses" attempting to take over women's spaces
in the name of patriarchy (Gamson 1996; Raymond 1979). Transmen,
in contrast, were positioned as "treasonous deserters" (G. Rubin 1992,
474) who transitioned in an effort to get male privilege (see Halberstam
1998b and Hale 1998 for a wider discussion of these "border wars").

This view of transgender people meant that some transmen felt
pushed out of lesbian networks once they openly identified as transmen
and/or as male. Describing his feeling of alienation after he decided to
physically transition, Winston says, "Lesbians are the worst! In terms
of people who were your friends [before you transitioned], they will
leave you faster than the average straight person. Which is sad. I mean,
someone living as a male in your camp? Keep the ally!" Thomas had a
similar feeling of alienation. Lesbians who were once his friends suddenly labeled him a misogynist. "I got tired of taking the rap for guys
who were assholes when I still had feminist politics. My ideologies had
not changed, just my comfort in the world. Suddenly it was, 'You have
male privilege.' And I was, like, wait a minute! How? I didn't get a plati-

num card in the mail, my credit rating didn't get better." Other transmen found support from their lesbian communities but felt it was inappropriate to stay in women's spaces once they were living as men.

Marginalization and exodus from lesbian communities contributed to the development of transmen-specific networks and support groups (H. Rubin 2003). San Francisco was a major center for this development. The city housed one of the largest and oldest gay enclaves in the Castro district and had been the site of much of the gay and lesbian activism of the seventies and eighties (Gamson 2004; Stryker and Van Buskirk 1996). It was also the home of one of the first organized networks of FTM-specific resources, started by Louis Sullivan. Sullivan's network morphed into FTM International (FTMI), an organization that continues to publish a newsletter for transmen (J. Green 2004). FTMI hosted the first conference organized by and for transmen in America in 1994. Wayne, who attended the conference after having been stealth for over ten years, was amazed to see three hundred transmen in a room together. Such a public gathering was unheard of in the gender clinic era, as therapists discouraged spending time with other transsexuals (Bolin 1988). Reflecting the public stigma aimed at transsexuals when he came of age, his first reaction was that this conference was actually a police sting designed to arrest sexual deviants. The comfort younger generations of transmen felt taking up public space in an expensive hotel spoke to him of the weakening of the hegemony of the deep stealth model.

FTMI ran ads for its newsletter in many gay and lesbian publications. For Aaron (b. mid-1970s), coming across this information was a major turning point in his life. He had found the space to be a masculine woman in the gay and lesbian community in his California hometown. Encountering transwomen, he began to wonder about the possibilities of transitioning from female to male. "I slowly started to gather what little information there was at the time. This was pre-Internet, when it was really hard to get information." He adds, "And a lot of it [the psychological literature] was really outdated. I remember reading numbers [at the time] that like transitions [from female to male] are something that happens one out of 250,000 live female births or something like that. And I'm going, wow, how am I ever going to find anybody!" In the early 1990s, he saw a small ad for FTMI and immediately wrote away for its newsletter. "[When it came], it was like kind of wow, wow! And I remember there was a little note from James Green, and they also had like a pamphlet or something."

From these resource networks emerged a new brand of activism, which offered a "reverse discourse" (Foucault 1978) on transsexuality. Inspired by the direct-action, confrontational tactics of AIDS activist groups (Crimp 1990), such as ACT-UP, a group of activists formed Transexual Menace to challenge the acceptance of violence and discrimination against transsexual people (Califia 1997; Stryker 2008).[3] Building on the success of the gay and lesbian movement, activists argued that "Gender Identity Disorder" should be removed from the *DSM*.[4] As one activist of the time put it, "Refuse the pathological medical model—we are not sick, just different" (Kaveney 1999, 147). The standards of care were positioned as infantilizing to competent adults. Illustrating this frustration, Thomas says:

> I was in therapy around gender issues because it was required. It was an adversarial process. I was paying someone money to convince them that what I wanted to do was right. I was twenty-nine, almost thirty years old, and I had put myself through [professional school]. I'd been able to function in life and make decisions for myself and take responsibility for those decisions, and I was pretty pissed off about needing somebody's permission.

Activists also questioned why the standards of care were developed with no input from transsexual people. This pressure led to the induction of WPATH's first transsexual board member, over twenty years after the organization was formed (Minter 2006).

This challenge further questioned the medical distinction between pre- and posttransition life for transsexuals, a distinction that set up genital surgery as the final step toward a "complete" sex change. The focus was put instead on creating bodies that were personally comfortable, not bodies that conformed to societal standards of "maleness" and "femaleness." Coming from the gender clinic era, Wayne was surprised at this shift:

> Everybody had [genital] surgery that I knew of back then. It was what you did. If you had to beg, borrow, steal money to have it done. If you didn't have it done, it was seen as an indication that you were literally wanting to be a freak. You were wanting to take T [hormones] and were kind of wanting to be like the bearded woman at the circus. You were wanting to make your body in this physiological middle state instead of going all the way. And boy, have things changed in that direction!

Activists and scholars interested in publicly adopting transsexual identities sought alternatives to the stealth model of posttransition life (Bornstein 1994; Stone 1991). Illustrating this shift, Henry (b. mid-1970s) notes, "Because FTMs have been such an invisible minority in this culture, I think it's important for people to self-identify [as FTM] or whatever terms they prefer to show that there is a visible transmale community." By the 2000s, an open identity model was held up as an alternative to the deep stealth model for those who could safely do it in their communities.

Activists and academics further problematized the pressure to conform to the classic *DSM* criteria to get access to hormones and surgery (Bornstein 1994; Stone 1991). These criteria share some elements with what I term an essentialist understanding of gender—a core feeling of internal maleness despite having a traditionally female body and being socially gendered as a girl. Yet these criteria ignored social and familial pressure for young people to marry and have children—pressure not all transgender people could avoid. They also reinforced the stereotype of the "tragic tranny" (MacKenzie 1994), a person with no ties to family, community, or romantic partners. Therapists' concern about any elements of a client's life that did not conform exactly to the diagnostic criteria forced many transgender people to lie about their pasts, the antithesis of a good therapeutic relationship. The hegemony of these criteria further delegitimized the myriad pathways toward transitions and the different understandings of gender identities that existed within transgender communities.

Illustrating a "transformable" understanding of gender that positions gender identity as changing across the life course with the impact of different life events, Trevor (b. late 1960s) noted that he "had no fucking clue" he wanted to transition until he was in his late twenties. "I think it was pretty abrupt in some ways. I met another transman. I was like, 'Oh? Oh! Oh, duh!' It wasn't like some big agonizing thing. . . . I just had never had any information about it before." About his current gender identity, he says, "Generally I go with being a queer man. . . . To simplify for people, I say I am a gay man looking for partners who are other gay men. But really, it is hard to stomach the man thing. I just think that I would have had to grow up with certain experiences of boyhood I didn't have." Henry (b. mid-1970s) says, "I typically say FTM (female-to-male). . . . I don't feel like I am strictly male or female on a biological level." Jake (b. late 1950s) de-emphasized a male/female binary, describing himself as a "permanent border zone dweller. . . . I don't think of myself as a woman, and 'not-woman' is something I would attach myself to. And I don't really think of myself as a man." While their personal gender identities varied, all of the men I interviewed who transitioned in the 1990s took testosterone and had chest surgery—decisions that afforded them social maleness in everyday interactions. Describing this distinction between personal and social gender identities, Devin (b. early 1970s), who transitioned in the 2000s, says, "I can have my own thing inside and feel like I am my own special gender inside but still want to be seen as a man [socially]."

Reflecting the increasingly acknowledged diversity in personal identities and decisions about body modifications among people classified as "transsexuals," new terminology emerged from people who saw themselves as differently gendered. *Transgender* had been in limited use (J. Green 2004), but by the late 1990s, it started to replace the use of *transsexual* in cities with visible gender activism, such as Los Angeles, San Francisco, and New York, particularly among white, college-educated people (Valentine 2007). The term was widely inclusive—all those who considered themselves differently gendered from a male/masculine or female/feminine model could fit under the rubric: feminine men, masculine women, drag queens, drag kings. *Transgender* was similar to the adoption of *queer* by young activists fighting sexual oppression in the 1990s. *Queer* could encompass anyone whose sexual identity and/or sexual practices put him or her outside of heteronormative norms, be that gay men, lesbians, bisexuals, individuals involved in S-M (Gamson 1996). Yet, while *queer* aimed to be confrontational by reclaiming an insult hurled at gay people—as was the use of *transsexual* by Transexual Menace—*transgender* removed the luridness of trans*sex*uality.

This shift in terminology and the push for the open adoption of differently gendered identities created some rifts between people who chose to openly identify as "transgender" and those who continued to identify as "transsexual" and often remained stealth. Roger, who transitioned in the gender clinic era, speaks to this divide: "I hate it [transgender]. To me, that is a political construct that has no practical meaning." He adds, "What that word is telling you is that it is your gender that's changed, and that's not who I am. My gender did not change. My gender was the one constant . . . I changed my physical sex to match my [internal] gender." For him, transsexuality was a medical issue, not an identity. "It is a background part of your life. It's like having diabetes. It is a chronic illness, and you always have to take medication for it for the rest of your life." Wayne, too, struggled with this new model of being openly transgender: "I am like a person of color before the civil rights movement . . . Before [in the eighties], you were seen as better if you could pass [go stealth] and no one would ever know . . . and now I think people kind of see that like you are missing a part of yourself." Christopher (b. late 1970s), who transitioned in the 2000s, felt in contrast that *transgender* was a more inclusive term and also a term more palatable for parents, as it did not have the association with mental illness and deviance that *transsexual* carried for him.

The activist and scholarly discussions of transsexuality, transgenderism, and gender identities coalesced into "transgender studies" (see Bornstein 1994; Cromwell 1999; Devor 1997; Griggs 1998; Hale 1998; More and Whittle 1999; V. Namaste 2000; Prosser 1998; Stone 1991; Stryker and Whittle 2006).[5] Transgender studies had connections to queer theory, a body of theory associated with poststructuralism that emerged in the late 1980s. Queer theorists emphasized that the positioning of biological sex differences as authentic was itself a social construction (J. Butler 1989; K. Namaste 1994; Seidman 1996). Challenging the notion of fixed identities, such as "man" and "woman" and "gay" and "heterosexual," queer theorists framed gender and sexual identity as performative— a citational act given meaning through its constant reproduction (J. Butler 1989, 1993). Theorists also deconstructed the assumption that sexuality followed from gender identity—an assumption that legitimated heteronormativity. This focus on exploding binaries and deconstructing heteronormativity had great promise for challenging the sociocultural frame of transsexuality. Yet it was short-lived. Many queer theorists reduced the complexity of transgender lives to mere allegory, creating stereotypes rather than inclusion (V. Namaste 2000; Prosser 1998).

Transgender critiques of queer theory began to filter into academic scholarship (Nataf 1996; Stryker 1998). Transgender scholars highlighted how many cisgender people—including feminists—were beholden to the cultural belief that gender identity was an offshoot of biology. Feminists put the focus on expanding the roles for men and women in society to make them more equal or more inclusive but did not question the assumption that "male" and "female" were fixed categories (see J. Butler 1989; G. Rubin 1992; Wilchins 1997). In contrast, some theorists conceptualized gender as a continuum or galaxy with a multitude of possibilities rather than as a simple binary (see Bornstein 1994; MacKenzie 1999;

Queen and Schimel 1997; Wilchins 1997). This gender diversity frame highlighted individual agency to create new gender possibilities by unseating a male/masculine or female/feminine model—a move that could be alienating to people who experienced their gender as unchanging and innate. Yet despite internal contestations in some transgender communities and among branches of theoretical scholarship, by the 2000s, transgender issues were integrated into activism, public policy, and sexuality research, at least in name, under the rubric of lesbian, gay, bisexual, and transgender (LGBT).[6]

Biological Diversity: Gender Variance and Political Rights (the 2000s)

Elliott (b. early 1980s) grew up in the Bay Area. As a little girl, he had a nagging sense of being different from other girls. "The closest word that I have to it is *awkward*. Like I felt really awkward in my body and in my [gender] presentation. There was something wrong, but I didn't know what it was." He adds, "I enjoyed feminine presentation and all that other stuff. So I did the girl thing really well. It was wrong, but it wasn't so wrong that I figured out what it was." Being attracted to masculinity, Elliott dated boys but did not feel comfortable with heterosexual power dynamics. In high school, he came out as a bisexual and then as a lesbian. At a conference for young queer activists, he met his first transman and began to question whether his sense of difference was about sexual identity or gender identity. Elliott gathered information about transmen from Internet blogs, online chat rooms, local FTM support groups, and LGBT-focused college courses. In college, he came out as transgender to his friends and family and began dating other transmen. Reflecting on his identity transformations, he laughs: "I've been the L, G, B, and T. I've done them all."

Elliott's story reflects a major shift from the 1980s and 1990s. Because he grew up in an urban area of California, the resources available to him were unimaginable to older generations of transmen: gay-straight alliances at many high schools, conferences for young queer activists, LGBT studies programs in universities. Even in a politically conservative suburb of Southern California, Robert (b. early 1980s) found an LGBT center that offered support groups for transgender youth. Attending the meetings, he learned it was possible to get free therapy and hormones from the Children's Hospital near his town until he was twenty-four. Casey (b. early 1980s) found a similar program as an eighteen-year-old living in New York City, another city with established transgender resources. Such programs provided an affordable way to get access to therapy and hormones. Within these growing resources was a wider acceptance of the diversity of gender identities in the transgender community. Some transmen felt that they made a transition from female to male (FTM) or from female to transmen. Others, such as Robert, who lived as male before he encountered the term *transgender*, felt they transitioned from male to men (MTM). Still others, such as Christopher (b. late 1970s), identified as "genderqueer": "Simplest way to put it, I am a guy, but I have . . . something of a fluidity. My gender and my gender expression changes moment to moment to moment. When I am in that moment, I truly am that gender."

This different cultural landscape on the West Coast was possible in some part because of the institutionalization of nineties grassroots activism. Organizations such as the Transgender Law Center and the National Center for Transgender Equality formed from smaller activist networks designed to address transgender discrimination on a national and local level. These advocacy groups argued that, along with sexual identity, gender identity (the internal feeling of being a man or a woman) and gender expression (the visible representation of gender identity) should be given federal protection in the areas of employment and housing, and in hate crimes legislation. These transgender civil rights issues came to be included under the umbrella of "LGBT activism," though transgender issues were and continue to be sublimated to gay and lesbian concerns—concerns that have a much longer history of institutionalized activism and political lobbying (Minter 2006). But even the nominal inclusion of the *T* increased the visibility of transgender lives, as reporters, researchers, policy organizations, and community resource centers increasingly began using *LGBT* as shorthand for anything to do with sexuality and gender. The media begin to pick up stories about transgender people with new intensity. As table 1.1 shows, the number of stories in major U.S. newspapers from 2000 to 2008 just about transgender people in the workplace doubled from a decade earlier. Transgender people long had been a staple of sordid daytime talk shows (Gamson 1998). In the 2000s, however, more legitimate talk show hosts, such as Oprah, Larry King, and Barbara Walters, began to feature transgender programming, as did the Discovery Health Channel and the Sundance Channel.

TABLE 1.1 **Transgender workplace stories from newspapers, 1971–2008**

	1970s	1980s	1990s	2000s
News stories	13	18	29	58

This new visibility increased the public focus on gender *diversity* rather than *perversity*. However, the nineties concept of gender diversity promoted a poststructuralist approach that challenged or queered the concept of a core, essential gender identity and a male/female binary. Though transgenderism has no established etiology—both psychological and biological theories are inconclusive—much of this new public discourse in the 2000s focused on possible endocrinological or neurological origins (see Rudacille 2005) and emphasized tolerance for *biological* gender diversity, comparing gender-variant people with the natural continuum of biological deviations from male and female in the animal world (Roughgarden 2004). Showing this change, a therapist interviewed in the *Dayton Daily News* dismissed the notion that transgender people are mentally ill: "There are a lot of things in the *DSM IV* that aren't really mental illnesses. We're moving away from an old school full of sexual folklore and myths to more of a new school of sexual science. . . . There are many different valid [gender] expressions once considered outside of the range of normal" (Warren 2008, A17). Gender Spectrum, a nonprofit organization that promotes educational programs about "gender variant" people, promoted a similar idea: "Our society is now at a crossroads. Our awareness of natural gender variance and gender diversity is expanding. . . . We must acknowledge, examine, and address the constrictions we place on gender . . . [to] work toward a world in which all of us are more free to be our authentic selves."[7] The move toward natural gender variance—and away from a social constructionist frame—parallels developments in the mainstream gay and lesbian movement (Lancaster 2003). Showing the political impact of this biological argument, seeing homosexuality or transgenderism as innate correlates with increasingly positive attitudes toward gay and transgender rights (Herek 2002; Landen and Innala 2000; Sherrill and Yang 2000).

The growing visibility of transgender lives in media outlets, in gay and lesbian enclaves, and in university curricula provided a wealth of information about transgenderism. Anthony (b. early 1980s), Brad (b. early 1980s), Christopher (b. mid-1970s), Dan (b. early 1980s), David (b. mid-1970s), Devin (b. mid-1970s), Ethan (b. early 1980s), Gabriel (b. early

1980s), Jack (b. mid-1970s), Kelly (b. early 1980s), Ken (b. late 1970s), Nicky (b. early 1980s), and Simon (b. early 1960s) were living as heterosexual, bisexual, or lesbian women in the 2000s. They were more likely than past generations to find information about trans*men* rather than just transwomen. Jack describes encountering drag kings—typically cisgender women who perform as men—as an important step on his pathway to identifying as a transman. While drag queens have a long history of performance (Rupp and Taylor 2004), drag king troupes became widely visible in the late 1990s and early 2000s (Shapiro 2007). After seeing his first performance, Jack started his own troupe: "I was mesmerized! It just opened the door for me to explore my gender identity." He describes his gender identity as moving from male-identified to FTM.

Kelly (b. early 1980s) was interested in transmen when he first came across them through one of the early documentaries about FTMs, *You Don't Know Dick* (Cram 1996). However, he felt that his life didn't fit the classic narrative. "I don't think that I was one of those people that [knew] when I was two or three or four or anything . . . I know some people that are like, no, when I was two, I was saying [I was male], but yeah, for me, 2001 is when I started really exploring [transitioning], and I was still kind of wishy-washy about it." While he had done "boy things" in high school, such as play sports, he had long hair and wore dresses because of his family's religious background. All the transmen he met online described past identifications as either male or butch. In contrast, he felt male-identified but also kind of "girly." At a transgender conference in California, however, he met a gay transman who had what he described as "femmy" gender expression. "I was getting online [from FTM blogs] that you have to be really butch. And then I met [a transman] just like being his big old flamey self. And I was like, 'I could do this!'"

While the 2000s offered more institutionalized and community support for transformable understandings of gender, many transmen who transitioned in the 2000s still had essentialist understandings of their gender identity—as table 1.2 shows. Preston (b. mid-1960s), Crispin (b. early 1960s), Colin (b. early 1970s), Julian (b. late 1970s), Scott (b. mid-1970s), Stephen (b. late 1960s), and Keith (b. early 1960s) all felt male in their youth. Several of them even looked into transitioning in the 1980s and 1990s. Colin says, "At that time, to start hormones and do surgery, it was something like twenty thousand dollars. . . . It just wasn't an option." Additionally, he realized he stood to lose support from the gay community, a space where he had found some acceptance. "And

TABLE 1.2 **Transmen's personal understandings of their gender, by transition era**

	1970–89	1990–2000	2000–2009	Total
Transformable				
Texas	0	0	10	10
California	0	6	9	15
Essentialist				
Texas	1	0	12	13
California	3	4	9	16
Total	4	10	40	54

the community [on the East Coast], like the gay community, it was not GLB*T*, you know, not accepting [of trans] at all. And certainly my family wasn't either. I made this conscious decision that I wouldn't go there." In the 2000s, Colin realized there were many new options. The Internet was a major source of information for him, just as it was for younger transmen with essentialist understandings of their identities, such as Peter (b. mid-1980s), who encountered transmen for the first time in an online chat room. This increase in online visibility also encouraged some transmen who had been stealth for many years to become part of their local transgender community. Describing the feeling of attending a transgender event after having been stealth for almost twenty years, Chris says, "Imagine if you were African-American and you had a white family and everyone around you was white. And then you saw someone who looked like you, and you were, like, '*Wow*'! I was so amazed!" While Chris remained stealth at work, he became involved in the burgeoning transman community.

In California, as the transgender community grew in visibility, the whiteness of the ever-expanding resources became harder to ignore. Keith described feeling unwelcome at his first transmen support group meetings as the only black man present. "Every time you go to a [transgender] event, there's no one like me. [I heard] they all go underground." Christopher, who wondered why there were so few other Asians in his transgender community, similarly heard they went "deep stealth" after transition—being invisible even to the transgender community. Showing the importance of regional context, I saw few discussions of race in Texas—though Eli (b. late 1970s) did feel like an oddity as a Jewish transman in the South. A network of transmen began to expand rapidly in Texas in 2007 that primarily focused on increasing transmen's visibility in the LGBT community and locating local resources. Luis (b. mid-1970s), Clark (b. early 1980s), Caleb (b. mid-1980s), and Trey (b. mid-1980s) felt that their transition experiences gave them commonalities with white transmen that surpassed racial differences. The newness of the Texas community was reminiscent of the networks Jamison Green (2004) describes in San Francisco in the 1980s and early 1990s, where differences among transmen were downplayed because there were so few resources.

Texas also offered a very different cultural landscape for transmen. The Rosenberg Clinic of Galveston, Texas, one of the few remaining private gender clinics, continued to promote a medical model of transsexuality. Brad (b. early 1980s) and Dan (b. early 1980s) both carried letters from the clinic in their wallets meant for potential employers or the police that stated they were dressed as men while being biologically female because they were undergoing treatment for "transsexualism," a "neuroendocrinological disorder." This medicalization is unsurprising due to the local context. While young transmen in California were attending queer conferences and taking LGBT studies courses and workshops, many Texas transmen born in the same years grew up in towns where the idea of even homosexuality was stigmatized. Tex (b. mid-1980s) says about his hometown, "There weren't any gay people that I knew of. No one is out there because it is too dangerous. The KKK is near. It is a scary place to be gay, much less trans. I didn't know what transsexual meant [until I was twenty]." With few visible local resources, Texas transmen looked for online help. But locating resources could be difficult because of the lack of familiarity with terms such as *FTM, transgender,* or *transsexual.* Clark (b. early 1980s) made several attempts in his late teens to find people "like him" online. It was not until he typed "I'm a girl who wants to be a boy" into a search engine that he found the word *transgender.*

Texas therapists had less experience with and exposure to the diversity of transgender lives, even in LGBT organizations. Not presenting the classic *DSM* criteria in an intake session could still carry penalties in the 2000s. Gabriel (b. early 1980s) was living as a feminine heterosexual woman when he approached his first therapist in 2003 about his sense of himself as a gay man. This therapist encouraged him to dress more femininely and gave him a prescription for Xanax. Christian (b. late 1980s) entered his therapist's office in what he described as "feminine drag" because he was still living at home as a female. His therapist told him that he would not be able to begin hormones until he was twenty-five because his personality was not fully formed until then—a "fact" she fabricated to justify her discomfort with his appearance, which did not match the *DSM* criteria. In contrast, Johnny (b. late 1980s), who presented the classic criteria, was given a prescription for testosterone at eighteen.

While important regional and local variations exist between Texas and California, once online, transmen in both states had unprecedented access to information about the possible outcomes of genital and chest surgeries, the potential risks of continued testosterone use, and the pros and cons of surgeons. In the communities in which I did my fieldwork, it was widely acknowledged that many transmen in the 2000s did not undergo genital surgery. Transmen with essentialist understandings of their gender identity were the most likely to express a strong desire for genital surgery, as having a penis was important to their sense of themselves as male. Clark, who identified as a gay man, says, "My body doesn't feel congruent [without genital surgery]. . . . I plan on having it if I can ever afford it. I might just sell a kidney online [*laughing*]." Other transmen wanted a penis but were too unhappy with the current technology to undergo such an extremely expensive surgery. Brad (b. early 1980s) describes making peace with the gap between his desire for a penis and the current state of the surgery: "For years, I thought I was going to have [genital] surgery. But then you get to a point . . . you might never have a penis, and it is just going to be okay. It is not going to define your gender or who you are. I am never going to have a penis, and I am still a man. I still do everything as male."

Transmen with transformable understandings of gender, particularly those who personally identified as genderqueer, expressed less interest in genital surgery, and in some cases chest surgery and hormones. Both Tex (b. early 1980s) and Anton (b. mid-1980s) were happy with their current genitalia. Tex notes, "I have never really liked penises at all. I am one of those guys who—I don't think the penis makes the man." Christopher (b. mid-1970s) wanted to keep his breasts, as they were an integral part of his sex life. Cole (b. mid-1970s), Jack (b. mid-1970s), and Ken (b. late 1970s) had all opted against hormone therapy or any surgeries for the present. Riley (b. late 1960s) and Xavier (b. late 1960s) had chest surgery and took hormones but personally identified as "two-spirit" and "genderqueer," rather than male, respectively. And several transmen decided against hysterectomies because they thought they might want to carry a baby later in life—a desire that would have resulted in rejection from Stanford in the gender clinic era.[8] For these transmen, the 2000s brought increased opportunities to bring their bodies in line with their personal gender identities—genderqueer, MTM, male, FTM, transman—in a way comfortable to them, not a way dictated by professionals.

These differences in identities and what I term "body projects" could create hierarchy among transmen—what many transmen described as a "trans-er than thou" attitude. Illustrating this, Tex and several other transmen generated ire in their Texas community when they participated in an all-transgender production of *The Vagina Monologues*. The issue was that a *real* man would not talk about his vagina. The conflict could also be generational. Expressing this, Roger says, "The guys that transitioned [in the early 1980s] knew that's what they wanted, they knew that's who they were. I have noticed now, it almost seems like it [transitioning] is just something new to try. Most of the people who are young, they are not going to have surgeries because it is too expensive." He adds, "It is just like saying, well, this is what I am now, and I am going to try this [identity] on, just to see. I can't relate to that because I can't remember a time when I didn't know what I was and how I felt." Wayne was surprised to see transmen avoid testosterone because of the possibilities of developing male-pattern baldness or certain types of female cancers. "In the past, there was much more rigidity about how you were just a guy, you just suck it up. You didn't get to be concerned about being short or not having hair. If the doctor gives you too much T and it bothers you, you just suck it up kind of thing [*laughs*]." Some younger transmen similarly felt that they could not relate to this older generation, whom they saw as hung up on conforming to hegemonic stereotypes of heterosexual maleness.

These generational issues were less pronounced in Texas because there was less generational diversity; only one of the men I interviewed had transitioned prior to 2000. When I asked if anyone had ever encountered transmen who had transitioned in the 1980s or 1990s, most of my interviewees could name only two people—the same two people. The explanation was that many transmen in Texas went deep stealth because the political landscape was less hospitable to transgender people than on the coasts. Yet, while uneven geographically, the proliferation of virtual transgender communities and resources, as well as the growth in media attention, brought unprecedented possibilities for transmen and highlighted the diversity of ways transmen understood their gender identities and their personal body projects.

Contested Frames

Cultural frames about transgender people have undergone enormous shifts since the 1960s. Yet, while the biological diversity frame has gained salience in the press, older understandings have not disappeared. Some evangelical Christian organizations adopt a version of the sociocultural frame that emphasizes the authenticity of sex over gender—making strange bedfellows with some feminist theorists. Echoing Janice Raymond (1979), Jerry Leach, head of an organization that claims to cure "gender identity confusion" through psychotherapy, argues, "Rather than cutting tissue by invasive surgery and starting a new life . . . [transgender] people need to find help psychiatrically. . . . The essence of who you are in your genetics, anatomy, chromosomes, and DNA does not suddenly change by surgical amputation" (Kennedy 2008, 2). This opposition to transgenderism garnered a great deal of discussion in 2008, when Pope Benedict made an allusion to the threat of transgender people to the gender and sexual order in his annual pre-Christmas address (Israely 2008).

Biological diversity can provide a compelling justification for tolerance: gender-variant people are born this way rather than making an active choice. But this frame does not challenge deeply held beliefs about the naturalness—for most people—of the male/female binary. The persistence of violence toward transgender people illustrates the precariousness of tolerance (Bettcher 2007). The resistance of many states to including gender identity in hate crime laws further legitimizes the belief that most people do and should experience a natural connection between genitalia, gender identity, and gender expression. This binary is institutionalized in governmental practices (Currah, Juang, and Minter 2006; Lorber 2005) and carries real-life consequences for people whose appearance and documents do not line up. In the mid-2000s, employers began receiving "no-match letters" from Social Security that informed them that the reported gender of one of their employees did not match his or her legal gender. The primary purpose of these letters was to identify undocumented workers. Yet these letters have unwittingly identified stealth transgender people in the process. These no-match letters show

how the institutionalization of a male/female binary regulates the legitimate options for gender identities. Transgender men, regardless of their
personal sense of themselves as male, genderqueer, transgender, or all of
the above, must still negotiate the legally sanctioned male/female binary
in order to avoid not just societal stigma but potential consequences in
employment, housing, and finances as well.

CHAPTER TWO

Self-Made Men

Culturally Navigating "Natural" Difference

Shortly after he began living as a man, Colin went to buy a pair of glasses. When he was signing his receipt, the salesperson told him she had a new grandson named Colin. She had been a little unsure about the name and wanted to know if he struggled with misspellings and mispronunciations. "I said, 'Actually, I picked that name,' not thinking of where this line of questioning would go. She said, 'Oh, what was your old name?' Because I was caught off guard, I said, 'It was Jane.' She kind of stopped and pulled back a little bit." He immediately understood her hesitation, as this response—a routine answer for thirty years of his life—failed to meet the expectations for his appearance as a man.

This disjuncture between biography and appearance illustrates the interactional difficulties that can accompany the transition from being viewed by others as women to being viewed as men—what I call achieving social maleness. Even when transmen experience themselves as male from an early age, their parents and guardians raise them as girls, the only culturally legitimized option for people assigned female at birth. Over time, many transmen develop a female-socialized habitus—a complex and embodied matrix of "perceptions, appreciations, and action" (Bourdieu 1977, 82) imparted over a lifetime by parents, schools, and peers.[1] Female-socialized people do not always think, feel, and behave in normatively feminine ways; however, they understand the consequences of rejecting the idealized expectations of femininity—

consequences that vary across other social locations, such as age, race, and class. Yet, while this habitus encompasses interactional flexibility in a wide range of contexts, it does not prepare transmen for navigating the social world as men.

Transmen start their transitions into social maleness with different understandings of their personal gender identity: it is innate, it is a diverse spectrum, it is a transformable pathway. What united the men I interviewed was a desire *not* to be socially gendered as female in everyday interactions. Hormone therapy, surgeries, and clothing can aid in this process. But natural differences schemas that position men and women as polar opposites bring expectations about gender-specific interests, knowledge, and abilities for men that are very different from the expectations for women. For new men, such as Colin, these expectations come to the forefront in interactions with people who do not know about their physical transitions. The interactional negotiations involved in achieving social maleness illuminate the cultural processes that underlie natural differences schemas as well as the hierarchical power dynamics behind those seemingly innocuous notions of difference (R. Connell 1987; Schippers 2007).

From F to M: The Attainment of Legal Maleness

Masculinity and femininity—the practices, interests, qualities, and abilities culturally associated with men and women, respectively—are commonly thought to derive from differences in chromosomes, hormones, and reproductive roles (R. Connell 1995; Laqueur 1990). Under this logic, people who have XY chromosomes, penises, and the ability to produce sperm are classified as men. Yet, in everyday interactions, chromosomes and genitalia are not visible. Instead, in most social interactions, the presence or absence of visual markers coded as male, such as facial hair, flat chests, and low voices, are used to classify people into the category of man or woman (Dozier 2005; Kessler and McKenna 1978)—a cultural rather than biological practice. Illustrating the importance of these appearance cues in determining social maleness, almost 95 percent of the men I interviewed were taking testosterone (T) or planned to take it in the near future because of its strong masculinizing effects. With T, voices typically lower, facial hair develops, and, depending on genetics, hair loss may start—though these changes can take several months to a year. These changes make transmen's personal sense of maleness, masculinity, and/or "not femaleness" visible to others.[2] That only five of the fifty-four men I interviewed had not undergone or made immediate plans to undergo chest, or "top," surgery also shows how a flat chest is an integral part of crafting social maleness. Fewer transmen opted for hysterectomies (less than 30 percent) and genital surgery (less than 10 percent), more invasive and expensive surgeries that impact parts of the body normally hidden under clothing. The visible effects of testosterone and chest surgery operate as "cultural genitalia" (Kessler and McKenna 1978), as, in most social interactions, transmen are seen as men regardless of whether they have a penis. Facial hair, in other words, allows them to "[do] sex in a gendered world" (Dozier 2005, 297).

Undergoing these body modifications can bring transmen's personal and social gender identities closer together but can also create a conflict with the legal gender indicated on their government documents. The procedure for changing legal gender varies by state. Texas and California require a letter from a medical professional stating that a transman has undergone a surgical "sex change." Showing how commonsense beliefs that gender identity must align with genitalia are institutionalized, *sex change* in this context is synonymous with genital surgery. Yet, as an increasing number of medical professionals recognize that many transmen do not have genital surgery, some transmen are able to get these letters after a hysterectomy or, in some cases, chest surgery. With this letter, transmen can change their gender on their driver's licenses and Social Security cards. Some states will issue new birth certificates that read "Male." Other states merely change the document to read "Female Amended to Male" or put a line through "Female" and type "Male" next to it.

These differences in laws mean that gender identity varies by state (Greenberg and Herald 2005). Transmen may be male in Texas (and thus legally able to be heterosexually married) but still female in Indiana. And an officially changed legal gender can always be trumped by judges' deeply held beliefs about the invariance of biological sex, as the case of Christie Lee Littleton illustrates. Littleton underwent genital surgery at a Texas state facility in the 1980s, legally changed her gender marker from M to F, and married a cisgender man. When he died due to hospital malpractice, she sued for wrongful death. The state of Texas dismissed her case, ruling she was male and therefore not legally married. The judge wrote in defense of his decision, "At the time of birth, Christie was male, both anatomically and genetically. . . . There are some things we cannot will into being. They just are" (*Littleton v. Prange* 1999, 9). The *Littleton* case is not unique. Transgender people's changed legal gender, physical appearance, genitalia, and social gender have been dismissed in favor of chromosomes in order to deny rights to an estate of a dead spouse (*Estate of Gardiner* 2002) and to deny custody of children (*Kantaras v. Kantaras* 2004), to name just a few cases.

Yet, while chromosomes may have sovereignty in court rulings, the actual process of changing gender on government documents is influenced by appearance—Suzanne Kessler and Wendy McKenna's (1978) "cultural genitalia." The belief that appearances are a stand-in for biological sex means that many people do not anticipate that someone who has a beard may not have a penis. When Sam moved to California, he applied for a new license. He never mentioned that his old license carried an "F." "You go into the DMV looking [like a man] and they are not gonna be, like, 'Well, did you used to be a woman?' Or, 'What does your birth certificate say?' They are going to go, 'Okay, male.' Which is what they did." Aaron had a similar experience. He went to the DMV to get a name change. While changing his name, the clerk noticed the "F." As Aaron had a significant beard, she assumed it was a mistake, apologized, and wanted to immediately process his gender change. Thomas had only recently changed his driver's license to "M," though he had transitioned in the 1990s: "I've been pulled over and the cops just didn't see it [the "F"]. But I also had a beard down to my belly. And so it is hard to get past those cues. That little 'F' in the box miraculously became an 'M.' The fix-it ticket I got said 'M.'" That transmen can be socially gendered as men—even by gatekeepers of legal gender—once they have facial hair suggests that the institutionalization of a male/female binary relies more on the logic of culture than on the science of chromosomes.

From Women to Men: The Achievement of Social Maleness

Physical and legal changes are only one part of the process of achieving social maleness. Transmen also must negotiate behavioral expectations for men—a negotiation that many transmen referred to as "passing." In our interviews, most transmen described worrying a great deal at the onset of their physical transitions about whether they were being read as

male in social interactions. Being able to interact as men with strangers, casual acquaintances, and, for stealth transmen, coworkers who do
not know about their physical transitions was taken as supportive evidence that they successfully passed physically and behaviorally. Yet,
while many transmen recounted high levels of passing-related anxieties
when they began their physical transitions, these concerns were time-
bounded. Once transmen gained embodied ease with being men in the
world, their anxieties about passing faded.

In an attempt to capture the transformation from passing to achieving
social maleness, I asked in my first few interviews, "How did you learn to
act like a man?" Anticipating long, nuanced responses, I was surprised
to get dismissive answers. Peter says, "I was always living the same way
I am now, but my appearance changed so it changed how people saw
me." Echoing this, Cole says, "I just have always kind of done it [act like
a man]." For Winston, the only difference was that looking like a man
gave more legitimacy to what he viewed as his innately male behaviors.
"For me, living as a female was constant self-editing. Don't walk like
that, don't talk like that, don't sit like that. Now, as a guy, I sit any damn
way I want to." For Devin, once he physically passed as a man, people
saw his actions as "manly": "Other people, society, and the world help
me be [a man]. It's really an interaction."

I quickly realized that asking transmen how they had learned to "act
like men" fails to capture the complexity of achieving social maleness—
an interactional, not individual, process. Testosterone gives transmen
the markers of a male appearance, but other people afford them social
maleness. In social interactions with people who do not know about their
physical transitions, transmen navigate systems of cultural meanings and
expectations about natural differences between men and women and adjust to a new position in the hierarchical relations of masculinities and
femininities. Negotiating these expectations as female-socialized men,
transmen can develop a gender "double consciousness" (Du Bois 1903).[3]
They simultaneously inhabit social space as men and maintain, to varying degrees, an internal repertoire of female-socialized interactional
strategies. This double consciousness can generate culture shock as they
struggle to synthesize two identities—a female history and a male social identity—that natural differences schemas position as opposing.
To gain gender competency, transmen study the idealized qualities that
make up a hegemonic understanding of masculinity. As their ease with
embodying social maleness increases, however, they can develop gender

literacy that allows for flexible responses to normative expectations of manhood.

Gender Culture Shock

Once transmen look like men, people evaluate their actions and behaviors by a male standard. This change can create a feeling of culture shock, as transmen struggle to understand how people are making new sense of once-familiar behaviors. In some cases, they get social approval for actions they were stigmatized for performing as women. Crispin gives one such example:

> [Now that I'm a man], stewardesses ask me to lift their bags for them. Girls drop things in front of me, and I'm like, "Oh, I'll get that for you." And . . . it is really amazing. All those things I desired. Before, I used to do them [as a female] anyway, but I always felt like I was making the person uncomfortable. . . . I used to love to open doors for women. . . . I would put my coat on the ground and step on water, the whole thing, but they thought, "This is weird. You are a girl." Now it feels comfortable.

As a chivalrous woman, Crispin disrupted gender relations that support heterosexual dominance. As a man, he is now embodying hegemonic masculinity, the idealized qualities and social practices defined as manly that reproduce and maintain a hierarchical and complementary relationship to femininity (R. Connell 1995; Kimmel 2004). Though the behavior has not changed, the recipients of his chivalry feel more comfortable because his actions are now read as gender-appropriate and heterosexual.

Once-comfortable behaviors can also carry negative new meanings. At a work-related conference, Winston, a stealth transman, remarked to a coworker that one of the conference attendees looked "like a dyke" and suggested they should recruit her for some LGBT programs they were designing. "She said, 'You really need to think about how you talk about people.' And I thought, 'Oh, man, she is right!' I mean she is sitting here looking at a middle-aged white man." A former lesbian, he adds, "Sometimes I tell stories about 'these dykes I used to know.' And that word was not negative to us [dykes] back then. It was like how some black people call themselves the 'N' word. But, as a [heterosexual] man, I have to realize I don't have those language privileges." This comment might not raise eyebrows in some settings, as hegemonic masculinity by definition devalues "pariah femininities" (Schippers 2007) such as lesbianism. Yet, in professional work settings that offer workplace protections to gay and lesbian employees, his comment is censured as inappropriate. Winston's comfort with this terminology, a holdover from a lesbian past, cannot be adapted for a heterosexual man without the accompanying assumption of intolerance for homosexuality—a disconcerting label for a former lesbian to face.

Bodies read as male also carry a different relationship to privacy and sexual intimacy than bodies read as female. Nicky stopped hugging women at work because this behavior from a man could be interpreted as predatory or degrading. Devin notes, "The women at work [who don't know about my transition], they slap me on the chest and stuff like that. They are in their fifties, and they just like to flirt with me a little bit. Like '[You are] such a nice young man.' It is still really freaky to me. [I have to tell myself,] 'You are not supposed to flinch!'" For a woman, having a coworker—man or woman—touch her chest is a violation, as this part of the female body is coded as sexual and private. In most workplaces, this action could be classified as sexual harassment or physical violence. Yet, for a man, this kind of touch can be a casual interaction, like a woman putting her hand on a man's shoulder, because his chest is coded as nonsexual. Other transmen had to adjust to arm punches from heterosexual men who know them as just one of the guys, as men rarely punch women in this jocular way. Devin's flinching reaction demonstrates the difficulty of adjusting to male expectations for bodily contact.

When they first start living as men, many transmen worried when men, seeing them as any other cisgender man, said to them, "Well, you know how men are. . . ." This statement highlights natural differences schemas. Men as a group are thought to share certain interests, experiences, and bodies of knowledge that women would never want or be able to understand—interests somehow embedded on the Y chromosome. Roger says that once he physically passed as a man, "It was like, 'Oh, you are male, you know cars.' No! My father was a mechanic, and I didn't learn anything by osmosis." Gabriel, one of only two men in his workplace, says, "When the computer breaks, everyone comes to me to fix it, and I don't know anything about this." Julian says, "I did a lot of [male] things naturally, but the social interactions and stuff, that is definitely a learning experience." Growing up, Scott learned a lot of "man stuff" from his father. However, he soon realized this was only a small part of what it meant to be a man. "It is just the mores and the subtle body language. I study men all the time. And you know, it's funny, I used to study women so I could be more like one."

A male-socialized habitus—what men are referencing in the statement about "how men are"—is fluid, embodied, and specific to age, race, class, and sexual identity. It is also flexible enough to provide appropriate behavior for a range of contexts and situations. This flexibility takes strategic practice. For cisgender men, this practice occurs in childhood. Little girls, however, are barred from participating in all-boy activities of childhood during which norms and expectations of maleness are transmitted (Messner 1992, 2000). The gender segregation of locker rooms and bathrooms precludes women's gaining firsthand experience with how men interact with one another in these locations. Transmen, then, face the task of learning how to enact social maleness while already being seen by others as men. This learning curve is heightened for transmen who transition later in life. Joseph, who transitioned in his forties, recounts, "There was nobody to teach me the ropes . . . no older guy to bring me up to speed. There was a big gap in my knowledge because I was an older man, just a different level of expectation." Because he was stealth at work, men his own age expected him to have shared biographic experiences. Younger men looked to him for advice, advice he was seeking from others. Wayne, who transitioned in his late teens, had a different experience: "At first, it was, like, how the heck am I going to learn [how to be a man]? In a number of settings, there were things that I just didn't know about." He soon realized he was at the age at which he was expected to be getting advice about what it meant to be a man (rather than a boy). "It was pretty age-appropriate stuff [that I didn't know]."

All-male spaces, such as the public men's restroom, present a particular challenge for new men. The segregation of public restrooms is a cultural strategy to reaffirm deeply held beliefs about men and women's natural differences in a gender-integrated society (Goffman 1977). Expectations for men's and women's bathroom culture are shaped by gendered assumptions. For women, feminine modesty demands a room divided into small, private stalls. Men's restrooms, in contrast, typically have one or two stalls and then a wall of urinals where men urinate in direct view of one another. These interactions are governed by heteronormativity—this open display of genitalia is acceptable only because men are not supposed to want to look at one other. Coming to the men's restroom with years of practice in the women's restroom can be a challenge. Describing his first experience, Brian says, "This man just walked up and pulled

his dick out, and walked forward [to the urinal]. I was so surprised! Especially being a lesbian, coming from that kind of experience! The look
on my face probably was so funny!"

Transmen typically retain vivid memories of the first time they used
a men's restroom. Transmen who had just begun T, such as Tex and
Anthony, worried about men challenging their right to be there. This
fear of surveillance came not just from anxieties about their appearance but also from an awareness of the high level of surveillance that
occurs in women's restrooms. As women are socialized to be vigilant
about sexual predators, they keep a sharp eye on who is entering or leaving the bathroom. People perceived as posing a threat to this gender-
segregated space are confronted about their right to be present. Many
transmen described being frequent targets of gender policing in the
women's bathroom prior to their transitions, a common experience for
masculine women (Devor 1989; Halberstam 1998a). Most respondents
told at least one story involving women or security guards challenging
their right to use the women's restrooms. Colin's story is typical. "A
couple of women approached me and said, 'Why are you in here? You
shouldn't be in here.' I said, 'Actually, [I am a woman].' My voice was
a lot higher, and I figured that would do it. They're like 'No, no, you
shouldn't be in here.'" Yet, while these experiences are irritating, transmen know what to expect from women because they have used women's
restrooms for typically twenty to thirty years. Over time, they develop
strategies for dealing with these situations, such as making their voices
higher when they interact with women, hurrying into the privacy of the
stall, or avoiding public restrooms as much as possible. For the men's
bathroom, however, they struggle with not knowing what to expect
if men challenge their right to be there. When Simon was unsure if he
physically passed as male, he continued to use the women's restroom. He
felt safer braving reactions he was accustomed to than facing unknown
reactions from men.

Physically passing as men is a big concern for many transmen when
they begin taking hormones. They measure success by what I call the
"sir" test—an informal count of the percentage of time clerks and wait-
people refer to them as "sir" at first sighting. The more "sirs" they get,
the more confident they are in their appearance. Until they are sir-ed
100 percent of the time, transmen can feel hypervigilant about their
personal safety. With a gendered appearance that newly transitioning
transmen describe as "awkward" or "in-between," they can be targets of

ridicule and/or violence in a society that accepts only male or female—as Eric found out when a car full of teenagers yelled at him, "Are you a boy or a girl?" While not all transmen I interviewed personally identified as male or as men, most of them preferred being seen by strangers as male to make their everyday interactions safer.

Transmen's feelings of vigilance about personal safety are also part of being socialized as females. Public spaces belong to men at night (MacRobbie 1991). Little girls are taught that dangers lurk in the dark in the form of rapists and muggers (Lees 1993). As the negative coverage of rape trials clearly shows, women are held responsible for their own victimization because they should have known better than to go out at night alone (MacKinnon 1987). Men, however, are allowed to take up public space, even at night (Duneier 1999; Vance 1995)—as Caleb learned once he developed confidence that he successfully passed as a man. When he was on his way out with a group of men, his mom reminded him to "be careful, lock your car doors, and don't talk to anyone." "I was like, 'Mom, we're a bunch of guys. It's not really gonna make that much difference. Nobody's gonna bother us.' It's so nice not to be freaked out. To have that kind of security." Showing a trade-off, however, Christopher described his sadness that women now perceive him—just another guy—as a potential sexual predator when he encounters them alone on the street at night. This freedom could be further complicated by the new risk of interactions between men turning violent. When Jake began T, he was living in a predominantly Latino neighborhood in California. Given his shaved head and the youthful appearance that came from the development of facial "peach fuzz" (an outcome of starting T), teenagers saw him as another young Latino. They yelled at him in Spanish and made gang signs, actions he was unprepared to negotiate as a white, thirty-something professional.

Rather than violence, physically passing as men could bring a new camaraderie with other men, a reaction some transmen described as being welcomed into the "men's club." While being one of the guys could be exciting, some transmen were uncomfortable with the relationality this change signified: men see themselves as not just different from women but better than women. As David notes:

An older man perceiving you as a younger man is just so happy to be in your presence. It is just bizarre. They are not like that to women. There is this distance, because there is some kind of sexual interaction they are facing—or

some kind of distance because they think you are a dyke or a masculine female. . . . But if they think you are a young guy, they are just so happy to be in
your presence. It just bothers me that there is just such a big difference based
on just subtle appearance issues.

Luis felt that salesmen were much faster to acquiesce to his demands
once he physically passed as a man. When Preston and Anton took their
cars in for minor tune-ups, mechanics did not try to sell them extra,
costly services—a markedly different experience from taking their cars
in as women. Describing his experience at the auto shop, Julian says,
"Male privilege is alive and well! There was this woman there. She's buying new tires, and I could overhear her interaction. I started talking to
the same guy about tires. And to me, he was, like, 'Yeah, man, you can
get those tires here, and I'll give you my employee discount.' And I'm
like, What the hell is this?" Joseph, like Julian, added that being treated
like a man by other men made him much more deeply aware of gender
oppression than he had ever been living as a woman. While Joseph felt
he was not always treated fairly as a woman, particularly working as a
professional in the 1980s, he never realized to what extent men gave one
another informal advantages over women until he personally received
such treatment.

Yet not all embodiments of maleness bring the same reactions from
men. If hegemonic masculinity is defined as different from and better
than femininity—a definition that is necessary to maintain hierarchical
heterosexual gender relations (R. Connell 1995; Schippers 2007)—then
men who come across as feminine in their behavior and demeanor can
be devalued. Some new transmen did not want to shed what they described as female-socialized habits, such as talking with their hands or
being physically demonstrative. Yet they realized these mannerisms in
a man were stereotyped as gay. While more than half of the transmen
I interviewed had lived as lesbians at some point in their lives and reported little harassment or violence, they worried that being seen as a
gay man—regardless of whether they identified this way—would bring
negative reactions. Elliott says, "I did the lesbian thing and was fine. I
didn't experience a lot of homophobia. But this [being a gay man] is just
an unknown." These reactions were not unwarranted. Paul notes, "I was
walking on the beach with my brother, and these boys walked by and
we heard one say, 'Are those queers?' And this is so interesting because
[in over thirty years,] no one ever yelled at me, 'Is that a lesbian?'" In a

more extreme case, Casey was the target of antigay violence while riding his bike in Texas with another man. Xavier, who had stopped T for a few months, remarked that he felt safer in Texas being seen as a masculine woman than as a feminine man. "I'm worried about people kicking my ass because I look like a Nellie fag. I actually feel less vulnerable looking female. I feel like most guys in Texas don't hit girls."

The experiences of transmen of color further show the hierarchical relationality between embodiments of maleness. Transmen of color can experience a loss of freedom as men. Jack, a Latino, and Trey, a black man, both realized they physically passed as men when women started clutching their purses tightly when they walked by. Trey notes, "On one hand, I was like, 'Oh, I am passing!' and then I was like, 'Oh, but you think I am dangerous.'" Keith, a black man, says, "It is interesting now to see it from both sides. I know why the black man is angry! I do. He doesn't start off that way. . . . It is just so weird to get that vibe from people. I just manifest . . . their fears, everything they fear. I am every black man who has been accused of something." He encountered frequent racist treatment, such as being pulled over by white police officers for driving in the "wrong" (that is, wealthy and white) neighborhoods and being followed in stores—all common experiences for black men in the United States (Bolton and Feagin 2004).

Trey faced a similar experience in Texas. Walking a friend's dog in a predominantly white, affluent neighborhood at night, he was stopped by neighborhood patrols and police officers three times in a span of twenty minutes. Shocked at this treatment, he asked his older brother how he dealt with it. His brother was surprised that Trey didn't realize "how it was" and told him that soon he would become accustomed to such treatment. Socialized as black girls, Trey and Keith did not have the same embodied strategies as cisgender black men for navigating this treatment. While schools and families socialize black boys into accepting and adjusting to stereotypes of black, masculine criminality (Ferguson 2000; Oliver 2003), black girls' socialization often focuses on regulating their sexuality and maintaining their self-respect (Kaplan 1997; Orenstein 1994). Becoming a black man means finding interactional strategies that address the expectations of black male criminality.

While transmen of color can experience a heightened sense of visibility, white transmen can start to feel invisible. Eli, who lived as a self-described masculine woman until he transitioned in his early twenties, adopted a confrontational attitude toward people who questioned his

gender identity. "It was like all of a sudden [after I passed], I was completely invisible. Which is what I wanted all my life. It's good, but it took
a while to get used to. When I'd walk around, I'd be like, [*snarl*] 'What
are you looking at?' and now it's like, 'Oh, you're looking at someone
else.'" Henry felt that he had to readjust his strategies for being assertive.
"I have always prided myself on being a strong woman and being outspoken and willing to take up space. In the same way, as a transperson, I
want to take up some space. I do feel like a guy, but I don't feel like a
'typical guy.' I hold a lot of female socialization." Yet, once he physically
passed as a man, his strategies for being assertive as a woman no longer
worked. "What people see is a white guy who is upper-middle-class at
this point. It is really a process. I am having to realize how people react
to me [when I am assertive]. I am stepping on their toes. And they are
perceiving it to be based on gender and ethnicity. And that makes me really sad." He adds, "All my life I have fought to take a step forward, and
now I have to step back."

Achieving social maleness also brings a change in everyday interactions with women. Seeing them as any other cisgender man, women often exclude transmen from their interactions on the basis that they "just
cannot understand"—the Mars/Venus distinction that characterizes natural differences schemas. This social distance from women was a relief
to transmen who had fought their whole lives not to be treated like one
of the girls. Elliott, in contrast, felt sad, noting, "I grew up surrounded by
women. And now to have them be leery of me, that takes some getting
used to." Brian, too, felt sad about this exclusion: "I have tried before to
get into conversations [as a man] where women are talking and . . . just
been shut down. Not being allowed to participate because 'I wouldn't
understand.'" While transmen's gender double consciousness may make
them feel more connected to women on a political level because they
suddenly see inequality so clearly, women assume that, as men, they are
unable to share "female" experiences and interests. This exclusion from
women's spaces highlights that natural differences schemas—schemas
that contribute to gender inequality—exist in part because women, not
just men, do interactional work to maintain them.

Gender Competency

Socially crossing the male/female binary puts transmen into the clas-
sification of unsettled lives, "periods of social transformation in which

established cultural ends are jettisoned" (Swidler 1986, 278). Similar to other major identity transformations—coming out as gay or lesbian (Stein 1997), becoming an ex-nun (Ebaugh 1988), publicly acknowledging positive HIV status (Sandstrom 1990)—transmen struggle with synthesizing an old social identity (woman) with a new social identity (man). As they learn at the onset, some behaviors can be carried over into social manhood while others no longer work. To adjust to the social expectations of maleness, transmen draw in a very conscious way on their "cultural toolkit" (Swidler 1986) of symbols, stories, and worldviews. Like anthropologists in a foreign country, transmen amass a vast amount of commonsense knowledge about the idealized qualities and behaviors of men. Armed with these guidelines, they develop gender competency in social maleness that eases the culture shock they can experience as female-socialized men.

The workplace can serve as a learning ground for gender competency. Scott describes how he got firsthand experience in how men act with other men when he went stealth in a blue-collar job: "The camaraderie at a male-oriented job. It's so funny. You're always like, 'Oh, thanks, man,' or 'Hey, dude.' And you make a fist and punch the other guy's fist or something like that [laughs]." Elliott, who openly transitioned in his retail job in his early twenties, experienced his interactions with men in a similar way. "[I got to learn] the way they greet one another. The little handshakes, all that kind of stuff. To get to participate in that stuff, to be in the inner circle of guys, it's fun." Not all transmen saw this learning curve as amusing, however. Crispin, who went stealth in his late forties in a blue-collar job, expressed much more anxiety about picking up these interaction nuances at work than transmen who transitioned in their late teens and twenties. "All my confidence is not quite there yet. If I was in college, I wouldn't care so much. But I am in a man's world. A good ol' boys' world."

Transgender community groups also serve as socialization agents. Louis Sullivan, the founder of FTM International, published the first handbook for transmen in the 1980s. The book gave tips for where to buy smaller men's clothes, how to wear men's clothes appropriately, how to shave (Garber 1997). The resources grew exponentially in the 2000s. During my fieldwork in California, one of the social groups for transmen in the area hosted a weekend camping trip. The trip included a series of instructional seminars designed to teach participants the "men basics": how to change a tire on a car, check the oil, tie a tie, pitch a tent, smoke a cigar. Most of the participants in the courses were "newbies," while the instructors were older generations of transmen. The "Tranny Boi Scouts" trip, as it was jokingly referred to, was a lighthearted event. But it also transmitted cultural knowledge about maleness. Support groups served similar functions, as older transmen give advice about navigating the world as men. For transmen who are not part of a local community, such as Nathan, social etiquette for situations such as the men's bathroom are available on transgender blogs and informational sites.

Adhering to rigid bathroom rules can ease the initial shock of using the men's restroom. Describing the rules he learned, Elliott says, "No one looks at each other. They walk in with their eyes on the floor and do their business and leave." Following these rules allowed transmen to feel that they were producing for other bathroom inhabitants the sense that "nothing out of the ordinary" was occurring—the baseline for a successful social interaction (Goffman 1963a). Urinals, however, present a unique challenge. Showing the limits of cultural genitalia, many transmen do not have the visible marker of belonging at the urinal: the penis. There are a variety of devices that enable transmen to urinate standing up. Negotiating these devices, however, can be awkward. Recognizing that fumbling with a device at a urinal could suspend the normal expectation that men do not look at one another in the restroom, many transmen opt for the privacy of the stall. This option, though, can create anxiety for transmen who believe that men use stalls only for defecation.

The longer transmen use the men's room, the more exceptions they see to these rigid rules. They see that some men prefer stalls, a realization that can be a great comfort. They also learn that rigid bathroom rules discount contextual variation. As Kelly notes, "Bathrooms in gay clubs are totally different! No doors on the stalls, more eye contact going on." Brian, who transitioned over fifteen years ago, laughs at how he clung to the rules of bathroom behavior at the beginning of his transition. He quickly learned that bathroom behavior was flexible, as men do talk in the bathroom in some workplace settings where they interact with the same men every day. Elliott, too, learned the need for flexibility: "I taught myself guys don't talk in the bathroom. And then one of my coworkers will come in and be like, 'Hey, dude, what's up?' And it's like, 'Oh God, I have to talk now.' I just have to try to be fluid with whatever comes up."

Mastering social maleness outside of the bathroom also seems at first to require following a set of rules. Henry notes, "I don't tend to do the gentlemanly things. Like I don't think to hold the door open or let the women go into the elevator first. And I am really expected to do it now [as a man]. But yet I was so against that when I was a woman. I really struggle with how much of that behavior to take on." Reflecting on his experience, Douglas says, "I felt a lot more pressure to conform [to masculine norms] at the beginning. Men don't talk about things being cute. You don't gesture with your hands." This pressure transmen describe toward conformity may seem, at first reading, to support the sociocultural frame of transsexuality—that transmen try to embody normative masculinity. However, to me, this initial conformity suggests more about the need to learn the potential penalties for failing to meet new social expectations, an outcome of an unsettled life, than about any investment in idealized masculinity. New transmen can opt to protect themselves by "butching it up" in some social interactions—a rational strategy in a society in which transgender people have no federal protections against violence and discrimination—until they learn the potential consequences of being perceived as transgender, feminine, and/or gay men.

Other men can be models for how to negotiate the expectations of maleness in flexible ways. Julian looked to his stepfather to find strategies for bypassing the sexism he felt expected to express as a heterosexual man. "He is just gentle in a lot of ways. I think that's a good way to be with people. It doesn't seem to matter what [someone's] gender is, he treats them the same way." David looked to an ex-boyfriend. "I learned a lot from him about just being yourself and not having to deal with the way that people expect you to act. He never felt that he had to talk about football. . . . He just modeled that some men don't care that they are a miserable failure at traditional male things." Douglas saw some of his gay friends as a model for crafting a particular kind of gay masculinity: "Like my friend Tim says, 'The Super Bowl? That's the game with the pointy ball?' I like fags. I like how they are. I don't have to be a stereotype of a guy." These role models also can be public figures. Joseph, who transitioned in the 1980s, a time period he describes as valuing chauvinism in men, was moved by Rosey Grier, a star football player, "coming out" as a man who did crochet. These role models challenge the rigidity of the so-called man rules by showing variation and flexibility.

Gender Literacy

Henry, who had been living as a man for almost eight years at the time of our interview, wished that he had kept a journal about his transition experience. "It is amazing how socialization works! I barely notice it [gender differences] now. But when I first started transitioning, I saw it all the time. I have just gotten so used to it. And it really was so blatant to me early on." Wayne, who has lived longer as a man than he did as a woman, says, "I even forget that I had chest surgery. It is like if you had an operation as a child or something. No one really talks about it, and you just forget." Brad, who transitioned eight years prior to our interview, adds, "When you first transition, you think about it a lot. . . . Maybe for like the first two years, you think about it every day. How is it different living as a man? And then it is not an issue anymore." Using me as an example, he added, "Like you identify as a woman. How often do you think, 'I am a woman.' You just are one." What these men are describing is the development of literacy in social maleness. As they find flexible strategies for negotiating social interactions as heterosexual men, men of color, gay or queer men, and/or transgender men, transmen find different ways to socially embody their personal gender identities.

The public men's restroom, once a major source of anxiety, shows this gender literacy most clearly. Now a few years into living as a man, Kelly says, "Men don't pay attention in the bathroom. Everyone told me that at the beginning, and I was like, 'No, that is not true.' But now, I have no issues. I walk in, walk out, no one looks. No one makes eye contact." Robert has grown comfortable using a urinary device at urinals in public restrooms: "Men are not going to look down at my crotch because this society is homophobic." Brian says about newly transitioning transmen, "They freak out and worry about feet pointing in the wrong direction. They just kill themselves with anxiety over issues that really no one is paying attention to and no one gives a damn." Yet this realization can come only with experience. New transmen can hear that men don't pay attention, but they cannot believe it until they have experienced it themselves over and over again—the kind of practice necessary for embodying social maleness.

Literacy also brings the development of cultural tools for potential challenges to bathroom behavior. Homophobia is a powerful social control mechanism, particularly in intimate, all-male spaces such as the bathroom or locker room (R. Connell 1995; Messner 1992; Pascoe 2007).

For Jason, homophobia was a cultural tool he could use to defend possible challenges to his use of the stall: "Guys are very prideful. They don't want to be gay. It is taboo. So they are not going to be looking at your penis. If you go in the stall all the time, maybe you just don't want anyone looking at your penis." Johnny goes further, saying he would call someone "gay" if they questioned him or looked at him too long in the bathroom. "It would shut him up really quickly because no guy wants to be questioned about their sexuality, especially in the males' restroom." Homophobia also justifies a refusal to urinate in front of other men outdoors or discomfort with being naked in men's locker rooms—all situations that can be challenging to navigate for transmen who do not have genital surgery. Being seen as men also brings more right to privacy. Transmen who have had chest surgery have scars that run the length of their chests. When I interviewed Sam, I met him at his gym, where he was known only as a man. I asked if any of the men, people who see him without a shirt on a daily basis, ever asked about his scars. He said that it happened on occasion, but he just gave a vague reply that it was from a surgery he had as a kid. When men asked Peter about his chest scars, he said they were intentional scarification—a subcultural form of body marking. He notes, "They thought it was cool and hard-core." These responses fit with idealized masculinity: stoically dismissing pain.

While transmen talk about their potential reactions to challenges, however, they were rarely put in such situations. Riley had been told to leave a men's restroom when he first started T and looked "in-between" in his gender presentation. With that exception, none of the men I interviewed had ever been questioned about their right to use public men's restrooms. This point emphasizes the interactional safety that physically passing provides—and illustrates the potential for harassment and discrimination that transgender or genderqueer people who cannot or who choose not to physically pass as men or women can face. Referring to the effects of testosterone, Roger says, "After what I call this awkward phase [in appearance], you really have to make an effort to tell people you are trans[gender]." Jake says that now when he comes out to people as transgender, people assume he is planning on becoming a woman. Because most people expect that biological sex differences are written on the body, they overlook any visible female cues when facial hair is evident. During our interview, Stephen and I took a break to get some coffee. He had not had chest surgery at that time and was not wearing a binder—a tight, flexible top that flattens breasts. Though he had visible breasts, everyone in the store called him "sir" because he had a goa-tee. Laughing about how concerned he used to be about passing, Brian notes, "With a beard and balding, no one is going to say, 'Oh, did that used to be a girl?'"

Literacy brings a lessening of accountability to idealized masculinity. Transmen who had lived as men for several years often raised and then dismissed stereotypical notions of how men should act. Trevor, a vocal feminist, noted that he took the feminist idea that there are many valid ways to be a woman into his transition—an inspiration for him to shape his own ideas of how to do masculinity. Almost ten years past his initial transition, Brad notes, "I used to think I was supposed to act a certain way [to be a man]. And I would try to act like that. I would feel like I am going to draw attention to myself if I don't act macho. But I am over that now." Winston says, "I didn't go through everything I went through just to be full of crap. I said I wasn't going to be afraid of my feminine side [as a man]." Johnny, who identifies as heterosexual, notes, "The femi-nine traits I do have add to my personality as a man." Transmen also re-alized that no man actually embodies idealized masculinity. Roger says, "Some guys know sports, and some guys don't. It doesn't matter." When people ask him if he knows about cars, he replies, "Yeah, I know you join the Auto Club." Wayne, too, rejects many of these expectations—a change from when he first transitioned in the 1980s. "My wife and I had to have our car fixed. This mechanic, he didn't want to talk to my wife. He wanted to talk to me. Right off the bat, women are perceived as having less information about car repair. And my wife is much more into that kind of stuff. Nowadays, I am much more willing to say I don't know and I don't care about that stuff." These discussions illustrate the achievement of gender literacy—being able to understand the qualities that make up idealized masculinity and, at the same time, understand that no one embodies these qualities in all contexts.

As transmen gain experience negotiating the world as men, they be-gin to see many different ways to embody their personal understandings of gender. Some transmen are comfortable with being what they describe as a "man's man." Others, such as Preston, maintain a commitment to being vocal feminists. Douglas and Trevor cultivated gay identities that rejected many expectations of heterosexual masculinity. Ethan high-lighted his female-socialized past as a point of pride. "For me person-ally, if I could go back and change it, I would not have wanted to be born male. I appreciate and value my trans identity. It is nothing I intend to hide. In conversations, I'm like, 'Hi, I'm Ethan, I'm trans!'" Other transmen, such as Roger and Wayne, were most comfortable being stealth, as this strategy gave them the best alignment between personal and social gender identities.

Transmen of color describe less freedom of choice in shaping their masculine identities, as they felt boxed into racialized and gendered systems of meaning in everyday interactions. For Keith, achieving black social maleness meant losing freedoms he had as a black woman. Making this point in our interview at a ritzy, predominantly white coffee shop in California, he said, "I could stand up right here and yell. And it would be 911! But if as a female I stood up here and yelled and screamed, I'm okay. As a man, if I get mad, it is like, 'Oh no, crazy black man in there!'" He felt that he had no choice but to adopt a strong, silent persona—worlds away from his self-described "loud black woman" behavior—to protect himself. Ken identified as mixed-race, part Asian and part white. "I get white male privilege for the most part. Like older white males will call me sir or young man." To distance himself from this white privilege, he legally changed his surname and first name to be unequivocally Asian. While this change connected him to his Asian heritage, he, like Christopher, found that Asian men were stereotyped as weak and unassertive (Fung 2004)—the antithesis of idealized masculinity.

For some transmen, being socially male for many years relegated "transgender" to a background identity. Trevor, who had been out for many years as a transman, noted that recently, "I have been much more in the space of, I just want to be a dude [rather than out as transgender]. . . . And it is interesting because I heard [older trans] guys talk about being at that stage, and I couldn't imagine it. And now here I am!" In contrast, Chris began to adopt a transman identity after being stealth for many years. Similar to homosexuality (Brekhus 2003), transgender may be a master status, a background part of life, or an identity that has more salience in specific contexts, such as transgender events. New identities can take on new importance with changing life experience. Douglas notes, "Having settled some of my gender demons, other things have emerged that now have more salience for me." Sexual identity, for example, may become more of a focus for transmen after they achieve social maleness. Clark always thought of himself as a gay man born in a female body. However, seven of the men I interviewed went from dating women to dating men—a big shock for people who had once identified as lesbians or heterosexual women. Brad notes, "All my life I was never attracted to men. Never, never, never, never! And then a few years ago, [I was]. It was like a whole nother world! I think that is more interesting to me than the trans stuff."

Different but Equal?

Transmen have diverse understandings of their personal gender, even when they share the desire not to be socially gendered as female. While not all transmen in this study conceive of themselves as male or as men, they understand that they are located within a culture that recognizes only two gender categories as legitimate. In some contexts, transmen who seek to blur this binary may feel a great deal of validation. However, in everyday interactions with acquaintances and strangers, they may feel more comfortable being read as men—particularly when they live in states where gender identity and expression are not covered by hate crimes legislation. Achieving social maleness requires a change in physical appearance and legal gender. Transmen also work to synthesize, to varying degrees, female socialization and male social identities—two identities that natural differences schemas position as innately opposing. While this social maleness may feel precarious at first, it can become embodied over time. Transmen retool their cultural toolkits, aligning their social and personal identities in ways that allow them to flexibly negotiate everyday interactions in a wide variety of ways.

Undermining the assumption that biology dictates gender, transmen achieve social maleness regardless of their chromosomes or their decisions about genital surgery. This new social identity as men can create distance from women, many of whom assume men do not and cannot understand their lives. Being treated as one of the guys by men, in contrast, can bring more recognition and camaraderie, particularly for white transmen read as heterosexual. These changes in social interactions can transform the double consciousness some female-socialized men have about gender difference into an outsider-within perspective on gender inequality, as transmen negotiate being treated as not just *different from* women but *better than* women. This outsider-within perspective is most visible in contexts where schemas about natural differences between men and women are institutionalized, such as the workplace.

CHAPTER THREE

Becoming Men at Work

The Unequal Outcomes of Difference

At nineteen, Chris went stealth in a blue-collar job. While it was exciting to be working as just one of the guys, he could not ignore how women were treated. "Girls couldn't get their forklift license, or it would take them forever. They wouldn't make as much money. It was so pathetic." Preston, who openly transitioned twenty years later in a blue-collar job, still saw similar differences: "They let the guys get away with so much stuff! And the women who are working hard, they just get ignored." Both men felt that these differences were visible to them because of their unique perspective. Chris notes, "I would have never seen [these differences] if I was a regular guy. I would have just not seen it. . . . I can see things differently because of my perspective. I am a lot like a guy because I transitioned younger, but, still, you can't take away how I was raised for eighteen years." Preston adds, "I am really aware of it [gender inequality] now. And that is one of the reasons that I feel like I have become much more of a feminist since transition. I am just so aware of the [gender] differences that my experience has shown me."

Because maleness is defined in opposition to femaleness (Chodorow 1978; R. Connell 1995; R. Connell and Messerschmidt 2005; Schippers 2007), transmen negotiate being viewed as not just different from but also better than women. The differences in treatment that can come from changing social location within a hierarchical system are particularly evident in institutions that allocate rewards and tasks on the basis of gender, such as the workplace (Acker 1990; C. L. Williams 1995). Transmen can benefit from the "patriarchal dividend" (R. Connell 1995, 79), the advantages men in general gain from the subordination of women. Yet not being born into it can generate an "outsider-within" (Collins 1986) perspective on how seemingly innocuous beliefs about gender difference translate into gender inequality.[1] But not all embodiments of social maleness carry the same advantages. White, tall transmen who can physically pass report greater returns from the patriarchal dividend than transmen who are short, gender-ambiguous, and/or racial minorities. The varying experiences of becoming men at work illustrate the hierarchical relationality not just between men and women but also between competing embodiments of maleness.

Before and After: Changes in Workplace Experiences

A large body of research shows that natural differences schemas impact the trajectories of employees (see Ridgeway and Correll 2004). White men are rewarded more than women for offering ideas and opinions and for taking on leadership roles (D. Butler and F. L. Geis 1990; Valian 1998). Both men and women view white men as more competent, more knowledgeable, and more able to command others than women (Elliott and Smith 2004; Olian, Schwab, and Haberfeld 1988; Padavic and Reskin 2002). My analysis of transmen's "before and after" workplace experiences brings these documented patterns to life. Two-thirds of the transmen in my study, both open and stealth, described new workplace experiences as men at work that line up with the workplace benefits associated with maleness: increases in workplace *authority*, perceived *competence*, *reward and recognition* for hard work, and *economic opportunities*.[2]

Authority

When I asked Henry if he noticed any differences in his workplace treatment as a man, he laughed and said, "Do you know how smart I am?" He went on to explain, "I'm right a lot more now. . . . Even with folks I am out to [as transgender], there is a sense that I know what I am talking about." Henry's experience illustrates the gain of a hallmark of social maleness: authority. He is asked to support his opinions and arguments with facts less frequently than when he worked as a woman, and he is sought out more often for his expertise on a wide range of subjects. Trevor, an open transman, also had a sense that his ideas were taken more seriously as a man. "I had good leadership skills leaving college, and . . . I think that those work well for me now. . . . Because I'm male, they work better for me. I was 'assertive' before. Now I'm 'take-charge.'"

Paul openly transitioned in the 2000s in a female-dominated profession. He attended large regional meetings where most of the participants, almost all women, were unaware of his transition. Being a man in these settings brought a new kind of authority:

> [At] some of the meetings I'm required to attend, you have lots of women there. There are [many times], mysteriously enough, when I'm picked [to speak]. . . . That [had] never happened [before transition]. There was this meeting . . . a little while ago where I appeared to be the only male between these thirty, forty women and everybody wants to hear from me.

Gabriel, a stealth man in a female-dominated job, had a similar experience: "[In meetings,] everyone will just get quiet and listen to me. But when this [woman expert] speaks, everyone talks over her. And I have no specialization in this area. I don't know anything, yet they are all listening to me." Xavier, too, openly transitioned in a female-dominated job: "[My colleagues] started paying more attention to what I was saying. . . . In meetings, someone would [raise an issue,] and when I would jump in and say, 'Have you thought of that?' everyone would listen like in a way they hadn't before." He adds, "I think part of it was like, 'Hey, the voice sounds different.' But part of it was also like this kind of creepy programming [for women], like, 'Hey, let's not interrupt the boy voice.'" Rather than being alienated by gender tokenism as women often are in predominantly male workplaces (Eisenberg 1998; Byrd 1999), stealth transmen can be given more authority from their women coworkers, a common situation for white men in women's professions (C. L. Williams 1995).

Some examples of increased workplace authority are more overt. Roger, who openly transitioned in a technology-related retail environment in the 1980s, found that once he physically passed as a man, customers assumed that he knew more than his supervisor, a woman: "People would pass her and go straight to me because obviously, as a male, I knew [*sarcastic*]." He adds, "We would play mind games with them. . . . They would come up and ask me a question, and then I would go over to her and ask her the same question, she would tell me the answer, and I would go back to the customer and tell the customer the answer." Show-ing how gender schemas that link maleness and authority are deeply in-grained, customers did not recognize the sarcasm behind his actions. Twenty years later, these schemas persisted, as Scott discovered when he went stealth at a blue-collar retail job: "It was me and three other girls [in that] department. We could be standing right next to each other and if some guy had a question about caulking or spackle or something, they would always ask me. And I had been there for two months, and these girls had worked there for at least a year." Gabriel found that people who came in looking for the supervisor in his workplace always assumed that he, one of two men, must be the person in charge. Even when he insisted he was low on the workplace hierarchy, he was asked to take charge of a variety of situations he had no institutional authority to command.

This new authority can be welcome. In his blue-collar job, Keith was relieved that he no longer had to couch his directives in social niceties, what he called "cuddling after sex." This authority also can be unwanted and disconcerting. Gabriel notes, "Sometimes [in meetings], I get flus-tered. I kind of start stuttering because it is so quiet and everyone is look-ing at me. It really confuses me because I could be saying something so dumb. It just doesn't matter; everyone is still, like, 'Wow!'" Joseph strug-gled with how this new authority came at the expense of women. "I'd al-ways known that women were oppressed, especially on the job. But now [as a man], I have learned so much more about white male power. I didn't really understand that [before]."

While Joseph transitioned in the 1980s, Trevor's experiences in a pro-fessional job in the 2000s show that men's workplace authority can still come at the expense of women: "A woman would make a comment or an observation and be overlooked and be dissed essentially. I would raise my hand and make the same point in a way that I am trying to reinforce her, and it would be like [directed at me], 'That's an excellent point!'" He adds, "I saw this shit in undergrad. So it is not like this was a surprise. But it was disconcerting to have happen to me."

Competency

Thomas saw little change in his treatment from his employers when he transitioned into working as a man in his professional job. Yet, once he passed as a man, people who were unaware of his transition began to view him as more competent. Illustrating this change, Thomas tells how a man who worked at an associated company commended Thomas's boss for firing "Susan" because she was incompetent. He added that the "new guy" (that is, Thomas) was great. The punch line of this anecdote is that Susan and the new guy were the same person. Trey had a similar experience in Texas. He applied as a woman for a professional job in a high-tech field in which he had an associate's degree. When he did not get an interview, he decided to take the time off from work to begin hormones. Three months later, he reapplied for the same job as a man and was hired. While he did not know if the same people evaluated his second application, he knew from his past work experience that men did not view women as being competent in this field. Marking the "M" box on the application made him a closer fit for the idealized image of a competent worker in this occupation.

Thomas's and Trey's experiences illustrate how men are evaluated as more competent than women in careers associated with stereotypically male skills and abilities, such as aggressiveness and technological "know-how" (Pierce 1995; Valian 1998). Brad, who worked stealth in blue-collar jobs for many years, says, "You don't see women as superintendents [on construction sites]. And it is nothing [women] can't do physically. It is just interacting with crews and managing things. But men view other men as more competent and more authoritative." Stephen, who went stealth in a customer service job staffed primarily by men, adds:

> Just because [the men I work with] assume I have a dick, [they assume] I am going to get the job done right, where, you know, they have to second-guess that when you're a woman. They look at [women] like, "Well, you can't handle this because, you know, you don't have the same mentality that we [men] do," so there's this sense of panic . . . and if you are a guy, it's just like, "Oh, you can handle it."

Caleb notes, "The male attitude [about women] is not that great. I've noticed so many guys are like that at work. They just feel like women are below them." Julian's experience in a blue-collar job with men who did not know he was transgender supports this observation: "[The site manager] was obviously saying things to me that he would never have said to a female. He was like, 'You have to help me! The other place I called sent me a bunch of women. . . .' And I was [thinking], 'Buddy, you don't even know the half of it!'" Anton found a similar devaluation of women when he went stealth in a professional job. He was warned by his women coworkers that his new boss could be demanding and overbearing. Yet, after only two months, he was treated as a respected peer. "He says things like, 'I know I can trust your judgment.'" Though he was a recent hire, Anton was told to double-check the work of the other office staff—all of whom were women with many years' seniority on him. "He'll have the staff put together a schedule, and then it's like, 'I want you to make sure this works, make sure everything comes off smoothly.' And the support staff *is* making sure everything runs smoothly. But he is saying, 'I want you to double-check these women's work.'"

Women coworkers also attribute greater competence to transmen in some arenas of the workplace, such as computer-related concerns. But women can also allow more leeway for assumed male incompetence, particularly in female-dominated jobs that men are not expected to have an interest in. Gabriel found that this new leeway meant he could get out of doing required workplace activities he found burdensome or boring: "I can play the dumb guy. [Women] won't get mad at me. Whereas before, when I worked [as a woman], I couldn't get away with that. If I played dumb, they would just get really pissed off. Now I can play dumb, and it's, 'Oh, Gabriel, you know, that's okay.'" This acceptance of male incompetence in arenas coded as feminine upholds gender inequality at work, much as it does within the family (Hochschild 1990), as men are relieved of the expectations of doing work outside their "natural" abilities. While women in male-dominated jobs are also assumed by their coworkers to be incompetent, they still have to go above and beyond to keep their jobs (Paap 2006).

This outsider-within perspective on gender differences in workplace competency is heightened because many transmen have experienced the reverse: being thought, on the basis of gender alone, to be less competent than men. This sense of increased authority and perceived competence was particularly marked for transmen who had worked in male-dominated occupations as women. In the 1970s, Paul faced open opposition when he applied to be a truck driver as a woman: "[Men] would tell [me], 'Well, we never had a female driver. I don't know if this works out.' Blatantly telling you this." He adds, "[I had] to go, 'Well, let's see. Let's give it a chance. I'll do this three days for free and you see, and if it's not working out, well, then, that's fine, and if it works out, maybe you want to reconsider [not hiring me].'" Stephen, who did blue-collar work as a woman in the 1980s, describes the resistance he faced from men when it came to even basic help, such as enforcing safety precautions for loading pallets. "[The men] would spot each other, which meant that they would have two guys that would close down the aisle . . . while you were up there [with your forklift and load,] . . . and they wouldn't spot you if you were a female. It was maddening, and it was because of gender." In the eighties and nineties, supervisors wrote up Crispin, a woman in a male-dominated job, for every small infraction, a practice used to drive away "outsiders" that Janice Yoder and Patricia Aniakudo (1997, 330) refer to as "pencil whipping." In the 2000s, Dan, still working as a woman, received implicit messages about the incompatibility of women and blue-collar work. "One of my foremen was always talking about his daughter and how he refused to let her [do this job]. He never specifically said anything to me. It was like a subtle hint that he didn't approve of women on the site." Whether the messages were subtle or overt, transmen who worked in male-dominated jobs as women understood that they were assumed to be less competent than men.

Respect and Recognition

Going stealth in a professional job, Nathan immediately noticed differences: "[The men] listen to more of what I say and respect what I say. I actually get a lot more respect from the men." Preston's experiences openly transitioning in a blue-collar job were similar:

> I was not asked to do anything different [after transition]. But the work I did do was made easier for me. [Before transition,] there [were] periods of time when I would be told, "Well, I don't have anyone to send over there with you." We were always one or two people short of a crew, or the trucks weren't available. And I swear it was like from one day to the next of me transitioning [to male], I need this, this is what I want. I have not had to fight about anything.

He adds, "The last three [performance] reviews that I have had have been the absolute highest that I have ever had. New management team. Me not doing anything different than I ever had. I even went part-time." Having achieved social maleness, he is rewarded for doing less work and has to fight less to get what he needs. Additionally, he receives more positive feedback for his work, demonstrating how men and women can be evaluated differently for the same tasks.

As with authority and competence, increased recognition for hard work was particularly noticeable for transmen who had worked in occupations in which they were gender minorities. Preston, who was an ROTC cadet, felt that no matter how hard he worked as a woman, his achievements were passed over: "I was the highest-ranking female during the time I was there. . . . I was the most decorated person in ROTC. I had more ribbons, I had more medals, in ROTC and in school. I didn't get anything for that." He adds, "There was an award every year called 'Superior Cadet,' and guys got it during the time I was there who didn't do nearly what I did. It was those kinds of things [that got to me]." Similarly, Crispin reports:

> I worked really hard. . . . I produced typically more than three males put together—and that is really a statistic—but it would come down to, "You're single. You don't have a family." And because I was intelligent and my qualities were very vast, they said, "You can just go get a job anywhere." Which wasn't always the case. It was still a boys' world, and some people were just, like, there aren't going to be any women on my job site. And it would be months . . . before I would find gainful employment.

Nathan notes similar treatment as a professional: "I went as far as I could go in management [as a female]. . . . I had reviews as a woman where I was told that I was not going to get promotions even though I was deserving because men had families to support." These experiences illustrate the hardships that women working in male-dominated jobs often face: being passed over for hiring and promotions, having their hard work go unrecognized, and not being socially accepted. Having this experience of being women in an occupation composed mostly of men can create a heightened appreciation of reward and recognition for job performance as men. Even if the changes in treatment are not vast, they are different enough to be noticeable to many transmen.

Another reward that some transmen gain is freedom from unwanted sexual advances, as men encounter less touching and groping and fewer sexualized comments at work than women. Brian recounts his experience working as a waitress, saying that "customer service" involved "having my boobs grabbed, being called 'honey' and 'babe.'" He notes that as a man, he no longer has to worry about these types of experiences. Jason reported a similar change: "When I transitioned . . . it was like a relief! [*laughs*] I swear to God! I am not saying I was beautiful or sexy, but I was always attracting something." This new freedom is limited to stealth transmen, however. Open transmen often are asked invasive questions about their genitals and sexual practices during their transition process, which they can experience as a new form of sexualized harassment.

Economic Opportunities

Some transmen did feel that becoming men brought economic advantages. Chris notes, "I transitioned at nineteen. I went from making feminine minimum wage to making eight hundred dollars a week. That was back in the 1980s. I don't know what kind of job I could have gotten as a female making that same amount of money at the time." Chris had almost twenty years of career history to reflect on, highlighting the importance of longitudinal data for assessing the issue of salary changes. However, while such overt financial changes were rare, some transmen did feel that achieving social maleness increased their *economic opportunities*. Henry says:

> I am really aware of having this [professional] job that I would not have had if I hadn't transitioned. [Gender expression] was always an issue for me. I wanted to go to law school, but I [would have had to] wear the skirts and things females have to wear to practice law. I wouldn't dress in that drag. And so it was clear that there was a limit to where I was going to go professionally because I was not willing to dress that part. Now I can dress the part and it's not an issue. So this world is open to me that would not have been before just because of clothes. But very little has changed in some ways. I look very different, but I still have the same skills and the same general thought processes. That is intense for me to consider.

As a man, Henry is able to wear clothes similar to those he wore as an "obvious dyke," but they are now considered gender-appropriate. Chris felt that he had different entrepreneurial abilities as a man than he would have had as a woman:

> I have this [professional] company that I built, and I have people following me. They trust me, they believe in me, they respect me. There is no way I could have done that as a woman. When it comes to business and work, higher levels of management, it is different being a man. I have been on both sides [as a man and a woman], and I will tell you, man, I could have never done what I did [as a female]. You can take the same personality and I would have never made it.

While he acknowledges that women can be and are business entrepre-
neurs, he felt that his business partners would not have taken his venture idea in a male-dominated field as seriously if he were a woman. Additionally, he would not have had access to the types of social networks
that made his venture possible.

Wayne achieved social maleness after many years of being gender-
ambiguous. As men and women always face accountability for being either definitively male or definitively female (West and Zimmerman 1987),
gender ambiguity can result in negative workplace treatment. Working
at a restaurant in his early teens, Wayne had the following experience:

> The woman who hired me said, "I will hire you only on the condition that you
> don't ever come in the front because you make the people uncomfortable."
> A couple of times it got really busy, and I would have to come in the front or
> whatever, and I remember one time she found out about it, and she said, "I
> don't care how busy it gets, you don't get to come up front." She said I'd make
> people lose their appetite.

Once he looked unequivocally male, his work and school experiences
improved. He went on to earn a doctoral degree and become a successful professional, an economic opportunity he did not think would have
been available had he remained gender-ambiguous. Wayne and Henry
highlight the power of becoming *normative*. Yet becoming normatively
male still plays an important role in these workplace outcomes. Illustrating this, both George and Trevor had self-described feminine gender expressions when they worked as women. While they did not feel
discriminated against as women, they still reported gains in perceived
competence as men.

Peter went stealth in the process of finishing an undergraduate degree in a female-dominated academic field. Professors and colleagues
told him that his gender would be a benefit, as employers were looking
for more men in this field. Devin, who openly transitioned in graduate
training for a women's profession, felt his gender benefited him in the
job market. "I think because there are so few men [in this profession],
they're like, 'Oh, let's bump up the number of men we've got here.' So
that kind of sets me apart in a weird way, just because of the field." Anton saw clear economic benefits to being one of the only men (aside from
his boss) in his professional workplace: "I was promoted immediately.
Within two and half months of being hired." When I asked if he would

still have been promoted as a woman, he said, "It's the guys that rise through the ranks, and they rise quickly. . . . The workplace is mainly women. These are Latino women who are ten years older than the men and have been in the same position for ten years." He adds, "When someone comes in at that same position and two and a half months later is given a fifteen-thousand-dollar salary increase, it pains them." In this situation, Anton benefits from both his race and his gender. In contrast, David, who transitioned while in professional training for a male-dominated field, worried that becoming a white man was a double disadvantage if hiring committees wanted to increase representation of gender and/or racial minorities. However, the persistence of the gender and racial gap in math and science (Schiebinger 1999), law (Pierce 1995), construction (Paap 2006), stock trading (Roth 2006), and finance (Blair-Loy 2003) suggests that white men are still viewed as more qualified for many male-dominated occupations.

Johnny went stealth in a retail job that involved working in the warehouse loading merchandise. He was promoted after two months to floor shift manager. "[As a female], I would not have been in the back. I would have been on the floor [with the customers] doing merchandise and stuff." The gender segregation of workplace tasks put him in a location where it was possible to move up the ranks quickly. When he went stealth in a blue-collar job, Brad was offered promotions over more qualified, senior women. "There was a girl who worked hard, just as hard as me. But they wanted someone to be assistant manager, so they asked me. She had been there longer." He adds, "I can't say that she shouldn't have had it more than me. I think guys are just like that between one another at work." Trevor and Jake, who both openly transitioned in professional jobs, remember women joking that they were going to "join the good old boys' network" and get promoted. While they discounted these comments, they were promoted soon after their transitions. They felt these promotions were related to their job performance, not their gender—a point I am not questioning. Yet these promotions show that while these two men were not benefiting undeservedly, transitioning did not interrupt the upward trajectory of their careers in these fields.

It is possible that the workplace gains that some transmen reported have a spurious connection to gender. Rather, such changes might come from a gain in education—a change that increases human capital. As table 3.1 shows, some transmen have higher degrees as men than they did as women because they transitioned in college. Others return to

TABLE 3.1 **Highest level of education attained, before and after transition**

| | Stealth FTMs | | Open FTMs | |
| | Before transition | After transition | Before transition | After transition |
Highest degree level				
High school / GED	12	7	4	3
Associate's degree	5	5	7	7
Bachelor's degree	3	6	14	10
Master's degree	1	2	2	5
PhD	0	1	2	3
JD	0	0	1	2
Other	0	0	1	1
Total	21	21	31	31

Note: In this table, I exclude Seth and Eric, as they had not held any paid jobs since their transitions. Seth was a homemaker, and Eric was living on disability. Therefore, the table totals to only 52 transmen.

school for higher degrees. Yet, while education level matters in accounting for workplace outcomes, men get a greater reward from their educational attainment (Valian 1998). Anton's experiences bear this out. He was hired in his professional job straight out of college. As a woman, he would have had the same degree. Yet, in his workplace, he observed that women did not advance in the same way that he and other men did. Trey had the same associate's degree in a high-tech field as a man that he had as a female. But the company that hired him as a man passed over his application when he initially checked the "F" box. As many transmen's experiences show, social maleness also influences views of competency. This change holds true even outside of the workplace where their education level is unknown. Crispin notes:

> I used to jump into situations [as a woman]. Like at Home Depot, I would hear . . . [men] be so confused, and I would just step over there and say, "Sir, I work in construction, and if you don't mind me helping you." And they would be like, "Yeah, yeah" [that is, dismissive]. But now I go [as a man,] and I've got men and women asking me things and saying "Thank you so much," like now I have a brain in my head! It's really nice.

As a man, Crispin is rewarded for displaying the same knowledge about construction—knowledge gendered as male—that he was dismissed for offering when he was living as a woman. These experiences suggest that transmen's reported increased authority at work relates to becoming socially gendered as men, not just to changes in education.

Transmen's descriptions of their "before and after" workplace experiences are self-report data, which can render them suspect. If they anticipated that men get better treatment at work, they might be over-reporting workplace gains as a way to shore up their maleness. However, I have reasons to doubt that the transmen I interviewed exaggerated these changes. First, few transmen whom I encountered in my interview study or in my fieldwork expected that transitioning would result in anything but negative changes. Unless they worked in LGBT-related jobs, they expected to be fired, ridiculed, and harassed. For those who reported more authority, .rewards, and economic opportunities, this change was a shock—particularly when they remained in the same jobs. Second, reactions to this shock are conflicted. While more authority and respect can be satisfying, transmen are aware that this change is an arbitrary result of looking male. This knowledge can undermine their sense of themselves as good workers, making them question the motivations behind any workplace rewards they receive. It can also show transmen that they were receiving less reward as women workers than they had realized, a deeply frustrating experience. Further, many transmen express resentment that these changes often come at the expense of women. Thus, while many transmen could identify interactional benefits associated with social maleness at work, they often retained a critical eye to how changes in their treatment disadvantage women—the outsider-within perspective on gender inequality.

Other Experiences as Men at Work

About one-third of the men I interviewed reported no changes or negative changes in their workplace treatment due predominantly to *occupational context, being transgender,* and *embodiments of maleness*

Occupational Context

Transmen who worked in retail jobs reported little change in their workplace experiences before and after their transitions. Elliott and Nicky both worked as open transmen in high-turnover retail jobs with a great deal of college student traffic. The jobs had regimented promotion schedules, and they felt it was hard to gain any benefit outside of these set boundaries. They added that none of the workers, regardless of gender, were treated by managers or customers as having much authority because these were entry-level jobs. As tasks in these types of jobs often are gender-segregated (Leidner 1993), transmen might do different jobs than they did as women, such as carrying heavy boxes or working the grill in restaurants, but they were not financially rewarded differently. Casey felt similarly that he could not see any changes in his treatment. As a stealth temporary worker who did his tasks in a service job alone all day, he did not have any other coworkers, men or women, to whom to compare himself. Transmen who described their workplaces as gender-equitable also reported little change from working as women to working as men. Ethan worked as an open transman in a high-level professional job that had equal numbers of men and women. He described his boss as going to great lengths to reward all her employees equally.

Being Transgender

Several transmen felt that they had more negative workplace experiences as openly transgender men than they did working as women or when they were stealth at work. Caleb felt that he was treated like one of the guys in his stealth retail job in Texas. However, when he changed jobs—and came out to his employers as transgender—he had a markedly different experience. In his initial interview for a retail position, human resources personnel assured him that being transgender was not going to be an issue. During his training, he was assumed to be a man and given heavy-lifting jobs. At the close of training, he was assigned to be a sales representative for the company, a position that required a great deal of client interaction. On his first day, he told his direct supervisor that he was transgender. "She moved my position from sales rep . . . to [working in the back of the store]." Dissatisfied with his new position, which came with early morning hours and no interaction with customers, he asked for his original assignment back. "She just said, 'We can't have you in the public. You don't fit the representation of what we consider appropriate.'" While his appearance had not been a problem when his supervisor read him as male, the knowledge that he was transgender changed her perception of his suitability. Scott, who openly transitioned in a semiprofessional job, also felt that his work experiences took a turn for the worse because his supervisor treated him in a transphobic manner. "She had had a bad experience with another person who was transgender . . . and

I think she already had a [negative] conceptualization of what happens to a person [when he transitions]." Both Caleb and Scott quit and went stealth in new jobs.

Transmen who worked in jobs that had a predominance of gay and lesbian employees and/or who worked primarily with LGBT clients described a distinct set of workplace experiences they attributed to being transgender. While Douglas was the only one who openly transitioned and stayed in the same workplace, the other four transmen working in these fields were hired as openly transgender. They had high expectations for these jobs, as they were working alongside people who were part of, or at least committed to, the LGBT community. Perhaps because of these high expectations, this group of transmen expressed the most reservations about their actual workplace experiences. They described being treated as "token trannies." Tokens stand out in their workplaces as among the only members of a certain group (Kanter 1977). As token trannies, transmen felt responsible for overcoming their colleagues' preconceived notions about transgender people. Douglas's workplace had once employed a transwoman whom his colleagues described as "flaky." "It created an organizational idea that trans people are sort of inherently unstable. . . . I felt a lot of pressure to be different . . . because I had to deal with the precedent she set and people's expectations." Transmen also became the "go-to" people for any issue related to transgenderism, regardless of whether they had any expertise beyond their personal experience. Having "transgender" forced upon them as a master status negated the relevance of other identities, such as gay or queer.

Embodiments of Maleness

Different embodiments of social maleness carry varying workplace rewards. Transmen who were or looked young, who did not physically pass as men, who were short, and/or who were racial/ethnic minorities reported fewer or no changes in workplace treatment than white, tall, "passable" transmen.[3] Looking first at age, the development of "peach fuzz" prior to the emergence of thicker, fuller facial hair can be an initial response to taking T. This youthful appearance works against transmen who are established in their careers. Thomas says, "I went from looking thirty to looking thirteen. People thought I was new [to the job,] so I would get treated like I didn't know what was going on." Other transmen remember being asked if they were interns or if they were visiting a parent at their workplace, all comments that underscore a lack of authority. Looking youthful, however, is a time-bounded state.

Transmen who did not go on T describe very different workplace experiences than transmen who did. Christian was hired for a retail managerial position in Texas in the 2000s. He came out to his employer as transgender during the interview. She told him it was fine to identify that way but until he changed his legal gender, he could not inform his employees. Since he had what he described as an "in-between" appearance, some of the people he supervised referred to him as "she" and some as "he." He found the experience frightening in a conservative town where customers often had angry reactions to his ambiguous appearance. Jack and Ken announced their identities as transmen at work, but their coworkers continued to refer to them with feminine pronouns. While they often passed as men in limited social interactions, they were not afforded social maleness by coworkers—a difference they attributed to not taking T (and thus not developing the visual markers of social maleness). Riley had a slow reaction to T, meaning he looked "in-between" for over a year. While his coworkers at his professional job in California were not hostile, they rarely used masculine pronouns with him. Tex, Simon, and Anthony openly transitioned in a professional training job, a women's profession, and a retail managerial position, respectively. At the time of our interviews, they had just started T. They felt it was difficult to speak to any potential gender differences in treatment because they passed as male only about 60 percent of the time. At best, transmen who did not pass as men were treated the same way they were as women. At worst, they were physically threatened and ridiculed at work.

Being over six feet tall is part of the cultural construction for successful, hegemonic masculinity (Hall 2006). However, several men I interviewed were between five feet one and five feet five, something they felt put them at a disadvantage in relation to other men in their workplaces. Winston, who managed a professional work staff who knew him only as a man, felt that his authority was harder to establish at work because he was short. While he was one of the highest earners in my study, he felt he lacked the interactional benefits of maleness, such as authority. Being smaller than many of the men and women he supervised meant that he was always being looked down upon, even when giving orders. Kelly, who worked often with children, felt his height impacted the jobs he was assigned: "Some of the boys, especially if they are really aggressive, they do much better with males that are bigger than they are. So I work with the little kids because I am short. I don't get as good . . . results if I work with [older kids;] a lot of times, they are taller than I am." Sam added, "I have been a part of male culture, but I also feel like an outsider. I have always felt that it was because I am a little man. Men look down on you when you are a little man." These experiences demonstrate the importance of the body in discussions of gender, as being short can impact the relationality among different embodiments of maleness.

The experiences of transmen of color most clearly highlight the hierarchical relations among embodiments of maleness. Christopher felt that he was denied any gender advantage at work not only because he was shorter than the other men at work but also because he was viewed according to stereotypes of Asian men (Espíritu 1997; Fung 2004; Hamamoto 1994). "To the wide world of America, I look like a passive Asian guy. That is what they think when they see me. Oh, Asian? Oh, passive. . . . People have this impression that Asian guys aren't macho and therefore they aren't really male. Or they are not as male as [a white guy]." Keith felt he could be more direct as a man, but being a *black* man limited his ability to express anger. "I went from being an obnoxious black woman to a scary black man." Reflecting stereotypes that conflate African-Americans with criminals (Oliver 2003), he was asked to play "a suspect" in training exercises in his blue-collar job.

Trey, who was stealth, was accepted at work as one of the only black men in a male-dominated field. However, his predominantly white coworkers joked that he was the "workplace diversity" hire and spoke to him in what they thought was hip, urban (that is, black) slang. He did not find these experiences discriminatory, but they were an irritation that his white coworkers did not face. Aaron, who was openly transgender at work, also felt achieving black social maleness negatively impacted his work life in a predominantly white organization. His supervisors repeatedly told him he came across as "threatening" to others. When he expressed frustration during a staff meeting about a new policy, he was written up for rolling his eyes in an "aggressive" manner. The choice of words such as *threatening* and *aggressive*, words often used to describe black men (Ferguson 2000; Oliver 2003), shows how racialized and gendered schemas impacted his workplace treatment in a negative way.

Human Capital, Gender Socialization, and the Persistence of Inequality

Gender transitions typically are understood as private events. Yet, because transgender people do not exist somehow outside of society, these transitions bring interactional changes. These changes are particularly visible in gendered locations, such as the workplace. Open and stealth transmen move from being socially gendered as women at work to being socially gendered as men. This change can result in increased authority, respect, and recognition, particularly in professional occupations. Highlighting the relationality between embodiments of maleness, however, white, tall transmen who can physically pass report greater gains in these areas than transmen who are men of color, short, and/or gender-ambiguous. These differences show that maleness is not a fixed construct that automatically generates privilege. Rather, there is a hierarchical relationality between embodiments of social maleness (R. Connell 1995; Messner 1997). These findings demonstrate the need for using an intersectional approach to gender inequality at work that takes into consideration the ways in which there are crosscutting relations of power (Calasanti and Slevin 2001; Collins 1990; Crenshaw 1989; S. Martin 1994), as different embodiments of maleness bring very different outcomes.

In many ways, workplace transitions reflect other forms of status changes—changes that have expected outcomes. We anticipate improved treatment to come with certain types of status changes, such as gains in education—medical students who become doctors, graduate students who become professors. In contrast, we often anticipate worse treatment to come with changes away from "normative" statuses—people who publicly identify as gay men, lesbians, and/or transgender people. Some transmen in this study report changes in workplace treatment that run counter to this negative expectation, an expectation that, again, many of them personally held. Having low expectations may make any slight change in treatment more visible. But this does not mean that improvements in workplace treatment do not actually occur. Putting transmen's workplace experiences in context with the changes in their casual social interactions as men suggests that, in some contexts, being gendered as men by others can bring different, and at times better, treatment than being gendered as women.

Comparing and contrasting transmen's "before and after" workplace experiences offers a challenge to rationalizations of workplace inequality, such as human capital and gender socialization. Human capital certainly matters in these situations, as transmen who are educated and work in professional jobs report the most gains at work. Yet, looking beyond education, transmen who report improved workplace outcomes typically have the same skills, abilities, and childhood gender socialization they had as women workers. But, once they achieve social maleness, employers and coworkers can view their skills and abilities in a different light. The improvements in workplace treatment some transmen experience, and the new disadvantages other transmen face, suggest that inequality persists, at least in part, because coworkers and employers rely on racialized and gendered cultural schemas to evaluate their colleagues' achievements and skills at work.

CHAPTER FOUR

Manufacturing Gender Inequality

Workplace Responses to Stealth Transmen

When Caleb (t. [transitioned] late 2000s) was eighteen, he responded to a Help Wanted sign at a service job.[1] Walking into the store, he was unsure how he should indicate his gender on the job application. His birth name was gender-neutral, but he was still legally female on his documents. He was relieved to find the quandary moot; he was hired on the spot as a delivery driver without filling out a formal application. He mentioned to his new employers that he had a friend who was also looking for work. He was surprised to hear that his friend would not be a good fit: "I told them that I had this female friend who was interested in working as a driver, and they said, 'No, we can't hire her; she is a girl.' I was like, what? Their policy was they don't let women do delivery because it is apparently dangerous." He adds, "When I got hired, I was unaware of this. I just thought I was being hired as a human." Through this exchange, Caleb learned two things very quickly. He successfully passed as a man. And he would not have been hired if he had checked the "F" box on an application.

Stealth transmen work with people who have only and always known them as men. As a result, their workplace experiences provide unique insight into the persistence of workplace gender inequality. Going stealth at work can bring increased respect, authority, and even economic opportunities. These individual changes are intimately tied to a mode of thought (Spelman 1988) or system of gender (R. Connell 1987) that advantages men. While one of the outcomes of this system—workplace gender inequality—is well documented, less attention has been paid to the mechanisms and processes that produce and maintain it (Fenstermaker, West, and Zimmerman 2002). The experiences of stealth transmen in the workplace illuminate that these processes are institutionalized, as cultural schemas about men and women's natural differences in skills and abilities shape workplace organization. The processes are also interactional, as men and women enact and reinforce these natural differences schemas at work in ways that naturalize a gendered division of labor. Taken together, these "gendered and gendering practices" (P. Martin 2003) maintain hierarchical relations between men and women, transforming gender difference at work into gender inequality.

Making Men at Work

Going stealth at work was the recommended workplace strategy for transgender people in the gender clinic era (Bolin 1988; Feinbloom 1976; Kando 1973; Lothstein 1983). Therapists and doctors encouraged not just a change in jobs but also a change to a more "gender-appropriate" occupation. Some medical professionals, for instance, encouraged transwomen to move from engineers to secretaries (Bolin 1988) or from lawyers to paralegals (Griggs 1998). Yet going stealth at work did and does carry risks. In the case of transmen, a former acquaintance can challenge their identity, as can a paper trail from health insurance marked "female" or an employment reference who refers to a male applicant as "she" and "her." In these situations, transmen run the risk of being fired for gender deception—a common frame cisgender people use to make sense of learning that someone they have always known as a man was raised as a girl (Bettcher 2007; Gamson 1998; Schilt and Westbrook 2009).

Almost half (44 percent) of the transmen I interviewed had been stealth at some point in their work histories (table 4.1). Going stealth can be circumstantial, as it was for Caleb, who was hired as a man on the basis of his appearance. Typically, however, it is a conscious choice. Despite the potential risks, transmen can see going stealth as an appealing workplace strategy even when they are part of a transgender community and openly discuss their transitions with friends and family. Going stealth at

TABLE 4.1 **Stealth employment by year of transition, by state**

	1980s	1990s	2000s
California	3	4	5
Texas	1	0	11
Total	4	4	16

Note: This table reflects the number of transmen who had gone stealth at any point in their career. See the methodological appendix for additional information on past and current workplace strategies.

work creates an unequivocal identity as a man with employers and co-workers rather than as a former woman or a transman—an important achievement for transmen with essentialist understandings of their gender identity. Peter (t. mid-2000s), who transitioned while in college, says, "I kept it [my transition] out of my business life. I feel like I don't want it to be something that follows me around from one job to the next." Brian (t. early 1990s) adds, "The thing that keeps me from coming out at work is that there is always a reminder. People watching you, listening for what you say, watching your gestures. Just trying to think of you as female." Transmen can also see going stealth as the only option after an unsuccessful attempt at openly transitioning and remaining in the same job.

The first time they applied for jobs as men, most transmen in this study were hired unproblematically on the basis of their appearance even when evidence that contradicted this appearance emerged—showing the interactional process of *making gender*. As men at work, some transmen are given jobs employers describe as unsuitable for women. Women exclude them from conversational topics men are assumed not to understand. Men engage them about cars, sports, and women. While the logic of natural differences seemingly justifies these institutional and interactional practices, these practices themselves are central forces in *creating gender difference*. And rather than being innocuous differences in conversational topics and job duties, these practices are *creating gender inequality*, as they provide many stealth transmen (and many cisgender men) with more workplace opportunities than women. Highlighting the resilience of these natural differences schemas that justify inequality, when some employers and coworkers learn that a stealth transman did not always live as a man, they put effort into *maintaining the gender status quo* by protecting him as just one of the guys or banishing him from the workplace.

Making Gender

Checking the "M" box on a job application for the first time is a high-stakes test of whether a transman physically passes as a man. Yet, in most cases in this study, transmen were hired unproblematically as men. Dan (t. mid-2000s) notes, "I have never had anyone question it [my gender]." Caleb says, "They never even asked me [my gender]. They just saw my appearance and assumed." Roger (t. early 1980s), too, was readily hired as male. "When you apply for a job, they ask you what your qualifications are. They don't ask you about how your genitalia are shaped." Yet Caleb's experience being hired as a delivery driver shows that qualifications are not neutral units of human capital. Rather, employers can take appearance as a proxy for qualifications, just as facial hair is taken as a proxy for maleness. Because Caleb looked like a man, his employers assumed he was qualified to be a driver in a way a woman never would be on the basis of gender.

This trust in gendered appearance eases the process of going stealth for transmen. Johnny (t. mid-2000s) did not plan to go stealth when he applied for a retail job. While he was on T, he was still legally female. "I applied as female. But the person that interviewed me and the general manager that interviewed me . . . both just said 'he' right away." When he injured himself on the job a few months later, the nurses at the hospital assumed he was a man. "I left it [the gender question] blank on the form. But there was this question that asked about the date of your last period. I said something to the nurse about it. He just kind of looked at me. I had shorts on, so he looked at my [hairy] legs and looked back at me. He was just, like, 'Why are you asking this question?'" When the insurance report came through, Johnny was listed as male.

Employers and coworkers often see but fail to register information that contradicts appearance. When Winston (t. early 1990s) was hired as a man, he easily passed. But, a few months later, he lost access to T, a loss that gave him what he describes as an "in-between" appearance. Though his coworkers continued to see him as a man, customers meeting him for the first time often referred to him as "she." "I decided I would tell people what I am before they got the chance. So I started to say things like, 'I am such a geeky *guy*.' I realized I had overdone it . . . when my boss said to me, 'Winston, stop saying you're a geek! It's boring, and we are sick of it!'" Worried that his strategy had backfired, he pulled his boss aside later and told her about his dilemma. "I said, 'I gotta tell you, a lot of times I get taken for a female, so I just felt that I needed to jump in.' And she said, 'If you think you're a woman, you need therapy!' [*laughs*]." When Gabriel (t. mid-2000s) went stealth, he had all of his legal documents changed. However, his female credit history came up on his background check. "I claim[ed] identity theft and just said, 'I don't know who that girl is.' And it worked! I just told them, 'I don't know anything about it.' And they were really cool. They gave me a number for all these identity theft solution places and credit bureaus." In this situation, Gabriel's potential employers find identity theft, a highly publicized social problem in the 2000s, a more plausible explanation than thinking that the man before them once lived as a woman.

Some information cannot be overlooked. In his forties at the time he started T, Crispin (t. mid-2000s) had accumulated a long work history in a blue-collar field—a history he needed to get a job with comparable authority and pay. "I had two really good leads. One of the guys flew me out and met with me and everything. . . . My license says male, my Social Security, I look like a male. But my past is still so close to me." After several interviews and an enthusiastic fly-out to another state, Crispin was told that all that remained was to get some references from past employers. His former employers, who did not support his decision to transition, had told Crispin not to count on them to use male pronouns and his new name if they were contacted for a reference. "I left the interview and thought, 'I guarantee you I will lose this job because he will call my references [and they will 'she' me].' And sure enough." A week later, he was sent a terse e-mail telling him his services were not needed. While he could not be sure what happened, it seemed that his potential employer found information that contradicted Crispin's social and legal maleness that was too blatant to be overlooked. He had to take lower-paying temporary jobs until he built up a new work history as a man.

That potential employers explain away contradictory information in many cases is not unexpected, as most people assume a natural connection between a male appearance and XY chromosomes (Dozier 2005; Garfinkel 1967; Kessler and McKenna 1978). In other words, there is no reason why people should assume that someone who looks like a man once lived as a woman—unless, as in Crispin's case, this person is being called "she" by a former employer. Seeing this appearance–identity–biological sex connection as natural, people consider themselves skilled enough to tell when someone is "faking" maleness or femaleness. John-ny's experience going stealth in his hometown illustrates this point: "This girl came up to me [at work] and said, 'We're friends, right? I have something to ask you.' As soon as she said that, I was like, oh God, oh no. . . . She finally told me she heard [I had been born female]. She was, like, 'Well, is it true?'" Wanting to remain stealth, Johnny denied the ru-mor. And his reassurance was all she needed. She explained to him that she knew this information had to be wrong because she could tell he was obviously a guy. "She even admitted to checking me out [sexually] and looking at my butt and stuff. She was like, 'There's no way Johnny could be female. I would know.'"

Certain appearance cues can even make people rethink their orig-inal gendering of someone. Nicky (t. late 2000s) took the summer off his retail job to start T and came back with facial hair and a flat chest. While his coworkers and employers knew about his transition, the cli-ents did not. He expected to face questions about his changed appear-ance, or at least about the new name on his nametag. Yet even long-time clients saw him as just a guy. One woman whom he had waited on several times in the past asked him if he had a sister who used to have the same job. Another frequent client confessed that she had an em-barrassing secret. "She said, 'I hope you're not offended by this, but I thought for the longest time that you were a girl.' I thought, 'What clued you off? That I had boobs?' What the hell!" Clients he interacted with for years as a woman asked Preston (t. early 2000s) if he had a sister on the job or if he knew what happened to the woman who used to work his route. These experiences show the power of appearance cues, as fa-cial hair and a low voice can lead people to not just rethink but actually change their original gender attribution without considering the possi-bility that the man before them was the same person they remember—an impossible consideration from the standpoint of a natural male/female binary.

The ease with which transmen can become men at work illustrates the social processes that make gender. While employers, coworkers, and clients may believe they are reading maleness from invariant biological facts, in practice they are relying on the cultural markers of facial hair and flat chests. These cues can override contradictory information— unless that information comes from someone who has what is seen as trustworthy evidence, such as a former employer.

Creating Gender Difference

Being hired as men often means being assigned tasks coded as male. Natural differences schemas justify this gendered division of labor—men and women doing different tasks, even within the same job titles (Padavic and Reskin 2002; Reskin and Hartmann 1986). Robert (t. early 2000s) was hired in a retail job to work the register. He was quickly reassigned to the warehouse, an area of the store employers assigned only to men because they were seen as better suited for heavy lifting. Johnny had a similar experience of being tracked specifically into the warehouse of a retail store—a job that generated a higher hourly income than female-dominated register work. Sam (t. mid-1990s) and Brian originally went stealth in female-dominated occupations. They noted that men were assigned tasks that required physical strength. Sam, who started working as a man in his teens, was excited about these tasks: "I did heavy-lifting jobs. The agencies would send me because they knew I was capable of doing those [jobs]. Whereas if they would have thought that I was a woman, they wouldn't have sent me. I was given harder jobs, lifting and stuff, because I was a man." Brian, in contrast, found the gendered division of labor offensive. "There is a real sexist bias in regard to responsibilities. [Women] were in charge of cleaning up, and the guys had to do all the physical parts."

Gabriel went stealth in a female-dominated job that required a great deal of interaction with children. He did similar tasks to women in most cases. "I do a lot of care work. I comfort the kids. . . . They still have accidents, and I have to take care of that." However, he acknowledged a new division of workplace tasks. "I handle the urine-stained clothing, not the children. . . . I have an assistant, and she takes care of all that stuff." While he felt that in many cases he had more freedom at work as a man, he envied the ease with which women could do bodily care of children without the assumption they were sexual predators. "They can hug kids, play with the kids, bathe them in the sink, and nobody will say anything. If I walked into the bathroom while a kid was peeing, oh my God! Watch out!" Though Gabriel was not specifically instructed to avoid these tasks, he felt informal pressure from both parents and his employers to let women take the lead in these areas. This gendered division of labor reproduces the idea that women are naturally more suited to child care than men (Chodorow 1978), an idea that in Gabriel's workplace was enforced by *women* coworkers and parents.

Women exacerbate the gendered division of labor by asking men to do all the heavy or dirty jobs at work. As the only man in his semiprofessional workplace, Casey (t. early 2000s) lifted boxes and changed tires—all things that were not part of his job description. Devin (t. mid-2000s) says, "The ladies in my office that do all the mailing and stuff, they are always like, 'Can you get that box? Would you carry this to the back for me?'" Caleb adds, "At my job, they [gender differences] are about doing things and fixing things. When a chair breaks, who fixes it? The men. Or when the radio doesn't work, who gets asked to take it apart and look at it? The men. It's one of those things where it's always the guys that [get asked to] do the guys' stuff." Winston felt he had a second set of unspoken job expectations as a man that he was unable to meet due to a longstanding physical injury. "It is really embarrassing to be a guy and to ask everyone else to do the lifting because my back is shot."

Transmen can see these requests from women as burdensome. Illustrating this, many stealth transmen laughed at the idea of male privilege, saying it was not a privilege to be asked to do heavy lifting and fix things. However, the logic behind these requests assumes that men are stronger and more skilled than women—an assumption that reinforces a hierarchical gender system. Other men also encourage this gendered division of labor, as they highlight male superiority. Caleb says, "[The men at work], they just seem to feel like women are below them. We have two bosses. One is a man, and one is a woman. The woman is even bigger than the guy, she is taller and more physically built. But if she tries to lift a fifty-pound bag, they go, 'No, you can't do that. Let me.' Even though she obviously could." He adds, "It just bothers me that this is the world that we live in. There is a fine line between being kind and being demeaning." Women can benefit from these arrangements, as they are relieved of certain duties. But this division of labor still reproduces inequality by casting women as helpless and men as able.

Transmen's inclusion in homosocial workplace cultures also changes. While many stealth transmen never thought of themselves as female, they typically were included in "girl talk" at work on the basis of their social identities as women. When they are seen as men, however, women often exclude them from such interactions on the grounds that they cannot understand distinctly female experiences. When asked about their relationships at work with women, stealth transmen recount story after story of being excluded from women's conversations specifically about menstruation. Brian notes, "If they [women] are talking about their periods or something, they just point-blank tell me that I wouldn't understand." As people who have menstruated, or may still menstruate, depending on their decisions about going on T, transmen are amused at these statements. Devin says, "I remember the first time at work a woman said something about being on her period. She was kind of being hateful to me that I didn't have to deal with that. And it was like, 'Oh my God, that is so weird!'" Roger adds, "I have had women say in really condescending tones, 'That's okay; you just cannot understand.' And I will laugh to myself, Yeah, I have no idea." This open discussion of menstruation serves as a "gender ritual" (Goffman 1977) that emphasizes differences between men and women. These conversations also are a form of boundary heightening (Kanter 1977) that excludes men who attempt to cross these boundaries—an exclusion that contributes to gender segregation at work. And it is this gender segregation that contributes to women's lack of access to men's social networks, a key factor in moving up the workplace hierarchy (Valian 1998).

While they are excluded from women's interactions, transmen typically are welcomed into men's homosocial workplace cultures. Stephen (t. mid-2000s) found his first stealth job through the help of a pretransition transman who worked there. "He hasn't come out to anyone as trans. [The men] think he is a big ol' dyke. . . . They know him as 'she.' He doesn't get treated like the boys, and it's strange how I've come in [as a man], and all of a sudden, I am part of the boys' club." Some transmen describe initial discomfort with this inclusion. Brian says, "Coming from a lesbian-type situation, I had never been involved with men. It was an interesting situation because I was thrown in working primarily with men [as a man] . . . a lot of hands-on interaction. . . . I was a little self-conscious." Other transmen enjoy what they experience as male camaraderie. At the warehouse Robert worked in, men would snap one another's support belts like bras and leave tampons and sanitary napkins pilfered from the women's bathroom in one another's lockers. I asked Robert if these types of jokes made him worry that his coworkers thought he was a female. He laughed and said, "No, it just proves to me that they don't know. If they knew, they wouldn't do that." Chris (t. early 1980s) related a similar experience: "One of my coworkers, he Photoshopped a picture of me as a joke. He put makeup on me, made me bald, gave me a feather boa and earrings. Everyone at work saw it." About his reaction, he says, "I thought, 'Oh, I will get you back!' I didn't think, 'Oh no, [these men] know that I used to be a girl.' It could have happened to any [of the men] at work."

Chris's and Robert's lack of concern about the content of these interactions shows the embodied ease transmen can develop after many years of social maleness. These interactions themselves further highlight that this particular ritual of teasing other men by calling them women or gay men—a common social practice of male bonding (R. Connell 1995; Halle 1984; Kimmel 2004; Pascoe 2007)—is successful only if all participating parties are believed to be biologically male. Gabriel tried to avoid such "guy talk" at work. "During our lunch breaks, I would go with the women and spend lunch with them. And the guys were like, 'Why don't you come hang out with us?' I was trying to find excuses because I realized that I don't really want to be friends with guys." Stephen also felt resistance to being one of the guys at his work after learning that many of their conversations centered on the sexual objectification of women (Prokos and Padavic 2002). "I did not realize how misogynistic men can be, just in private company. It is almost like they are not aware of what they are saying. To me, it is like, 'Did you really just say that?' [They are] not even trying to be shocking."

Navigating inclusion in all-male conversations that transmen deemed sexist or homophobic could be difficult. Brad (t. early 2000s), who went stealth in a series of blue-collar service jobs, says, "I hated the guys I worked with. I really did. It irritated me to see how they acted. They were . . . ignorant. A lot of them were racist; a lot of them were sexist." Henry (t. late 1990s) had a similar experience: "I went to a [technical school] when I first transitioned. It was a very macho culture. That was my first introduction to what I was getting myself into [as a man]. And that was really hard. Learning how guys talk about women when they are not around. . . ." While he initially thought these conversations just occurred in "macho," blue-collar workplaces, he found similar discussions when he changed occupations. "Even guys at [professional] jobs, some of the stuff they will say just floors me." The surprising element was the vast differences between what men will say to women and what they will say to other men. Describing this change, Nathan (t. mid-2000s) says, "The good ol' boy talk . . . they just use a lot more vulgar language between men." Brian adds, "Oftentimes I just don't want to participate in what men are talking about. Either I don't agree with it, or I have something negative to say. When men say things about how women are, I *really do* know better [*laughs*]."

These experiences illustrate the social creation and maintenance of gender difference. Transmen are incorporated as men at work based on their appearance, which is taken as a proxy for biological sex. As men, they find that cultural schemas about their natural differences from women are embedded in workplace structures, translating into a gendered division of labor. Men and women can justify this separation by encouraging certain people to do certain official and unofficial duties at work. These divisions also play out in workplace interactions, as women exclude men from "girl talk" and men exclude women from "the boys' club." These homosocial interactions can create a sense of pleasure for included participants, a sense that they are engaging in natural gender camaraderie with others "of their kind."

Creating Gender Inequality

The homosociality of gendered workplace cultures has institutional consequences. Because men, particularly white men, tend to have the most workplace power (Padavic and Reskin 2002), men benefit from the sponsorship of other men (Bird 1996). Anton (t. mid-2000s), who was promoted two months after starting his professional job, says, "The fact that I have [the male] director's blessing is kind of helpful because he likes me to handle a lot of stuff he feels he can't really give to the support staff [who are all women]." Women, in contrast, stand to lose out for being excluded from men's workplace cultures, particularly in male-dominated professions. Julian (t. mid-2000s) recounts, "I get lots of calls [at my blue-collar job] that are, like, 'Don't send women here.' Or they will say, 'Why send a woman? Is she going to be cleaning the women's room? Because that is the only reason you would ask for a woman.'" Men also benefit from the idea that they are better suited to "men's jobs," jobs that tend to carry more respect, more authority, and more pay (Valian 1998). Describing his experience in blue-collar jobs as a man, Brad says, "Since guys are traditionally the breadwinners, if you have to cut someone, you cut a woman before a man. The guy has a family to support, and the women are assumed . . . to have a husband. I think guys are just like that. It is a good ol' boys' club. The only reason they have women [at blue-collar jobs] is because they have to legally." As these experiences show, institutional and interactional boundaries between men and women serve to maintain not just difference but also inequality.

As with cisgender men and women, not all transmen see these gender differences as unequal. For those who do, however, they find that disrupting *unequal interactions* between men can be very difficult. Brian says, "It is very frustrating. A lot of guys say something they don't really mean. They are just saying it to enhance their masculinity. And the sad thing is that it is really unnecessary because it seems like no one really wants it. Not the men or the women." Peter similarly saw these types of interactions as an unnecessary performance: "[Men] just think that is how guys are supposed to talk to one another. They don't even really believe it. It is like this male lingo: 'I'm your chum, I'm your friend.' Like this is going to be something we can connect on even though it has nothing to do with reality. It is like a script." Seeing this kind of talk as a way of shoring up masculinity, however, did not make it less frustrating. Stephen, who had been stealth for only a few months at the time of our interview, said, "It sucks. I'm not in the position to kind of get irate about this 'cause I have to blend in right now. If I overreact, I'm marked. I can't go there. It's dangerous." Having been very outspoken about gender inequality and homophobia at work as a lesbian, he added, "That [silence] is a strange place to be."

Being stealth is not a synonym for being *in the closet*, the term used to describe gay men and lesbians who pass as heterosexual (Seidman 2002; Woods 1993). Closeted gay men have a disjuncture between their heterosexual work identity and their homosexual home identity. Stealth transmen who personally identify as male have no such division, as they are men at work and men at home.[2] Yet, in some situations, being stealth can feel oppressive, as transmen can feel less leeway for offering opinions that go against the grain of the workplace culture. With no federal workplace protections, stealth transmen worried about inviting unwanted scrutiny by openly critiquing men's devaluation of women—part and parcel of the interactional enactment of hegemonic masculinity (R. Connell 1995; Schippers 2007). These concerns are not unfounded, as Joseph (t. late 1980s) discovered when he was fired after confronting his boss about his sexually harassing treatment of women. "I didn't want to hear it, I didn't want to be around it. A lot of times, I had to keep my mouth shut because I was afraid to lose my job. But I could only tolerate that kind of behavior up to a certain point." Brad felt similar pressure to keep quiet among his coworkers: "A few times, if they made racist comments, I made a point to say something. And it is like you could see they did not think lower of me [as a white man]. But on a few occasions, I confronted them about things they said about gay men, and they started thinking I was gay . . . and they started to treat me differently."

While many stealth transmen worried about unwanted scrutiny, particularly when they first went stealth at work, they expressed consternation at cisgender men's lack of reaction to other men's blatant homophobia and sexism. Stephen says, "It is just casual talk about women. Like, 'I saw this snatch at the bar the other day.' And I am like, 'You did not just say that in front of me!' It is just so completely casual, though. None of the other guys react." Like Stephen, many transmen expect that cisgender men should feel at ease confronting sexism and homophobia because they have a "biological claim" to manhood. However, the specter of homosexuality is a powerful regulatory mechanism that encourages men to be complicit in the devaluation of women and gay men (Hennen 2008; Kimmel 2004; Messner 1997; Pascoe 2007). The pervasiveness of this accountability in men's homosocial interactions at work makes alternative modes of behavior difficult to devise—illustrating why the interactional mechanisms that support workplace gender inequality are so slow to change. While transmen find role models for being different kinds of guys—guys who know cars, guys who hate sports, guys who crochet—they see few models for being men who openly challenge other men's sexist and homophobic behavior in the workplace.

Eventually, transmen discover that cisgender men use a variety of nonconfrontational strategies to excuse themselves from these interactions, strategies many stealth transmen adopt. When Scott (t. mid-2000s) wanted out of talk about women that he found sexist, he invoked a heavy workload as an excuse. "If any guy ever started a conversation that was degrading to females or whatever, I would gracefully find my way out of it. I would be, like, 'Okay, I got to go do this, or whatever.' I don't want to engage in that . . . talking in terms of degrading women." As devotion to work is a cultural schema associated with men (Blair-Loy 2003), professionalism can be an opting-out strategy that does not challenge heterosexual masculinity. Crispin cited his religious upbringing, developing a "saintly persona" that allowed him a graceful exit from talk about women and gay men he found degrading. Another cultural tool was crafting what I term a "gentleman persona." Johnny says, "If there is a female around, I'm, like, 'Hey, guys, kind of like chill. We got a lady in the room.' The girls know I am a gentleman. The guys laugh at me for it." While they may laugh at him, however, he is not held accountable in the way Brad was when he openly challenged antigay comments. Rather, Johnny is labeled a gentleman, a heterosexual man who expresses chivalry, another acceptable masculine behavior.

The gentleman persona was the most commonly invoked cultural tool for opting out of interactional misogyny. Describing this, Chris says, "If [my coworkers] went to a strip club, I absolutely will not go. They know that I have my opinions. Sometimes they would say something [tease me], but I don't care. . . . I would be, like, 'That could be your daughter up there.' My dad's the same way." Stephen describes his reactions:

> I play it off. I kind of shake my head or look at them or give them an eyebrow. They say, "Oh, you are a gentleman." I get that a lot. Yeah, I am a gentleman, and I don't appreciate that kind of talk. That is not how my parents raised me. My dad is a gentleman . . . and I just follow his lead. I've seen my dad in uncomfortable situations, and I just do what he did. Like, that's nice, but I need to get my work done.

Yet, while these opting-out tools free cis- and transmen alike from personally participating in the devaluation of women and gay men, they do not challenge these practices. These strategies are easily disregarded, as other men can see their gentlemen colleagues as simply paying lip service to political correctness—similarly to how white supremacists can believe that all white people are racist, even if they say they are not (Blee 2003). These strategies transform resistance to sexism and homophobia into individual preferences rather than into challenges of unequal interactional practices.

Stealth transmen found more leeway for disrupting unequal *institutional practices*. Chris describes such a challenge: "There was a girl who worked at the cash register. I told [my bosses] she would be really good in our department. And she ended up being damn good. And she made way more money." He adds, "But if I didn't go out of my way to tell the manager I wanted her— I was his assistant—she would have stayed at the cash register." Julian assigned women to blue-collar jobs even when his clients let him know they preferred men. "I never break it down in legal terms, as that makes people back off. I just send women to their sites." He adds, "I've had people that I've sent women to be skeptical. They will call and be, like, 'What did you send a woman out here for?' Then they call me at the end of the day, and they are, like, 'Holy crap, that woman was amazing! She just did three days of work for me.'" Brad turned down a managerial promotion he felt should have been offered to a more senior woman—and then encouraged his boss to offer her this position. Yet, while some transmen were able to help an individual woman, they felt they had to continually intervene into the gendered division of labor in their particular workplaces to effect similar changes for other women. In other words, no matter how well an individual woman did in a "man's job," it did not seem to change men's minds about the suitability of other women for such positions.

These experiences show how schemas about natural differences justify unequal interactions and institutional practices. Men are encouraged to actively participate or at least be complicit in the devaluation of women, as there are high stakes for heterosexual men in disrupting this seemingly natural attitude. Challenges to unequal institutional practices show that boundaries between men and women can be permeable, as women can be brought over to do jobs stereotyped as better suited for men. However, "men inviting women to cross a boundary or vice versa will not necessarily lead to lasting structural change" (Gerson and Peiss 1985, 323), especially if there is no accompanying change in official workplace policies or in the ideologies underlying such a division of labor. Individual women may benefit, but the inherent assumptions about men's and women's natural abilities, assumptions that are embedded in workplace structures and interactions, do not necessarily change.

Maintaining the Gender Status Quo

Stealth transmen achieve social maleness at work on the basis of their appearances. Being gendered as male means, however, that situations in which they decide to tell their employers and coworkers about their gender transitions, or in which they are unwittingly outed, have the theoretical potential to disrupt the gender status quo. Sociologists theorize that such a disclosure, whether intentional or not, will lead to stigma (Feinbloom 1976; Garfinkel 1967; Goffman 1963b; Kando 1973), as it challenges naturalized attitudes about static male or female classifications that derive naturally from XY and XX chromosomes, respectively. Drawing on this body of theory, I expected that in these situations, transmen would immediately be fired or at least marginalized by coworkers and employers. And some transmen did face such responses. In the mid-1980s, Chris encountered a former classmate at one of his stealth retail jobs. "She told the manager [about my transition]. I came into work the next day, and they started talking like a gay guy [*making a limp wrist gesture and adopting a lisp*] and acting weird. They treated me like a complete freak." In the early 1990s, Brian disclosed to a coworker, a lesbian to whom he had become close. "It basically ended our friendship. She just kind of put a lot of distance between us. She stopped talking to me." Over ten years later, Gabriel disclosed to a gay man he had become close to in his first stealth job. While there were no immediate negative consequences, his coworker informed their employers about Gabriel's transition after the two men had a personal disagreement. Gabriel's employers sanctioned him, telling him, "You did this to yourself; you brought your gender issues into it." His employers responded to this information by unexpectedly accusing him of sexually harassing women in his workplace. He quit in response to the allegations, which meant abandoning an important part of his employment history.

These responses reveal two interesting points. First, despite the unity suggested by the *LGBT* acronym, gay men and lesbians are not always allies to transgender people—a point that goes back to the long history of "border wars" between these two groups (Califia 2002; G. Rubin 1992). Gay men and lesbians can still hold a deep belief that there are two and only two genders, even while they challenge assumptions that heterosexual desire is a natural outcome of this male/female binary. Second, when stealth transmen are outed at work, people do not necessarily interpret this information to be about gender. Chris's coworkers begin to treat him like a stereotypical homosexual (notably a *male* homosexual), suggesting they interpret his classmate's gossip to be about sexual identity rather than gender identity. Gabriel, too, faces sexual charges (sexual harassment) rather than gender charges (gender misrepresentation or gender fraud). While it is unclear whether he was being viewed as a woman sexually harassing women (a lesbian), a man sexually harassing women, or in a different way entirely, his gender was not made the central issue. Regardless of how these disclosures are framed, however, transmen are discredited (Goffman 1963b), a strategy that maintains the naturalness of a heteronormative male/female binary.

Other stealth transmen experienced different reactions, particularly if they purposefully came out to their employer, coworkers, or the human resources (HR) person at their workplace. In many of these incidents, employers and HR personnel offered what I call "protective responses." As with the blindness toward any information that contradicted transmen's male appearances in the interview process, employers and coworkers did not immediately believe that someone they knew as a man could have once lived as a woman. In another stealth job Chris held early in his transition, he again encountered a woman with whom he had gone to high school. She promised that she would not tell anyone about his past. However, this promise was soon broken. "Basically, for the first time in my life, I had girls like, like [be sexually attracted] to me. And I think what happened was that she was thinking, 'Oh, that is sick. I better warn them.'" He found out that his past had been shared when a coworker asked him if he had a twin sister—a more plausible explanation for this coworker than that Chris had not always lived as a man. A group of friends eventually pulled him aside to tell him the rumors flying around the workplace. "I said, 'Well, it's true. That is just the way my life is.' The next day, I brought it up [transition] again, and they were like, 'Oh, we thought you were joking.'" He adds, "When you tell people, they just don't get it. They don't really think about it. Nothing changed. I still did [men's jobs,] and there was never a situation where I felt I was treated a certain way [like a woman]." He continued to work there for several years, consistently getting promotions and raises.

In some cases, stealth transmen purposefully tell an employer about their transitions. This type of disclosure is a risky proposition. Discussing these risks, Roger, who had been stealth for over twenty years, says, "You can never predict how a person is going to react. And then, after you tell them, it is too late to say, 'Oh, just kidding. I just wanted to see what you would do.'" Wayne (t. mid-1980s), who had built a successful professional career, also worried that such a disclosure would significantly alter his work experiences:

> There is something to be said about being male-bodied or a male-perceived person in [an all-]male space. Unless you have done it, it is hard to explain. Having that knowledge that I wasn't always this way might take away from that. I know that for me, it is important to be viewed as just a guy, not as a person with a particular past.

While Wayne did not worry about stigmatizing or violent reactions, he feared being "regendered," being returned, at least in people's minds, to the female side of the binary. Chris expressed similar concerns: "[My employees] would probably be fine with it. But I wouldn't like for them to know. Sometimes I get emotional at work. I don't get any more emotional than [the other men], but if they knew about me, it would give them a reason to say, 'Oh, well, he used to be a girl.'" These fears are not unwarranted. When Winston was outed to some coworkers at his professional job, ironically by an employee he had come out to because she was beginning a gender transition, he told his boss about his transition in order to head off any negative repercussions. She was very supportive, and he saw no change in his job duties. But sometimes she joked with him when he got upset at work to "stop being such a girl."

The benefits of coming out, such as being able to explain when a female name comes up on a credit check, can outweigh the potential risks of marginalization or regendering. Henry wanted some record that he had disclosed his transgender identity at work in case he ever encountered problems on the job. Under California law, if he was harassed or fired for being transgender, he would have a case against his employer. He decided to come out to the head of HR. The response was underwhelming. "He asked me why I was telling him . . . like why I thought that was important." Sam told his boss in a blue-collar job about his transition because he had participated in a documentary about transgender people and was worried his boss, whom he highly esteemed, would see it and feel betrayed. "He said, 'I'm waiting for the punch line.' I told him there wasn't one, and he started laughing. I knew that it blew his mind. He was, like, 'Man, I would never have known.'" He rushed to assure Sam that he still saw him as a man. "He said, 'You're a dude to me. I don't care. You are Sam. You have always been a guy to me. For five years, you have worked your butt off like a guy. . . . You can run circles around [the other men]." Yet he immediately cautioned Sam not to tell any of the other men at work, as he did not feel that they would understand.

Stephen was hired in a male-dominated service job while he was still in the process of changing his legal gender. He told the owner during the hiring process about his transition: "He didn't really understand what I was saying when I told him that my name on the driver's license, my passport, my Social Security, it was not going to look the same as who I am. It kind of shocked him a bit. But he was like, 'Okay, no problem. I don't care what you do as long as you do your job.'" He adds, "It took him a few days to get used to it, to forget that privileged information. But now the way he interacts with me, I'm just a guy." As the workplace had a very macho culture, the owner initially worried about other employees finding out this information. "He took me aside and said, 'Look, if anyone asks you anything [about your gender], you let me know. You tell them to go fuck themselves if you don't want to answer their questions. And you can tell them I said so.'" Brad's female name came up on his background check for a blue-collar job. After he showed his doctor's letter to the HR employee, she told him it was fine. "She kept my file separately so the manager could not see it. She didn't want anyone to make an issue out of it."

When Scott applied for his first stealth job at a retail workplace with a macho culture, one of the HR employees contacted him about a problem with his background check. "I flipped to the page in the application [where you have to disclose other names you have gone by]. I closed the door, and I pointed and said, 'This [female] name is the name I used to be known as. So you are going to have to run that one, too.' He was kind of quiet, and I said, 'Does that make sense to you?' He said, 'Yes.'" Scott added, "He never spoke of it again. He always called me 'Scott' and never treated me any differently." The HR person in Trey's professional workplace called him in to discuss his female name, which emerged on his background check. "I didn't know what to say. And he all of a sudden said, 'I know what this is.' I was thinking, 'You do?' He said, 'You are one of those people who are born with both [genitalia].' I was, like, 'Uh, yeah, something like that.'" He assured Trey he would never bring it up again—and he never did. These protective reactions transmen describe do not mean that employers and HR personnel forget this information. In contrast, my interviews with coworkers of open transmen suggest this information stays in people's minds for a long time. What these situations do illustrate is that, in these cases, employers are willing to be facially supportive of transmen as men—affording them social maleness at work.

This protection is precarious, however. In his current job, Gabriel anticipated his potential employer asking him about the female name on his background check. While he planned on being stealth with coworkers, he decided to disclose to his immediate supervisor. "She said, 'Can you tell us what is going on?' I said, 'I'm transgender.' And she's like, 'What?' I said, 'I'm a girl who became a guy.' She said, 'Oh, we thought it was a big deal, like you killed someone in a different name.' She didn't care." Yet this information became a "big deal" when the computer technicians did a review of the work computers and found that someone had gone to a Web site with *trans* in the title. The Web site no longer existed, so it was impossible to see what type of information was on it. It was also impossible to know which employee had gone to this site. But Gabriel was called in. "She [his supervisor] said, 'We found this Web site, and you can't look at surgical pictures and transsexual pornographic images here at work. You can be fired for this.' Just because they know I am transgender, they immediately assumed I was looking at something inappropriate." He admitted to having used the computer, but only to read an online invitation for a transgender community fund-raiser. Gabriel kept his job. However, with no law in Texas protecting gender identity, he had no recourse if he was wrongfully terminated.

Robert's immediate boss, a friend from a youth group he attended, knew about his transition. Though Robert was still legally female, this friend secured him a job working as a man at a retail store he managed. Yet, when this boss was fired, the protection vanished. The new manager seemed uncomfortable with Robert being listed as female on the work records but looking like a man. While she never made a direct comment to him, he was laid off for being "slow" two weeks later, the first performance complaint he had ever received. Because his layoff was technically about job performance, not gender identity, he felt he had no legal case under California law. As he wanted to remain stealth in the future, he also was not willing to bring legal action—a very public endeavor. These experiences show that protective responses offer very little real protection to stealth transmen, as they can be rapidly transformed into marginalization at the whim of employers.

Protecting Transmen, Protecting Gender

The workplace experiences of stealth transmen illustrate how gender difference is manufactured at work. Based on their appearance, transmen are given jobs men are assumed to have a natural ability to do. While they may have wanted these types of jobs when they worked as women, they often were denied them even when they had the same skills and abilities. Similarly, transmen are enlisted into men's workplace cultures and excluded from women's interactions. The sharp contrast of this inclusion/exclusion shows how both men and women participate in creating and maintaining gender distinctions at work—distinctions that are justified on the basis of natural differences schemas. Rather than innocuous differences in job duties and conversational topics, these divisions provide stealth transmen and cisgender men with more powerful homosocial networks than their women coworkers—networks that can bring more authority, economic opportunities, and in some cases, financial rewards. These differences suggest that cultural schemas about natural differences between men and women naturalize interactional and institutional gender inequality.

The protective responses some stealth men find when they are outed or when they come out at work raise a paradox, as these reactions contradict theoretical assumptions about how stigma works (Goffman 1963b) and how people respond to a challenge to their everyday reality (Garfinkel 1967; Kessler and McKenna 1978). Yet a closer analysis shows that these two reactions—marginalization or protection—do the same structural work. On an individual level, protection responses are much more beneficial to transmen, as they head off any potentially negative reactions from coworkers. Yet this protection is always precarious, particularly when there are no federal workplace protections for transgender people. These protective responses do enable stealth transmen to remain one of the guys, an important identity for many stealth transmen. However, on a structural level, protective responses maintain a male/female binary by ignoring the implications: that appearance, genitalia, and gender identity do not always line up as expected. While the type of employer reaction matters a great deal to individual transmen, the end result for the workplace is the same regardless of the reaction: the male/female binary, and the resulting gendered division of labor based on men and women's seemingly natural differences, remains unchanged.

CHAPTER FIVE

Business as Usual

Workplace Responses to Open Transmen

While Julian (t. mid-2000s) applied for his blue-collar job as a woman, he was already planning his transition. Based on his appearance, he was frequently referred to as "he" by clients meeting him for the first time. Julian's boss always jumped in quickly with a "she" under the assumption that this misgendering was embarrassing. After a few months on the job, Julian decided it was time to raise the topic: "I said, 'Hey, I need to talk to you about something. I know you've heard people say 'he' when they are referring to me. You've corrected them in the past. I just don't think we need to correct them anymore because that is how I am going to be more comfortable.'" He added, "I am taking steps to transition [and changing my name to Julian].' [My boss] said, 'Great, I can respect that.'" After the official announcement at work, another supervisor told him, "As far as your career goes, this is not going to affect it one bit. If it does, it will be over my dead body." A coworker left a supportive note on his computer. While these responses were comforting, he retained concern about how the Texas "good ol' boy" clients would respond when they heard the news. These fears were allayed when a longtime client ran into him on a field site and said, "So, it's Julian now?" "He caught on to the gender part on his own. When I went out to the [field] to meet him, he introduced me to his staff and said, 'He is the *guy* who does all our whatever.' Just roll[ed] with it."

Open workplace transitions present a potential challenge to the gender order of the workplace. Institutional actors have several possible avenues of responses, such as problematizing the existing social order (Raeburn 2004) or embracing a new way of doing things "naturally" (Dalton and Fenstermaker 2002). As transitions stand to disrupt deeply held natural differences schemas, a third, and more likely, choice could be marginalizing transmen as a way to smooth over the threat (Goffman 1963b; Garfinkel 1967)—a reaction some transmen face. Yet Julian's story shows another workplace reaction: incorporating transmen as one of the guys at work. In such situations, employers and coworkers frame gender transitions as a natural solution for someone who is trapped in the wrong body. Incorporating these rare cases into being one of the guys at work places transmen into what *should have been* their correct place in the male/female binary. Transmen who are incorporated as one of the guys have very different individual workplace experiences than transmen who are marginalized. Yet both reactions minimize potential challenges to employers' and coworkers' natural differences schemas and maintain workplace gender hierarchies as business as usual.

Becoming Men at Work

Openly transitioning and remaining in the same job became a more viable possibility for transgender people in the 2000s. Social science research from the gender clinic era shows that some people attempted to transition and remain in the same jobs, typically with negative outcomes (Feinbloom 1976; Kando 1973; Perkins 1983; Bolin 1988). Doctors and therapists and many transgender people themselves discouraged this strategy (Feinbloom 1976; Bolin 1988). The concern was that employers and coworkers would never be able to accept a transgender colleague's new social gender as authentic. Yet table 5.1 suggests a historical shift away from the deep stealth model as the only acceptable workplace strategy. The majority of the thirty-one transmen in this study (77 percent) who attempted to openly transition and remain in the same job did so in the 2000s. Of these transmen, twenty-four met my criteria for a successful transition: they were given employer support for their transitions, they felt that their employers and coworkers made an effort to address them by a new name (if necessary) and by male pronouns (if asked), they did not feel they experienced harassment related to being

TABLE 5.1 **Open workplace transitions by year of transition, by state**

	1980s	1990s	2000s
Transitioned openly			
California	1	6	13
Texas	0	0	11
Hired as transgender			
California	0	0	5
Texas	0	0	3
Total	1	6	32

Note: This table reflects people making attempts to openly transition and remain in the same jobs, and/or apply for a job as openly transgender. As three people used both strategies, there are 39 cases representing 36 people. See the methodological appendix for information about how stealth and open strategies vary across careers.

transgender,[1] their workplace duties were not cut or curtailed, they were given access to a bathroom they were comfortable using, and, if they left this job, this decision was reported as unrelated to their transitions. Also in the 2000s, eight transmen came out as transgender in their hiring interviews. All of these transmen were hired—though one transman was never formally scheduled.

Open workplace transitions have many potential benefits. While Nicky (t. late 2000s) wanted to go stealth eventually, he did not want to be looking for work in the midst of his transition. "I just didn't have the money to lose my job." For transmen such as Paul (t. mid-2000s) who transition well into their careers, they can retain their employment histories. "I had two choices: eliminating everybody in my life so far or telling the world and just moving on. And eliminating, that just wasn't an option because I had just started building a reputation [in my field]." Other transmen, such as Colin (t. mid-2000s), openly transition at work because they view it as activism. "I want to maintain an openness about my transition. Being openly trans[gender] so that I can educate people." Yet, regardless of their motivations, transmen cannot guarantee how their employers and coworkers will react to the announcement that they are changing names, pronouns, appearance, and, ultimately, social gender. Some employers and coworkers reject the transition, thereby *neutralizing challenges to the male/female binary*. Others anchor transmen to a legal female gender, *policing the male/female binary*. Some workplaces transform transmen into "transgender workers"—*creating transgender tokens* who can feel marginalized. In still other cases, employers and coworkers reshape gender boundaries, *incorporating transmen as just one of the guys*.

Neutralizing Challenges to the Male/Female Binary

All of his life, Winston (t. early 1990s) had a long-standing sense of him-self as a man. When he approached his direct supervisor about his inten-tion to transition, he had no desire to make "gender trouble" at work. Rather, he had been at his professional job for several years and hoped to continue building his career there as a man. He left the interaction with a feeling he had been told "no" without the word actually being ut-tered. "She told me she was supportive, but she couldn't speak for the owners. It was a small company, and reputation and appearance were very important." While he was waiting for the verdict, he received his regular six-month evaluation, which, for the first time, was negative. "I saw what was coming, and my [professional] reputation meant more to me than keeping that job. So I left with good references." Aaron (t. late 1990s) transitioned almost ten years after Winston. He had worked for several years in a semiprofessional job with only a handful of employees. He considered his workplace "prescreened," as his mascu-line clothes and short hair as a woman employee had never been a prob-lem. His initial conversation with his boss went well. "I told her I was planning on transitioning . . . and she said okay. Never had any questions or anything." Yet, after this conversation, his job was not the same. "Ba-sically, she kind of slowly pushed me out. Didn't want me working there. I no longer had a work history in that field. I couldn't use her as a refer-ence because I knew she wasn't respectful of my transition. . . . I knew she would use my old name and refer to me with feminine pronouns." Though he was never fired, Aaron "decided" to go elsewhere.

Winston's and Aaron's experiences demonstrate how employers who do not want to support open transitions can neutralize potential chal-lenges to the gender order. Rather than directly saying no, employers overscrutinize the workplace contributions of transmen or make subtle, negative changes to workplace tasks. For Winston, receiving his first neg-ative evaluation was a harbinger of what was to come—a slew of nega-tive evaluations that, taken together, would justify punitive action on the part of his employer. Nathan (t. mid-2000s) experienced similar treat-ment when he openly transitioned in a professional job he had held suc-cessfully for over ten years. He was never overtly harassed, but he felt his employers began to treat him "with kid gloves." On the surface, they supported his transition, asking him to present a "What Is Transgen-der" workshop to his colleagues.[2] At the same time, he began to receive negative evaluations. He left the job two years after his transition, going stealth in another professional job.

Neutralizing responses to open transitions are not always subtle. Tex (t. mid-2000s) began his transition the summer before he entered a professional degree program. At the time, he worked in an athletics-based summer program for elementary school children in a politically conservative suburb in Texas. He had always had a good relationship with his boss, as well as with the parents and children who were clients. He approached the topic of his transition expecting a positive reaction. "[My boss] said, 'If any of the kids or the parents think you are gay or trans[gender], you don't have a job here. You do what you need to do. I respect you. But this is a business, and that [a transition] doesn't work in a conservative city.'" He added that once the generation of children and parents who had known Tex as "she" had aged out of the program, Tex would be welcomed back. This reaction from his employer, similar in some ways to what Winston had experienced twenty years before, asks him to recognize a higher loyalty to business and professionalism rather than to make a demand for workplace recognition of what is framed as his "personal issue."

Crispin (t. mid-2000s) experienced overt neutralization when he announced his intention to transition in a blue-collar job. As one of the only women on his job site, he had strained relationships with his employers and coworkers. In the midst of a meeting with human resources about gender discrimination he had experienced on the job, he announced his transition. "I said, 'This is a good time to tell you guys. I am a transsexual person. I am getting ready to go through with a transition.' . . . They were all just sitting there going, 'Okay.'" While his employers did nothing to stop the transition, they did nothing to support it, either. "There was a supervisor who thought I was a joke because of my transition. And people overheard him say, 'Crispin doesn't [need any help]. Let's see how much of a man he really is.' He would make me stay out there on the job all by myself." The harassment was short-lived, as Crispin's entire team was laid off under the pretext of labor cutbacks. He resisted seeing this layoff as related to his transition until the rest of his team was hired back the next month and he was not. Scott (t. mid-2000s) had good relationships with his coworkers and his boss, a lesbian. Immediately after he announced his transition, however, this relationship with his boss changed. "She kept asking me, 'When are you going on testosterone? What is your dose?' She wanted medical information that she did not have a right to have." Her reaction stemmed from a negative experience she had a few years prior with another transman. Scott felt that she was using this past experience as a model for his transition—an evaluation he felt was unfair. Though he had been given a substantial raise prior to his transition announcement, he began to face constant censure from his boss. He eventually put in his two-week notice. She responded by asking him to leave that day and had him escorted off the premises by security. "She told my clients that I was fired because I was on testosterone and couldn't be trusted to be appropriate."

These experiences show how employers can neutralize the potential threat to the gender order that open transitions present, in ways both overt and subtle. Transmen's decisions to leave the workplace look like personal choices or, in the cases of overt firing, the result of being bad workers. The institutional discrimination underlying these personal "choices" is rendered invisible, ensuring the reproduction of business as usual.

Policing the Male/Female Binary

A small group of transmen found that employers wanted to retain them, or were willing to hire them, as long as they worked as women. To this end, employers policed the male/female binary, holding transmen accountable to workplace expectations and standards for women workers. This enforcement typically included an appeal to the binding status of a female legal gender. Because Riley (t. early 2000s) was legally female, his boss expected him to conform to a feminine dress code. "I wore an outfit one day during the summer that had shorts. It was still very professional. My boss had a really hard time with that. He made me go home and change into long pants. . . . But there are other men at work who wear shorts all the time." Taking cues from supervisors, his coworkers were slow to call Riley "he." "They would still try to overlay language that just didn't fit me. I would say to them, 'Could you just look at reality for a second and see that I am not feminine?'"

Overwhelmingly, these policing reactions occurred in Texas with transmen who worked in service jobs—occupations with high turnover rates in which employers have less investment in responding to what can be dismissed as an employee's personal issue. Brad's (t. early 2000s) employer in his food service job supported his transition and changed names and pronouns with him. "Everything was great until [that manager] changed stores. A new lady came in. She was Baptist, really Christian. . . . She had heard about it [transition]. She made it an issue right away." The application Brad had initially filled out had not asked for gender information. His new boss began to push the issue, asking Brad to fill out a demographic sheet on the computer. "When I got to the question about sex, she was standing right there, looking. She said, 'Remember, if you put the wrong one [sex], it can be considered lying.'" Brad, who carried a doctor's letter stating that he was under treatment for "transsexualism," marked the "M" box. "I took that letter to mean I could work as a man. She was really upset that I checked male but was biologically female. She considered it wrong [from a religious standpoint]. She started calling me female and 'she' all the time." Brad put in for a transfer to another store. His new manager was supportive of Brad's transition, but he asked if they could keep the information from coworkers, a request that effectively made Brad stealth.

During his job interview for a managerial position in a service industry, Christian (t. late 2000s) told his potential employer he identified as transgender. While he had not started T, he asked to be referred to with masculine pronouns. She informed him it was illegal for him to be referred to as male and to use the men's bathroom when he was legally female. His female name was kept on the schedule, though he used "Christian" with the staff. He ended up in a situation in which most of his staff referred to him as "he" and his supervisors referred to him as "she." He eventually quit the job, as lacking a fixed gender generated harassment from coworkers. Johnny (t. mid-2000s) began his transition in a service job that had a high level of client interaction. His employers expressed support for his transition until a customer complained about seeing a woman using the men's restroom. "It was a big issue. I fought them over it. It almost got to the point where I was going to sue them. Then I got my [doctor's] letter, and everything just calmed down." Johnny's experience demonstrates a potential counterstrategy to the enforcement of legal gender—the production of a doctor's letter. This letter can be taken by employers to mean that someone with medical authority is validating and taking responsibility for the transition. Yet these letters are not always effective, as Brad's experience with his religious supervisor demonstrates. For this employer, God's law overrode man's law.

Caleb (t. mid-2000s) sought employment in a retail job that was known for employing gay men. His logic was that a store that would hire gay men would not balk at hiring a transman. As he applied during a

holiday season, he was hired immediately—but as a man based on his appearance. When his female name came up on a background check, the
store manager told him that being openly transgender was not a problem
because the company had a nondiscrimination policy. However, he was
never put on the schedule. When he confronted his boss, he was told,
"We can't really keep you on payroll because we have a policy about any
male that works here can't wear women's clothes and any woman that
works here can't wear men's clothes." Caleb, who wore men's clothes but
was still legally female, had no rebuttal. "It was in their handbook [this
policy]. He wasn't lying. But it was a dumb excuse for why they didn't
want me there." Caleb faced two choices he found equally coercive: wear
women's clothes or find a new job.

These experiences show how male/female distinctions can be written into organizational policy in a way that counteracts facially inclusive
nondiscrimination policies. Appealing to the dress code or laws about
bathroom use allows workplaces to police who can belong to the categories of "man" and "woman." The emphasis on legal gender removes
the responsibility from employers—they are not discriminating against
transgender people, they are simply upholding preset rules or laws. And
unless transmen can produce a counter to legal gender, such as a doctor's
letter, or have the legal possibility and financial resources to sue, they
have few options beyond leaving these jobs. It also shows the precariousness of acceptance of an open transition in states such as Texas that
do not have gender identity protection laws. While individual employers may accept the transition, there is no guarantee that incoming bosses
will maintain this support.

Creating Transgender Tokens

Transmen who openly transitioned or who sought employment as out
transmen in workplaces that worked closely with LGBT clientele describe a third type of workplace reaction. All of these men worked in
California in professional and semiprofessional occupations with a focus on LGBT-related issues. Transmen in these fields described a sense
of being boxed in as "transgender" rather than accepted as "queer" or
"gay"—identities that had equal or more salience for them. After his unsuccessful attempt at openly transitioning in his professional job, Aaron
got an LGBT-related job. Identifying as a queer man, he thought he

would be incorporated as just one of the gay guys. However, his gender transition was made central to his workplace experience. "[When anyone had questions about transgender], they just told them, 'Go talk to Aaron.' Not 'This is how we work with transgender clients here.' It was 'Go talk to Aaron.'" Aaron complained about his coworkers repeatedly telling clients that he was a transman when the information was not relevant to their interaction. "[My supervisor] told me I needed to be more open with myself. . . . I couldn't believe they fucking said that! You can't make my personal business part of my job. You can't force me to do that." Aaron wasn't trying to be stealth at work, but he did want control over what he viewed as personal information.

As the only transman in a workplace composed primarily of gay men, Christopher (t. mid-2000s) also felt his transgender identity was continually highlighted. He was hired to be the liaison to the transgender community, a job he began to feel symbolized a theoretical commitment to transgender clients that fell short in practice. "When it came to transgender clients, I was expected to encourage them to pursue certain types of [expensive medical treatments] that they didn't necessarily need in my opinion." Reflecting on this job, he notes, "You would think that people in the gay community, people who are gay men, would not necessarily treat other people in the queer and trans community poorly. But that was just one of those things where I was, like, 'Well, I guess shit flows downhill!'" When he was fired from his liaison position, he felt it was because his loyalties lay with other transgender people rather than with the monetary interests of his employer.

In these occupations, transmen felt their coworkers did not quite know how to incorporate them into workplace cultures—illustrating the distance that can exist between gay men, lesbians, and transgender people (Minter 2006). Though Jack's (t. mid-2000s) workplace served transwomen clients, his coworkers—predominantly gay men—were unfamiliar with the concept of a transman. "I told my coworkers I was FTM, and some of them were like, 'I have never heard of that before.' They mess up on pronouns, and what really bothers me is that they don't correct each other." While his coworkers often referred to him as "she," he felt that he was seen as some type of "gender other." "They definitely interact with me differently than they do with lesbians. It's different. I notice that difference. I don't know what I must be to them. They just must think I'm some weirdo or freak or something." Aaron expressed a similar feeling. He wasn't one of the girls, but neither did he fit into his coworkers' conceptualization of a gay man. "They just treat me like an other. Like, 'I don't know what to do with you.'"

Not all transmen experienced being a "transgender worker" as marginalizing. Ken (t. mid-2000s) was aware he was selected for transgender-related jobs in his semiprofessional career. However, as he wanted to work with transgender clients, he did not experience this selection as alienating. Douglas (t. late 1990s) also was willing at the onset of his transition to be the go-to person on transgender issues. He notes, "I would say, in the aggregate, it got me more speaking engagements, more attention, and, as a result, I am now getting to talk more about other political issues I am interested in." However, these requests could become tokenizing when transmen felt no control over how employers and coworkers deployed their identities. "Transgender" became a master status—an identity that overrode all others—even when they personally felt that other identities, such as gay or queer, had more salience for them. The identity becomes static, as "doing transgender" (C. Connell 2006) is built into their occupational role. Transmen who worked in these jobs did have the highest expectations of workplace support, as they anticipated that an LGBT organization would be trans-inclusive. These high expectations may account for some of the reported negativity. Illustrating this, transmen who worked in non-LGBT-related jobs typically expected that their coworkers would have difficulty changing names and pronouns with them. Yet, while expectations frame reactions, transmen's experiences in these occupations are still suggestive of the ongoing lack of knowledge many gay men and lesbians have regarding transgender lives—a lack of knowledge that is problematic when considering the transgender inclusion the acronym *LGBT* suggests.

That gay men and lesbians can treat their transgender coworker in a way that makes him feel like an "other"—not quite male, not quite female—suggests that gay and lesbian people may be more willing to entertain an alternative to the male/female binary. Yet, rather than opening up new space for possibilities of gender identities, this "othering" can box transmen into being "token trannies." And transmen felt that when they defended their personal identities as queer and/or gay men, their coworkers, particularly gay men, positioned them as extreme versions of butch lesbians—relegating them to social femaleness. With the exception of Douglas, the four other transmen working in these jobs were transmen of color in predominantly white organizations, which suggests this "othering" may reflect assumptions not just about gender but also about race. These experiences demonstrate that the mere creation of a third gender category is not necessarily transformative in regard to a hierarchical, racialized gender order (Fausto-Sterling 2000).

Incorporating Transmen as One of the Guys

The fourth reaction open transmen reported was what I frame as a reshaping of gender boundaries, both institutionally and interactionally, that incorporated them as one of the guys at work. These responses typically occurred in professional workplaces.[3] On an institutional level, employers treat the transition as a logistical problem to be handled through a series of directives. Employers framed the transition as a private, oftentimes medical, issue that should not be widely discussed in the workplace. Brian (t. early 1990s) describes the reaction to his open transition in his semiprofessional job in California: "I explained the situation and told [my boss] what my plans were. She was supportive. [I could tell] she was a little freaked out, too. She didn't really want to ask any questions. It was like, 'Okay, we can do this, but I don't want to hear anything about it.'" Expecting to be fired, he adds, "It wasn't a negative situation, though. It was positive." Preston (t. early 2000s) experienced a similar reaction in his California blue-collar job. "[My boss] said, 'This is a personal issue for you. We don't make announcements when people get married. We don't make announcements when people get divorced. This is a business." While his boss wanted official documentation, including his new driver's license and Social Security card, he told Preston he would do everything in his power to make sure that the transition went smoothly.

Beyond relegating open transitions to being a private matter, employers emphasized professionalism. To achieve this end, they typically offered directives to employees about how to handle the transition. Colin (t. mid-2000s) says about his transition, "I met [with the head guy]. He was really great about [my transition]. He even made some jokes. He said, 'Do you know how hard it is to shave every day?' He met with all his directors and told them how to handle the transition." Clark anticipated a supportive reaction, as he had been in the job for over six years. However, shortly after he started hormones, he decided to move to a different branch of the same store. He worried that his new employer might react negatively to him. "I said to my old manager, 'For you, this transition is natural. You don't think about it anymore. But is the new manager aware of my situation?' He said, 'Yeah, he knows.' And he said, 'As long as Clark comes in and does his work, I don't care what he does [in his personal life].'" Cole, Anton, Clark, Anthony, and Nicky all transitioned in retail jobs in the mid-2000s. Their employers agreed to the transitions and made an effort to bring others on board with changing names and pronouns. While this support was not always effusive, employers still offered it and enforced it.

In some instances, this incorporation was institutionalized. Preston's employers told him that he might have to be rehired as a man and get another physical. He also had to start complying with the men's dress code: "I used to have long hair [on the job]. I like long hair. But as a male, you are not allowed to have it at my workplace. And I used to wear one earring to work. I had to take out my earring and cut my hair." Keith (t. mid-2000s), who transitioned in California in a blue-collar job, was moved to a new locker room. "[The day after my official announcement], I got to work and my supervisor was waiting for me. He said he was coming to help me move out of the women's locker room and into the men's locker room." Elliott (t. mid-2000s) also moved from the women's locker room to the men's locker room, though he waited until he felt he passed as a man to make this change.

This support was echoed in interactions with coworkers. Ethan recounts, "Everybody in the office was exceptionally cool about it. [One of the women], she made a point to tell me personally that she didn't understand it [my transition], but she loved me and thought I was amazing. She was proud of me for following my heart." Preston adds, "I have not had any negative comments. . . . People have been more like, 'We are proud of you. We think this is great.'" While Nathan felt pushed out of his job by his direct supervisors, he made a point of saying that his coworkers were not the problem. "A few of them were shocked, but the majority were not. After [my announcement], some of them actually congratulated me or made a comment about how brave they thought I was." Simon (t. mid-2000s) notes, "My coworkers, they definitely notice changes [in my appearance] and stuff. And they comment on it in a really positive way." Coworkers may, of course, be making negative comments about the transition out of their transgender colleague's hearing. However, in my interviews with coworkers, they, too, commented on the lack of discussion about the transition at work. This silence was a source of consternation to several of them, as they had expected to see negative reactions from other people at work who they expected would label the transition "strange." Only one coworker reporting hearing a "joke" about her colleague's transition—a situation that was stopped by upper-level management.

Most transmen could think of one or two coworkers who verbally opposed their transition or who began to avoid them after they announced they were becoming men. One of Jake's colleagues asked him if this was internalized misogyny. Scott and Douglas worked with women who grieved for the loss of a female coworker. Nicky and Trevor recount two men in their workplaces going out of their way never to share a bathroom with them. When transmen's descriptions of these encounters are analyzed, gay men and actively practicing Christians were described as the most likely to voice open resistance to the transition—a pairing that makes strange bedfellows of two groups typically in opposition with each other (Fetner 2008). Scott's Baptist colleague sighed and rolled her eyes throughout his coming-out speech to the workplace. Eli (t. early 2000s) had an older gay manager who opposed his transition. "He would always say 'she' in reference to me. And it was bizarre because as more time passed [and I looked like a man], people would be looking at him like he was a nutball." Showing the role employers can play in countering this opposition, Elliott's supervisors held an information session on transgender issues after two religious coworkers complained about his use of the men's locker room. The workers were told to come voice their complaints or forever hold their peace. They did not attend, and Elliott continued to use the men's locker room.

Changing pronouns is a visible display of coworkers' willingness to be supportive. Simon and Xavier (t. mid-2000s) did not expect their coworkers to use male pronouns immediately because they did not yet physically pass as men. Both men found that their coworkers began to check in with them to find out, "Is it time to change pronouns yet?" While this question suggests coworkers' commitment to upholding a male/female binary, both transmen took the question as a sign of support. This change can be difficult, however. Often during our interviews, coworkers would shift back and forth between *he* and *she* when discussing their colleague. They expressed their dismay at how many times they had used female pronouns with their colleague after the announcement of the transition. One woman says, "I find myself saying 'she' [a lot]. I always try to catch myself and correct myself because I don't do it on purpose. I think that has been the hardest part. I just do it out of habit, and I hate it." Another woman echoes these sentiments: "He was 'she' to me before. So it took some time. I would slip up in front of him and feel a little embarrassed and apologize. That was the hardest part for me. I was afraid he would think I hadn't bought into it, that I wasn't in support of him." Her use of "bought into it" suggests she does not necessarily see her colleague as a man. However, she is still expressing her willingness to perform as a visibly supportive colleague by calling him "he." And while coworkers' responses demonstrate how difficult interactional regendering can be, they also show how much effort some coworkers make. Highlighting this, several transmen recounted one or two coworkers taking on the role of pronoun police, calling out other colleagues who persisted in using *she* and *her.*

The men's restroom is another symbol of support. At most of the workshops I attended at transgender conferences that focused on workplace issues, how to handle the question of the bathroom was a focal point. For transmen who face policing of their legal gender, the bathroom is a major battleground. When transmen receive employer support, however, access to a men's bathroom was not reported as an issue. Some transmen sidestep this issue by seeking out individual bathrooms or bathrooms on other floors, a decision they described as personally comfortable to them—though it can also ease coworkers' tensions. In some cases, however, men went out of their way to invite transmen into the closest men's room. Colin says, "Two of the heads of the workplace pulled me aside and said, 'We just want you to know that we heard you are using a unisex bathroom. Use the men's bathroom. We don't care." As he transitioned more than fifteen years before our interview, Brian did not recall many of the comments he received from his coworkers. However, he clearly remembered men telling him to feel free to use the men's restroom. The men in Douglas's workplace held a mock ceremony to present him with the key to the men's room. Trevor (t. late 1990s) felt that his men coworkers went out of the way to make him feel welcome in the bathroom. "There was one guy at work, if I was in the bathroom with him, he would chat and make jokes. Like clearly trying to make me feel like it was normal to see me there." Elliott describes his coworkers making a similar effort to make him feel comfortable in the men's locker room: "The guys walk in and are, like, 'Hey, Elliott, what's up?' They just do their usual thing. That has helped."

Being incorporated as one of the guys at work brings a change in workplace interactions. Sociological research on stealth transgender people highlights how they consciously manage their behavior to create a new gender identity that does not line up with their bodies (Garfinkel 1967). While the theoretical import of this research has been to show how everyone—not just transgender people—actively produces gendered behavior (West and Zimmerman 1987), transgender people still come across as overdoing gender to "prove" their authenticity. Some open transmen did express a sense that they should change some of their workplace behaviors, worrying, as Nicky and Preston did, that hugging and touching women in a friendly way was inappropriate behavior from a man. Other transmen felt that openly transitioning allowed them more freedom not to change their behavior, as coworkers should not have different expectations of them. Most coworkers also mirrored this assessment, describing their colleague as "the same as before"—though one woman felt her colleague used more "macho" slang after his transition. Yet, while transmen may feel they are the same, they often noted the ways in which coworkers started to change their behavior toward them by enlisting them into "gender rituals" (Goffman 1977), ritualized interactions that display normative expectations about masculinity and femininity.

Discussing how his workplace experiences changed after his transition, Kelly says, "No one really asked me to do anything [physical] before I transitioned. Now, this one coworker, she is always asking me, 'Can you move this? Can you hang this up?'" He adds, "It took some adjusting. At first, I thought she was picking on me, but then I realized that it was just that she saw me as male, and it was like, 'Oh, now you can do this.'" These new physical requests can be exciting, or they can be seen as sexist. Trevor describes his reaction:

> I had one supervisor that just kept asking me to move fucking furniture, and to handle all the electronic issues. And I would have to say over and over again to her—because it happened several times a day—that I have a hand problem, and I can't do it. . . . And, meanwhile, there were a couple of big, strong women who were much bigger and stronger than me. And she asked me! I am kind of a little guy! I pointed out to her that this was a sexist assumption. Repeatedly, I pointed that out.

Trevor's description of this interaction with his supervisor illustrates the rote quality of gender rituals. Because he looks like a man, his supervisor expects him to fix computers and move furniture. Her gender schemas preclude her from recognizing that women in the workplace might be better suited to this type of work than Trevor, a "little guy." Trevor's open contestation of his treatment also highlights a clear distinction between open and stealth transmen: while stealth transmen might find these types of requests sexist, they can feel less leeway to directly confront them as they fear they might invite unwanted scrutiny. When open transmen feel secure in their jobs, they can, in contrast, feel more leeway to draw attention to the implications of what they see as unequal interactions. Open transmen who sought to trouble normative gender ideology also found ways to disrupt the seeming naturalness of these gender rituals, such as making references to elements of a distinctly female past, such as being in the Girl Scouts or menstruating—their way of challenging these restrictive gender norms.

Some men try to take transmen on as "gender apprentices," offering them unsolicited advice about clothing and hygiene issues. Simon, who felt boxed in by this apprenticing, notes, "Men feel like it is their job to tell you what a man is. . . . They totally think they are helping me be a man." Colin, in contrast, recalls the following encounter fondly: "I was wearing a tie, and the director came in, and he was like, 'Oh no, that's not a good tie knot!' He showed me how to tie a Windsor knot." Keith, too, appreciated feedback from other men. "[One of my coworkers], he told me, 'Stop wearing open-collared shirts with a jacket. Put a tie on. . . . He gave me pointers on shaving, and we talk about skin care." In these situations, men are passing on knowledge stereotypically handed down from father to son or brother to brother. However, as many open transmen believe that there are many ways to embody maleness, they can experience this apprenticing as gender policing, as Simon did. These reactions from men suggest rigidity about doing maleness "right"—rigidity usually attributed to transgender, not cisgender, people.

Jake recounts few changes in his workplace treatment after his transition except one: "A lot of male colleagues, at least at first, started kind of slapping me on the back [*laughs*]. But I think it was with more force than they probably slapped each other on the back." He adds, "It was not that I had gained access to male privilege but that they were trying to affirm for me that they saw me as a male. . . . That was how they were going to be supportive of me as a guy. Slapping me on the back." Clark was invited to play tackle football with the men—an invitation he had not received working as a woman. Kelly's workplace was female-dominated. After he transitioned, he received much more friendly attention from the few men who worked with him: "Guys now will say, 'What's up?' more than they used to. They will say stuff to me that I know they wouldn't have said before. . . . One guy, he didn't really talk to me before. He told me that he used to be homophobic and he was working on that." He adds, "Recently we were talking about working out, and he made a comment that he was going to go home and work it [have sex] with his girlfriend for exercise. I know he never would have said that to me before." Julian, who transitioned in a blue-collar job, found that one of his employers made an effort to include him in "guy talk" about women—talk he saw as devaluing women. He notes, "I think he would like to treat me like one of the guys. But, for him, that means making jokes about women and stuff. And I cut him off."

While Julian resists the incorporation into men's joking culture, a culture that often is based on the denigration of women (Halle 1984; Kimmel 2004; Willis 1977), other transmen saw such inclusion as a sign of acceptance. In some cases, this inclusion addressed elements of transmen's transitions. David (t. mid-2000s) notes, "We had a pull-up bar [in the office]. We had a contest. . . . And I did way more than my [male] supervisor [as a woman]. When I told him about my transition, he just said, 'So, does that mean that you are going to beat me even more than you do now?'" Scott had a running joke with the only other man in his workplace about whether the toilet seat in the men's room should be left up or down—a joke that reflected Scott's decision not to have genital surgery. Keith was asked by men in his blue-collar job if he was "gonna grow a dick." He responded, "No, I am not going to have the add-a-dick-to-me surgery. . . . Why would I have that? I'm Snap-on-Tools! I can be whatever you want me to be. I don't even have to be awake. There are two words that will never fall into my vocabulary: *erectile dysfunction*." While he was joking around with another man at work after that discussion, this coworker called him a "dickless wonder." "I fell out of my chair laughing! I told him in response, 'Your breasts are bigger than mine ever were, dude!'" Transmen do draw a line between joking together and being made the butt of a joke. One of Peter's coworkers told him that his manager had been making jokes to her about Peter's transition and that she had complained. Highlighting the power of top-down support to stop harassment, the manager was sanctioned by their direct boss and forced to take a sensitivity training course.

Coworkers also reported on these changes. One of the coworkers I interviewed told me about making a trip to Hooters with his colleague because they shared a desire to look at scantily clad women. While they might have shared that desire prior to the transition, this trip happened only after they both looked male. One of the women coworkers described her surprise at seeing men sitting around her transman colleague's desk. "They can all be talking about something, and then I walk up and it just goes quiet." These changes do not mean that coworkers forget about the transition. In contrast, I posit that coworkers think about the transition a great deal for a long time. Prior to conducting my research for this project, I did an ethnographic study of a workplace that incidentally had a transman employee. While he had openly transitioned at this workplace, the transition had occurred several years prior to my arrival. Yet it was still a source of discussion, both by new coworkers and by those who had witnessed the transition. I never observed any negative comments made about him. But even several years after the transition, coworkers wanted to tell me—a new person—that our coworker "used to be a woman." This experience suggested to me that a workplace transition can become an open secret in the workplace—something passed on to new generations of workers in the hallways—even when no one directly engages about it with their transgender colleague.

In my interviews with women coworkers, they expressed both curiosity and concern about their colleague's decision about genital surgery. One woman noted, "I've asked him about, as I like to put it, 'What is going on downstairs [with his genitalia]?'" Almost all of the women also brought up their questions about chest surgery. "I can just imagine it and think, why would I want to cut my breasts off? It just strikes me as mutilation." Another woman said, "I was kind of horrified, at first, about the chest surgery. . . . I think it was a similar feeling that I would have to a friend getting breast implants. You just don't want them cutting themselves up." Women also expressed hesitation about accepting transmen as men. One woman noted, "[His gender] feels like a middle-of-the-road thing for me. I mean I have a lot of gay male friends, so I feel like in some ways there is a similar characteristic. . . . At the same time, it feels like friendships I've had with women. So, it just doesn't feel the same as just a typical straight guy that I am friends with." Another woman said, "It is not like I see him as a girl. It is more just that knowing about his transition, it is kind of an aura I pick up on." Their hesitation related to how to locate transmen in a male/female system.

Heterosexual men presented themselves as placing less emphasis on the reality of transmen's gender—though one man noted that he felt self-conscious at times when interacting with his colleague. "[I worry] if there is anything that I should or shouldn't say. But it is just kind of a small background thing for me." Men also had questions about surgeries, particularly genital surgery. However, while women's concerns were baldly inquisitive, men framed their concerns as relating to an interest in "science" or "biology"—highlighting the social strictures on a heterosexual man expressing interest in the body of another man. One man said, "I think the whole [transition] process is interesting. Just the whole biology of how it happens." Another man added, "I had some specific questions. . . . It was more like from a scientific approach. Transgender surgeries just fascinate me from a scientific approach." As heterosexual women have a right based on sexual desire to be interested in men's bodies, they expressed less hesitation about direct questions. Heterosexual men, in contrast, adopt a "forgetting" strategy in which they do not publicly address the transition after the initial announcement unless it is in joking interactions. Describing this strategy, one coworker gave his impression of how other men in his workplace approached his colleague's transition: "They would rather forget. . . . The problem is they've got only two categories. They've got 'normal' and they've got 'freak.' In order to avoid having to deal with a freak, they put him in normal." As heterosexual men typically hold the most workplace power, treating transmen like "normal" on an organizational and interactional level creates the increases in authority and respect that some open transmen report. Further highlighting this point, transmen who report being neutralized, policed, and tokenized were the most likely to work under heterosexual women and gay men. I am not suggesting that heterosexual men have fewer qualms about transmen's gender identity. Rather, I posit that when an open transition is given workplace support, heterosexual men feel more social pressures to "forget" about the transition—as questioning another man about his body makes them potentially suspect in a way that heterosexual women, lesbian women, and gay men are not.

Regardless of their questions about the transition, or their qualms about their colleague's gender identity, this incorporation reaction suggests that coworkers will socially comply with regendering their colleague, at least passing as supportive colleagues, even if they internally question the transition decision. While they may be unsure of their colleague's "real" gender, they are still willing, in many cases, to change names and pronouns, and, if they are men, to share a bathroom. Part of this compliance comes from employers' top-down directives about how the transition should be handled at work. The power of this top-down support for easing the process of open workplace transitions is similar to the workplace regulation of sexual harassment: employers that demonstrate a zero-tolerance policy toward sexual harassment have fewer incidents than employers that adopt a laissez-faire approach (Deux and Ullman 1983; Eisenberg 1998; Gruber and Bjorn 1982; Paap 2006; Welsh 1999). The reactions to these employer directives are clearly seen, as many open transmen who get support from employers note that coworkers who are uncomfortable with the transition avoid them rather than directly confronting them.

Top-down support does not fully account for incorporation, however, as some transmen, such as Scott and Nathan, who lacked strong employer support still find support from coworkers. The missing piece of the puzzle is the biological frame of transgenderism. The coworkers whom I interviewed overwhelmingly viewed their colleague's transition as a result of a medical condition, or a biological error that placed a man in a woman's body. In this frame, the pretransition state was viewed as one of torture or agony. One woman said about her colleague, "He always felt that he should have been a guy. That is probably one of the hardest things I could think of going through, what he is going through." Another woman said she saw transgenderism as "primarily biological and cultural." She added, "I am not as worried about where it [transgenderism] comes from but more about how it is accepted in the environment. Because I think it must be complete torture to have to battle with it and not get support from anybody." Coworkers also emphasized their beliefs that their colleague's experiences leading up to the transition had been a lifelong struggle. One woman says, "He never felt a sense of self-identity as a female. He always leaned more toward being male and wanting to create that sense of self-identity as a male." Another woman said, "This [a transition] just isn't something you decide. It is something that takes years of therapy, and you have to go through this process to be approved to be able to do it." One man noted that this transition was natural for his colleague: "Growing up, he never thought of himself as a female. He never functioned as a female." For him, the gender transition, then, was similar to a colleague "having cancer surgery or having teeth pulled or something"—a medical procedure done for the good of one's health. As many branches of Christianity reject the biological frame of transgenderism (Kennedy 2008), seeing it instead as a violation of biblical law, it is not unexpected that open transmen would find the most vocal opposition to their transitions coming from evangelicals.

Some transmen reinforce this frame of transgenderism as a biological medical condition, because they share this frame and/or because this understanding of transgenderism can ease workplace acceptance. Paul showed his childhood pictures in which he looked like a little boy being forced to wear a dress to his coworkers to illustrate his lifelong sense of misgendering. Luis presented his workplace with information from the *DSM* about the treatment for gender identity disorder. Simon told his coworkers that he had "gender identity disorder, and since there is no cure, I have to go on hormones." Yet other transmen offered different or no explanations for their transitions. Devin framed his transition as an activity—"I am taking hormones"—and left the interpretation up to his colleagues. Eli asked to have a nametag that said "Eli" and offered no explanation. But even when transmen do not present an essentialist understanding of their gender to explain their transitions, coworkers can still view the transition as biological. Illustrating this, one coworker noted that she had been surprised at her colleague's account that he had enjoyed his life as a woman for many years. He told her that his transition was a new stage in his identity development, not something biologically determined. However, when I later asked her how she personally understood transgenderism, she replied, "[It] is basically comparable to a birth defect. Like, 'I am supposed to be male, and yet my body is female. That's wrong, and I am going to repair it.' To me, it would be like someone repairing a cleft palate or getting a birthmark removed." Highlighting the importance of this narrative, Riley emphasized to his coworkers that he identified as "two-spirit," a blend of masculine and feminine. And he faced the strongest coworker resistance to adopting a new name and male pronouns.

Seeing a transition as a remedy for a biological error provides a strong rationale for being supportive of transmen's decisions to transition—decisions that could potentially challenge the easiness of a natural male/female binary. Transmen are remedying a private, medical condition rather than introducing a political issue into the workplace or asking for "special rights." Highlighting this distinction between personal and political, one woman emphasized that she appreciated that her colleague did not make his transition into a "political issue." Scott, who had a supportive reaction from coworkers when he told them he had always felt that he was in the wrong body, received some negative comments when he put fliers about a transgender political event in mailboxes at work. These experiences suggest that transitioning at work is more readily accepted when it is seen as a private, biological issue. Transmen should become the men they were *meant* to be, not hold on to "transgender" as an identity. Incorporating these rare cases as men also gives transmen their correct place in the male/female binary without challenging the idea that most men and women develop naturally from XY and XX chromosomes, respectively. It also suggests, however, that there is less institutional support and incorporation for individuals who want to blur the male/female binary and/or politically advocate for transgender rights.

Individual Transformation, Structural Reproduction

Organizations have several choices for how to adjust to a challenge to business as usual—change their practices, incorporate the challenge into existing practices, or defuse the challenge by marginalizing the challengers (Dalton and Fenstermaker 2002; Garfinkel 1967; Raeburn 2004). While not all transmen seek to make "gender trouble" at work, open transitions theoretically present a challenge to the hierarchical gender logic that underlies workplace interactions and practices—a logic justified by belief in a naturally occurring male/female binary that creates inevitable differences between men and women. Employers and coworkers adopt a variety of strategic responses. Employers push transmen out of the workplace, formally in some cases, covertly in others. They marginalize transmen as token trannies in LGBT-related organizations. In service jobs, employers try to coerce transmen into working as women through the threat of potential legal consequences. Or they incorporate transmen as one of the guys—a response that overwhelmingly occurs in professional workplaces.

These incorporation responses to open transitions seemingly contradict theoretical notions of how people respond to breaches of deeply held gender schemas (Garfinkel 1967). Yet this reaction is another form of repair work. Transmen who are incorporated as one of the guys at work clearly benefit on an individual level over transmen who are pushed out of jobs or marginalized as token trannies. On a structural level, these four workplace responses—neutralizing, policing, marginalizing, and incorporating—are similar mechanisms for maintaining the gender status quo. Transmen are banished, kept "female," made "male," or put in a third, marginalized category. In all of these responses, the potential threat to the stability of the male/female binary—and, by proxy, the hierarchical gender order—is neutralized. What these incorporation responses do show is that gender boundaries can shift for individuals—former women can be accepted as men—without making workplace gender trouble and without causing a change in structural gender relations.

CHAPTER SIX

Transgender Matters

The Persistence of Workplace Gender Inequality

For Ben Barres, the Stanford professor whose story opens this book, a name change from Barbara to Ben and the development of facial hair brought more authority to his scientific work (Barres 2006). His experience is echoed in some of the workplace outcomes reported by both stealth and open transmen. The willingness of some employers and co-workers to treat transmen as one of the guys suggests that being openly transgender has become more socially acceptable. Yet the transition experience of Barres's colleague at Stanford, Joan Roughgarden, provides an important counterpoint. As Jonathan, Roughgarden was a well-regarded scientist. As Joan, however, she found that she had to "establish competence to an extent that men never have to" (Begley 2006, B1), as men in the science field spoke over her, disregarded her research, and saw her ideas as carrying less value. Of this experience, she says, "At first I was amused. I thought if women are discriminated against, then I darn well will be discriminated against, too. Well, the thrill of that has worn off!" (ibid.).

Both Ben and Joan are publicly acknowledging being transgender, an identity that has long been theorized as discredited (Goffman 1963b; Kando 1973). The open acknowledgment of the same act—a gender transition—should theoretically yield similar reactions. Yet Ben gains respect and authority while Joan is marginalized. These gender differences in workplace experiences are not anomalous. The workplace is not a gender-neutral location that equitably rewards workers based on their individual merits (Acker 1990; P. Martin 2003; Valian 1998; C. L. Williams 1995) but rather "a central site for the creation and reproduction of gender differences and gender inequality" (C. L. Williams 1995, 15). My research suggests that transitioning within this hierarchical context means that transwomen are more likely to face workplace barriers than transmen. Highlighting these gender differences is not meant as a cautionary tale to transwomen about the impossibility of transitioning on the job, as some transwomen do find workplace support for their transitions (Schilt and Connell 2007). Nor do I mean to suggest that no transmen face employment discrimination—a point that experiences in this book contradict. Rather, comparing these experiences suggests a gendered *pattern*, a pattern that illuminates the cultural, interactional, and structural practices that contribute to the persistence of workplace gender inequality in ways that impact transgender and cisgender people alike.

Transgender Differences at Work

While conducting ethnographic fieldwork between 2003 and 2008, I attended or led over fifteen workshops about transgender workplace experiences in four states. What I immediately noticed was the palpable nervousness of the attendees who were making plans to come out at work as transgender. They worried about maintaining job security, having access to a bathroom that fits their gender presentation, and keeping good relationships with coworkers and employers. Yet when attendees who were in the midst of open transitions began to share their experiences, a gender division emerged. Transwomen typically reported resistance from their employers. Regardless of industry, they told stories of being barred from using the women's restroom, being subjected to workplace harassment, and being told that they could not come to work dressed in traditionally feminine clothes. Even when they found support from their employers, their competence was questioned in a way it had not been when they worked as men. Some transwomen who worked in blue-collar jobs that required teamwork described fears for their physical safety. Transmen, in contrast, typically shared supportive responses from employers and coworkers, even in industries that would seem potentially fraught with opposition, such as religious-based occupations and occupations whose mission statement included empowering *women*. While not all transmen had smooth workplace transitions, they did not report nearly the same level of organizational opposition and coworker harassment as transwomen in these conference settings.

In interviews, transmen overwhelmingly agreed that their workplace experiences bore little relationship to those of transwomen they knew. Preston praised his blue-collar workplace for its professional response to his open transition. He had anticipated such a reaction because the corporation he worked for had a nondiscrimination policy. Yet when I asked him how his workplace would respond to a male-to-female transition, he said, "I think it would have been very, very difficult. It is really difficult for gay men to be [at my workplace]. . . . It is dyke-friendly [not gay-men-friendly]." This comment assumes that transwomen would be transitioning from gay men to heterosexual women—a pathway I encountered much less frequently in my fieldwork than transwomen who transitioned from heterosexual men to lesbian or bisexual women. Yet his comment is still suggestive of an important difference: based on his experience with this company, an openly gay man, or a man perceived by others to be gay, would face resistance long before he announced his intention to work as a woman—a very different experience than Preston recounts as a self-described masculine woman in a "macho" job.

Coworkers made similar distinctions when I asked their thoughts on how their workplaces would react to a trans*woman*. A coworker in Texas said at the start of the interview that she had heard that her new colleague was transgender before he started work. Describing her workplace as interested in diversity of all kinds, she says, "People were like, 'Oh, that's great that this company knows [about transgender people] and they have hired someone [trans]." However, at the end of the interview when I asked her how the same workplace would have responded to hiring a transwoman, she said, "I think it would have been more difficult. . . . Someone who's male going into a women's restroom probably feels more threatening than someone who's female going into a male restroom." Other coworkers said it would just be "a different situation" but could not elaborate on the rationale for this difference.

These responses are speculative. However, transmen who worked alongside transwomen witnessed differences in their treatment. All of these men worked in LGBT-related organizations or workplaces that served LGBT populations. While they often felt tokenized, they received better treatment than their transwomen colleagues, particularly from gay men, who have a long history of identity skirmishes with trans-

women (Meyerowitz 2002; Perkins 1983; Rupp and Taylor 2004).[1] Eli
notes, "The gay guys, they always refer to me as a guy to my face and to
other coworkers. They respect [transwomen clients] to their faces, and
then it is 'he' as soon as she is not around." Aaron found similar attitudes
toward transwomen at his workplace. "We have a coworker who [is transitioning,] . . . and one day [my supervisor] said to me that she was nothing more than 'a faggot with no class.'" This incident was not an isolated
one, he added. "Two years ago, we had an MTF woman working here,
and during a staff meeting, [this supervisor] kept sending me notes like,
'Do you think she is supposed to be a woman?'" While transmen might
be tokenized in these workplaces, gay men's attempts to include them in
these interactions suggest that they can be more socially integrated at
work than transwomen.

Legal cases and news stories about transgender employment problems support these speculative responses about transgender differences
in workplace outcomes. Table 6.1 shows the gender breakdown of legal
cases and news stories that include transgender people facing some type
of employment discrimination, such as wrongful termination, gender-
based harassment, and unlawful withdrawal of a job offer. The number
of news stories about transwomen could be a questionable indicator, as
male-to-female transitions long have received more spectacular coverage than female-to-male transitions (Meyerowitz 2002). Yet seeing the
same patterns in the legal cases suggests that transwomen report more
employment barriers than do transmen. While the exact parameters of
the transgender population are not known, the recent visibility of FTM
communities suggests that the gender breakdown of transmen and transwomen is more equal than previously assumed (J. Green 2004; Meye-

TABLE 6.1 **Gender breakdown in legal cases and news stories about transgender employment
barriers, 1971–2008**

	MTF		FTM		
	Legal	News	Legal	News	Total
1970s	4	4	0	1	9
1980s	9	6	0	1	16
1990s	10	15	2	1	28
2000s	20	18	3	3	44
Total	43	43	5	6	97

Note: See the methodological appendix for details on how this content analysis was conducted.

rowitz 2002). Assuming a closer parity in proportion, table 6.1 shows a gendered pattern in reported negative workplace experiences for transmen and transwomen.[2]

The "before and after" questionnaire data I collected reflect similar patterns. The thirty-six transmen and twenty-five transwomen who participated in the questionnaire had similar demographic characteristics: they were predominantly white (63 percent), and almost half of the respondents (42 percent) had a BA degree or higher. Only three transmen and three transwomen reported leaving a job involuntarily due to their transition. However, in the open-ended portion of the questionnaire, transmen describe few workplace barriers—often to their surprise.[3] As one white transman in a government job wrote, "I am one of the lucky ones. My job was extremely accommodating, thanks to the liberal attitude at my job and [in my town] in general." Another white transman in a similar field wrote, "I applied for the job as a female but submitted a status change form as male. I provided a Trans 101 workshop with [my] boss's blessing. To my face, all coworkers are professional." A white transman in a private job added, "My transition with the company went very smoothly. I came out to 250 employees in '99. All have been very supportive." A white transwoman working in the private sector wrote, in contrast, that she left her job because she was "uncomfortable with the clients and coworkers." Another white transwoman who was self-employed wrote that she lost clients and experienced "intolerable harassment and threats." A white transwoman in a private-sector job added, "I was fired three months after [I came out as transgender] and told it was because I am trans." Finally, a white transwoman in a similar job wrote, "I only came 'out' [as trans] since I lost my job. I have yet to find new employment." No transwomen wrote about a smooth transition, though two highlighted finding ways to improve their negative experiences.

Changes to salaries reported in the questionnaire suggest that transwomen can face steeper economic penalties than transmen after transition (see Schilt and Wiswall 2008). Transwomen who participated in this before/after salary questionnaire were, on average, ten years older at the age of transition than transmen, suggesting they had more time to accumulate workplace experience. Illustrating this, ten transwomen had worked in their job for ten years or more prior to their announcement of their transition. In contrast, seventeen transmen had worked in their job two years or less when they announced their transition. Yet transwomen lost on average nearly a third of their salary after their gender transition, while transmen saw no change or a slight increase in salary (ibid.). These findings come from a very small sample size (ibid.). However, similar examples abound in the news stories and legal cases. Diana Schroer's three decades of experience in government work put her at the top of a list of eighteen contenders for a job in the Library of Congress. However, when Diana—who applied as a man—informed her new employer of her impending transition, the offer was rescinded (Dvorak 2005). Philicia Barnes served over twenty years as a man on an Ohio police force. She had just scored in the top 20 percent on the sergeant's exam when she began her transition. Yet she was demoted, rather than promoted, once she began to feminize her appearance (*Barnes v. City of Cincinnati* 2004). Allen Stehlin had an exemplary record during his decade in the Tampa fire department (Testerman and Malone 1990). When he transitioned to become Alice in the late 1980s, he was making thirty-two thousand dollars a year. Alice left the department but then sought to be reinstated a few months later. Because she had been outed as transgender by the papers, she could not find a new job. With her prior experience, she was the most qualified potential candidate for her old job. And she was offered the same job—with a two-thousand-dollar pay cut (Testerman 1990). A comparison of two Associated Press articles from 1982 also is suggestive of gender difference in workplace experiences. The article "Sex-Change Cop Files Suit" (Franck 1982) features a twenty-two-year-old transman who claimed he was fired from the police force because of his transition from Linda to Scott. "Transsexual Loses Sex Bias Suit" (Associated Press 1982), in contrast, covers the story of a twenty-four-year-old transwoman who made a similar claim that she was fired from a bill collection agency when she transitioned from Roger to Sharon. Scott found a new managerial job in a retail company, however, while Sharon entered the adult entertainment industry as a dancer.

As Joan Roughgarden's experience shows, transwomen can also be considered less competent as women workers. Reflecting this, a white transwoman employed in the private sector wrote on her questionnaire, "My boss still calls me 'he' and regularly asks me if I know how to do specific jobs she knows I handled exclusively for ten years." Other studies have shown that when transwomen remain in jobs they held as men, their men colleagues and supervisors can question whether estrogen limits their abilities to effectively handle male-coded tasks, such as managing employees and programming a computer (Schilt and Connell 2007).

These examples suggest that transwomen's human capital—which does not change when they start taking estrogen—can carry less value as women. While becoming men brings a resulting stereotype of incompetence in some arenas, such as emotional expression and child care, it can bring newfound respect and recognition in the workplace—as the experiences of Ben Barres and some of the transmen in this study illustrate. These patterns I identify reflect different workplace experiences for transmen and transwomen, even though they both undergo a gender transition—an action assumed to carry a discreditable stigma (Goffman 1963b).

Accounting for Difference

What accounts for these patterns of difference? Three explanatory frameworks can be brought to bear on the situation: innocuous *individual differences* between transmen and transwomen, such as personality differences or differences in workplace productivity; systematic *between-group differences*, such as differences in being physically passable in one's destination gender; or systemic gender bias that results from and upholds *the cultural logics of gendered organizations*, such as the workplace.

Individual Differences

Open transmen who received employer and coworker support for their transition offered an individualistic frame to account for this reaction. Typically, they attributed their incorporation as men at work to their value to the workplace as "good workers" and "productive workers." Thomas, who transitioned in a professional job in the 1990s, said, "I don't think that my bosses were particularly enlightened. I think I worked cheap and I worked well and I got a lot done, and that sort of guaranteed my job." Reflecting on his transition in a service job in California in the 2000s, Peter echoed this sentiment: "I had a good attitude, so [I knew] people would treat me well, and that is basically what happened." About his success in his blue-collar job, Preston offered a similar account: "I'm a really good worker, and I have a good attitude at work. People know I like to work hard. And that really greases the palm of so many people because they know I am going to work. When push comes to shove, it doesn't really matter what kind of personality you have [if you are a good worker]."

Being a valued part of the workplace is important in an open transition. As one workplace consultant who had facilitated hundreds of transgender workplace cases told me, "If your workplace did not like you before the transition, they will not like you any better after you make the announcement." Yet a closer look at work histories suggests this explanation does not always fit the facts. Several transmen announced their intention to transition in jobs they had held for only a few weeks or even mere days—arguably little time to establish themselves as indispensable. Kelly expected to be laid off from his semiprofessional job, a job he had held for only a few weeks, when he told his employers he planned to transition. "I just assumed that when you say 'transsexual' or anything, people go, 'Ugh,' and don't want to deal with it . . . especially since I was working with kids." However, his employers made it clear he still had a job if he wanted it. "They thought 'transitioning' meant leaving for a new job. We eventually got this [miscommunication] worked out, and they said, 'We don't care [what you do] as long as you are not quitting.'" When Ethan applied for his professional job, he was in the midst of transitioning. He used his initials on his résumé—initials he intended to keep once he changed his name legally. During his interview, his potential employer asked him what his "real" name was. "I explained to him that legally I am Ellen, but I prefer to go by Ethan.' And that was it [I didn't go into details]. He offered me the job and had business cards printed up for me that week that said 'Ethan.'" Ethan had yet to even work at this job, highlighting the unlikelihood that being a "good worker" accounted for his employer's willingness to hire him as a man.

Transmen could become *better* workers after their transitions because they are happier when they are able to work as men. While their human capital remains unchanged, their personal characteristics—attitude—could change. Or they could become more productive because they are freed from the worry and anxiety that can result from planning their transition announcement. Supporting this theory, some transmen do describe themselves as happier workers after they start working as men. But this did not mean that they had bad job performance or negative attitudes as women. In contrast, working as a woman in male-dominated fields did not allow much leeway for being unproductive. Rather, they describe themselves as working two or three times harder than men with less reward. This description, of course, is self-report data. A more compelling refutation of this changed performance and attitude argument comes from the comparison with transwomen. Transwomen should experience the same type of happiness increase as transmen because they, too, finally gain a social gender identity that lines up with their personal sense of themselves as female. Yet, as women, their workplace experiences can take a turn for the worse (Griggs 1998; Schilt and Connell 2007; Schilt and Wiswall 2008). This pattern suggests that something beyond individual difference is at work in these situations.

That transmen adopt the individualistic frame of "good worker" or "better worker" to account for their incorporation as men at work is unsurprising, as this frame provides some agency in an alienating process of negotiating organizational and interactional constraints. However, seeing workplace experiences as the result of individual characteristics means that transgender people who face workplace barriers make their own bad experiences. While transgender people can be "bad" or "unproductive" workers, trans*women* overwhelmingly face this label from employers who are attempting to justify disciplinary action. In *Emanuelle v. U.S. Tobacco, Inc.* (1987), a transwoman who worked in a factory as a man for six years was stripped of her union leader duties and then fired after she began working in traditionally feminine clothes. Her employers argued that her termination was unrelated to her gender. Instead, this decision stemmed from her poor production quality, a complaint she had never received before, and her decision in the prior week to leave work "one minute early." In *Lie v. Sky Pub. Corp* (2002), a transwoman with four years' experience as an editorial assistant was fired one month after her open transition for having a "hostile" attitude and "abusing the office email protocol." A transwoman who participated in the before/after questionnaire wrote about her experience, "I was laid off from my ten-year management position for having a 'bad attitude.' Coincidentally (!), I was given notice the first week I began presenting as female." She added that she was eventually rehired but for a lower-paying job. These patterns suggest that employers begin to see transwomen as a detriment to the workplace, regardless of their past performance or their potential new happiness. If there were only one or two cases, the "good worker/bad worker" theory might hold. However, viewing transgender workplace experiences in grouped patterns is more suggestive of systematic, not individual, difference.

Between-Group Differences

While transmen and transwomen are grouped together under the transgender rubric because they share the experience of gender transitions,
strong between-group differences could make them noncomparable
populations. Listening to transmen discuss their transition experiences
in relation to transwomen supports this idea of between-group differences in two areas: what I term "passability," and the gap between what
I term "before and after" appearances. Passability refers to transgender
people's abilities to achieve their desired social gender: men for transmen and women for transwomen.[4] Looking at the experience of passing
empirically, 56 percent of the transmen in the before/after questionnaire
described themselves as "always" passing, as compared to 17 percent of
transwomen—even though this sample of transmen had fewer years of
living as men on average than transwomen had living as women (Schilt
and Wiswall 2008). In response to the question "Did you tell your employers and coworkers in your new job about your gender transition?"
several transwomen wrote next to the fixed responses of "yes" or "no,"
"only if asked"—suggesting that their female social identity was questioned at work. No transmen wrote similar comments, though the one
respondent who had not taken testosterone noted that customers and coworkers "were confused" about his gender. Further, some transwomen
who had been living as women and taking estrogen for over ten years
prior to completing the questionnaire described themselves as "never"
passing as women. No transmen who had been on T for several years described themselves in similar terms. This distinction supports prior research that suggests that physically passing is more likely to remain a
concern for transwomen, not transmen (Griggs 1998).

Cultural norms about gender and appearance contribute to this passing differential. As "man" is the default assumption for attributing gender (Kessler and McKenna 1978), transmen can face less appearance
scrutiny than transwomen. Men also have a wider range of acceptable
heights—from the extreme height of basketball players such as Shaquille
O'Neal to the shortness of men such as Napoléon. While short men may
receive less respect than taller men (Hall 2006), they are still seen as
men in social interactions. Women over six feet tall, in contrast, come
under more scrutiny, as they stand outside of female body norms (Kessler and McKenna 1978). The differing effects of testosterone and estro-

gen widen this passing differential. Transmen develop facial hair, thicker body hair, deeper voices, and, in some cases, male-pattern baldness with the use of testosterone. This transformation typically occurs over a six- to eight-month period. Many times during my fieldwork, I had the experience of seeing but failing to recognize someone I had interviewed only two months before because the changes to his appearance were so great. Estrogen can stimulate breast growth, but it cannot stop the development of facial hair or raise the tenor of voices. Further, the changes brought on by estrogen are not as readily visible as those brought on by testosterone. Illustrating this difference, one transwoman who responded to the questionnaire wrote, "I started hormones and electrolysis a year before [I was hired], but I still lived/presented as male when I got the job." I also met transwomen in my fieldwork who had taken estrogen for years but were still working as men—typically because of the fear of losing their employment history if they came out as transgender at work. In contrast, transmen who started taking testosterone while still working as women quickly faced questions from coworkers about their deepening voices.

Passability matters at work because it is tied to appearance. Prior research has shown that appearance and attractiveness impact workplace outcomes (Biddle and Hamermesh 1994, 1998). More attractive people, this research suggests, get more workplace rewards than unattractive people. Transwomen who do not pass as women, following this logic, should anticipate facing appearance discrimination—as should transmen and genderqueer people who opt not to take hormones. On a theoretical level, this discrimination can seem unconnected to gender. Yet, in making sense of transwomen's workplace experiences, appearance discrimination is intimately tied to cultural expectations about how "men" and "women" should look. In other words, when transwomen face appearance-based discrimination at work, it is not because they are ugly or because they are badly dressed; it is because they fall outside the realm of acceptable appearances for women. Appearance discrimination in these cases *is* gender discrimination.

Doe v. United Consumer Financial Services (2001) highlights the gendered aspect of appearance discrimination. Jane Doe transitioned in the 1970s. In 2000, she was hired as a woman by a temp agency. Two months into her assignment, the agency called her current employers to check on her performance. During the conversation, Doe's employer asked the agency if they had ever noticed anything "strange" about Doe. The employer noted that several employees had begun referring to Doe as "Mrs. Doubtfire," in a reference to a film in which Robin Williams plays the role of a man pretending to be a woman. The temp agency began its own investigation of Doe, going as far as to call her high school to request her yearbook. That this organization would go to such lengths for a temporary employee suggests a strong anxiety about the authenticity of her gender. Doe was called in for a meeting, in which the director allegedly asked her, "What gender are you? Just looking at you, I can't tell. Are you a man or a woman?" She was told to produce medical evidence that she was a woman or face termination. The "Mrs. Doubtfire" reference and the questions from the director show that the issue at stake is not Doe's attractiveness but her gender. This case suggests that when transgender and genderqueer people do not pass, voluntarily or involuntarily, the resulting discrimination they can face is intimately related to normative expectations for appropriately gendered appearances.

The passing differential between transmen and transwomen is important to consider when making broad statements about "the transgender experience." Yet it is an unsatisfactory explanation for divergent workplace outcomes because it refers to an average rather than an absolute. The staff of gender clinics saw the ability to physically pass as a woman as the strongest indicator that someone was a "real" transwoman (Billings and Urban 1982; Bolin 1988; Feinbloom 1976; Kando 1973). After undergoing genital surgery, some transwomen married men who were unaware of their transitions (Perkins 1983), a move strongly suggestive of achieving social femaleness. News stories and legal cases also demonstrate that transwomen go stealth—a strategy that requires passability. In *Rentos v. Oce-Office Systems* (1996), Rentos worked as a field manager for over a year. When she filed an insurance claim to get transition-related procedures covered, her employer learned she had once been insured as a man. She faced a swift, punitive reaction: "[The] plaintiff was terminated, her belongings were packed up, and employees of the defendant were warned not to talk to the plaintiff any further." In *Lopez v. River Oaks Imaging & Diagnostic Group, Inc.* (2008), Izza Lopez's job offer was rescinded after a male name emerged on her background check. She had listed this name on her initial application, but it had gone unnoticed because she looked like a woman. In these cases, transwomen lost their jobs not because they *could not pass* as women but rather because they *did pass* as women.

Transwomen also face employment barriers before their appearance as women becomes an issue. Rachel Bonura was fired in 2005 from the pharmaceutical company where she had worked for several years as a man after she announced her intention to transition. Describing the experience, she says, "It felt like I was praised and everything was fine and then the next week I was crucified" (Mason-Draffen 2005, A56). When David Warfield, a nine-year veteran of high school teaching who had won several distinguished teaching prizes, announced his intention to become Dana, he was put on administrative leave and then fired. While only four out of fifteen hundred parents raised concerns about the transition, the school board decided that such an action would be traumatizing to students (Nieves 1998, A12). In *Holt v. Northwest Pennsylvania Training Partnership Consortium, Inc.* (1997), a transwoman's employer told her coworkers to treat her respectfully and gave her access to a unisex, single-stall bathroom. However, her employer also told her that if she came to work dressed as a woman, she would be disciplined for a violation of the employee dress code. In these cases, passability is a moot point, as transwomen are disciplined and/or terminated merely for the intention to adopt traditionally feminine attire.

These disparate reactions to transgender people's apparel could stem from another between-group difference: the gap between "before and after" appearance. Working as women, many transmen in this study describe themselves as having short hair, eschewing makeup, and wearing traditionally masculine clothing. Transwomen I met during my fieldwork, in contrast, typically described themselves as a "man's man" before they announced their transition. Several of them had visible army or marines tattoos, a testament to their time as men in a hypermasculine setting. News stories about transwomen highlight similar participation in military careers and masculine-coded activities such as football, kayaking, and carpentry (Dvorak 2005; DeFao 2005; Schafer 2001; Sloat 2001).[5] That many transwomen in legal cases and news stories as well as in my questionnaire worked in blue-collar jobs for years as men without incident also is indicative of masculine gender expression as men. Since men in blue-collar occupations can face gender harassment from other men if they are not "manly" enough (Talbot 2002; Welsh 1999), it is unlikely that a man could have an exemplary work record in these occupations if he advertised femininity via clothing or behavior.

These differences in before and after appearances are shaped by social norms about gender-appropriate clothing: in many occupational contexts, women can wear some traditionally masculine clothing, such as pants and button-down shirts, but men can never wear any traditionally feminine clothing, such as skirts and dresses, unless they are employed as drag performers. This difference in clothing norms means that many transmen can apply for jobs as women wearing a more masculine style of clothing. Their workplaces can be considered almost prescreened for their likely acceptance or rejection of an open transition. In other words, an employer who would hire a woman who obviously prefers men's clothes should theoretically be less likely to balk when that employee announces her desire to work as a man. This masculine appearance can be a "coming attraction" for employers and coworkers, as this clothing puts transmen's personal identity as men or as "not women" on the body in a visible way. That transmen in this study were hired as masculine women in professional jobs, blue-collar jobs, "women's professions," and retail/service jobs suggests that such an appearance does not always preclude being hired—though they can still face gender and sexual identity harassment from men and women who view them as "dykes." Illustrating this, Gary Johnson, the first transman to file an employment discrimination claim under the California state law protecting transgender workers, faced wide-scale harassment in his nonprofit job when he masculinized his appearance, as his employer and coworkers began to read him as a lesbian (Yeung 2001).

The rigidity of acceptable clothing norms for men means that regardless of occupational context, men cannot ease into wearing skirts or dresses at work without making a stir. This social norm about gendered appearance and clothing explains why some transwomen might hide their personal identity as women or as feminine under a veneer of hegemonic masculinity at work. Yet being hired as one of the guys means that their workplaces are not prescreened. In other words, employers and coworkers have no advance cues that the man before them identifies as a woman or as feminine. Without this prescreening, transwomen have a greater risk of encountering workplace barriers once they begin an open transition. One way to interpret this difference, then, is that moving from *masculine to men* creates less cognitive dissonance (Festinger, Riecken, and Schachter 1956; Festinger 1957) for employers and coworkers than moving from *masculine to women*.

Cognitive dissonance is a useful framework for making sense of these divergent outcomes. Yet this process does not occur in a vacuum. Rather, the dissonance is intimately related to cultural schemas held by social actors. In open transitions, coworkers and employers are resolv-

ing not simply their colleague's change in social gender but also the va-
lidity of a reality in which there are two and only two sexes (Garfinkel
1967; Kessler and McKenna 1978). To assume that transmen's appearance as masculine women eliminates cognitive dissonance ignores the
strength of many people's belief in a male/female binary. When transmen are hired as women, they are read as *women* until they explicitly tell
coworkers about their transition—regardless of their clothing or hair-
cuts. Many transmen describe being called "miss," "young lady," and
"ma'am" by coworkers as unbearable because it shows them that their
efforts to inscribe maleness on their bodies were being overlooked or
misread. Coworkers see them as women who are not meeting normative appearance expectations for femininity rather than as men. Illustrating this, one coworker described his transman colleague's pretransition appearance as being "an unattractive woman" rather than "manly"
or "masculine." To see transmen *as men* when they are hired as women
requires a much more fluid understanding of gender than cultural schemas about the male/female binary provide.

In interviews, coworkers raised the sense of dissonance they had about
their colleague's before and after appearance. Most of them had not met
a transman before the workplace announcement and had little prior experience with transgender people in general. They fluctuated between
describing themselves as surprised by the transition and always knowing that there was something "different" about their colleague. Making sense of their coworker's transition within a male/female binary required considerable mental acrobatics—even when transmen dressed in
traditionally masculine clothes prior to the announcement. One woman
said at the start of the interview, "He was already very malelike. You
know, he dressed like a boy, and he just didn't have the deep voice. So
it wasn't a big shocker when he started talking about actually doing the
surgery." Yet, at another point, she noted, "I was surprised at our initial
conversation that he preferred the pronoun *he* and associated himself
more as a man than as a woman. I was, like, 'Wow, okay.' It is not an everyday conversation that I have had before." While she recognized that,
as a woman, his dress was more masculine than other women at work,
"his résumé said 'Miss,' so I assumed he was a woman. Even though the
clothing could have been considered more manly." This surprise is reflected in a newspaper article about Deputy Tony Barreto-Neto, a transman who openly transitioned on the police force in Florida in the 1990s.
In an interview, he even noted that he "dressed, acted and thought like

a man" for years, but his coworkers continued to gender him as female (Shaver 1995, 2).

Seeing gender transitions as a solution to a biological condition can resolve this cognitive dissonance. This resolution is not immediate, however. Coworkers recount having long discussions with their spouses and friends about what they see as an unusual situation. Yet, as transmen begin to develop facial hair, coworkers face social pressures to treat them like men. In the workplace, open transmen often interact with people who know about their transitions and people who do not. Being in mixed company gives coworkers an incentive to use male pronouns with their colleague, as otherwise they would look foolish for calling someone with facial hair "she." Even though coworkers might be merely passing as supportive colleagues, their willingness—and the willingness of others—to change their workplace interactions with transmen naturalizes the situation. Exemplifying this naturalization, one coworker I interviewed said, "I chuckle to myself every now and then, just how natural it seems. [It] took a while for the pronouns to catch on, but now it just comes out naturally. It just seems like a natural fit." While he initially felt surprised at the announcement, he came to see his coworker's desire to live as a man as something he recognized early on: "It just seems like my inclination or my intuition at the beginning was correct; it just seemed, like, natural that she should go through with something like this because she was gonna be more comfortable as a man than as a woman." In an attempt to resolve inconsistency, coworkers reread their colleague's "before" appearance as a new sign or clue. They come to see the transition as something they knew about all along rather than something that challenges their understanding of a static male/female binary. This resolution is a classic example of incorporating and rationalizing new information to resolve cognitive dissonance (Festinger, Riecken, and Schachter 1956).

In news stories and legal cases, transwomen's decisions to transition also are framed as solutions to "a medical situation—an inborn imbalance of hormones" (Associated Press 1979, A3), or a "biological problem" (El-Bashir 1998, 6). Yet many transwomen still face obstacles when they feminize their appearance at work. This resistance cannot be fully explained by the gap between before and after appearance, as feminine men are not always readily incorporated into the workplace as women (Schilt and Connell 2007). I met several transwomen in my fieldwork who worked as men with long hair and manicured nails in professional jobs—and they recounted being ostracized by coworkers. A woman's letter to her local newspaper advice columnist illustrates this situation. She writes about working for the last three years with "Frank," who is a "bit of an odd duck" because he "has a strange appearance for a man, with obviously manicured fingernails and plucked eyebrows" (Curry 2007, F1). She adds that in the last week, Frank came out to the workplace as Frances. Yet, rather than feeling that Frances's previous appearance now makes sense, she describes the situation as going from "odd to surreal" (ibid.). Her reaction suggests that while working with a feminine man is uncomfortable, working with a feminine man who identifies as a woman is even more so. Another editorial written in response to a transwoman suing for her right to wear a skirt to work brings this point home. The author notes, "What, one is tempted to ask, is wrong with telling a man that wearing a pink skirt to work is not OK? All the sensitivity training in the world is not going to alter the fact that, outside the confines of a drag queen bar, a grown man in a pink skirt is a preposterous sight" (Campos 2000, A23). Concerned Women for America (CWA), a politically conservative organization that has been an outspoken critic of the Employment Nondiscrimination Act (ENDA)—the bill that would, in its most inclusive form, give federal workplace protections for sexual identity, gender identity, and gender expression—plays upon the cultural discomfort with "men in dresses" in its critiques. Illustrating this tactic, CWA sent to members of Congress an e-mail opposing ENDA that ended with the following statement: "Corporal Klinger, the crossdressing character from *M.A.S.H.*, might have been pleased to see congressional offices with men in dresses, but we don't think your constituents would be so happy. We strongly urge you not to sign this 'Klinger Pledge'" (A. Smith 2002). While CWA mocks transmen (Barber 2007), it does not use the specter of "women in suits" as a scare tactic.

A man purposefully adopting behaviors and appearance cues stereotyped as feminine creates cognitive dissonance that is not as easily resolved—regardless of "before" appearance—as a woman purposefully adopting masculine-coded behaviors and clothing styles. Illustrating this point, the legal cases show a difference in the attention given to transmen's and transwomen's changing appearances. In *Broadus v. State Farm Insurance, Inc.* (2000), K. Broadus left his job at State Farm because his employer gave him strange looks on account of his transition. In *Maffei v. Kolaeton Industry, Inc.* (1995), Daniel Maffei brought harassment charges against his employer, James Wong, alleging that Wong made comments that Maffei's transition was "immoral." In neither case does transmen's changing appearance warrant much attention in the court documents. In contrast, transwomen's "after" appearance is documented in close detail—and often offered up by employers as the reason why a transwoman was terminated. The issue is not that transwomen are not passable as women; it is that their feminine appearance allegedly creates workplace tension. An accounting firm fired a transwoman accountant because her "red lipstick and nail polish, hairstyle, jewelry, and clothing . . . created personnel problems" (*Holloway v. Arthur Andersen and Company* 1977). A health care facility fired a physician because she "shaved her beard and removed all vestiges of facial hair. She sculpted and waxed her eyebrows, pierced her ears, started wearing emerald stone earrings, and began growing breasts" (*Enriquez v. West Jersey Health Systems* 2001). In one case, personnel reported a transwoman's feminizing appearance to the U.S. government as a potential risk to national security (*LaFleur v. Bird-Johnson Company* 1994). In another case, a police chief ordered the vice squad to follow a transwoman police officer when she was off duty, as her feminine appearance seemed suggestive of engagement in an illicit lifestyle (*Barnes v. City of Cincinnati* 2004). The different reactions to their changing appearance that transmen and transwomen can face at work suggest that the cognitive dissonance raised in open transitions cannot be untied from the larger gender order that produces and maintains hierarchical relations between men and women. Transmen's move up this hierarchy makes cultural sense, while transwomen's step down does not. Fully accounting for these differences requires locating transitions within the cultural logic of gendered organizations, such as the workplace.

The Cultural Logic of Gendered Organizations

Differences in institutional and interactional responses to transmen and transwomen occur within the cultural logic of the workplace. Rather than a neutral setting that rewards workers for productivity and skill, the workplace is a gendered organization that maintains and produces gender hierarchies and heteronormativity (Acker 1990; Britton 2003; C. L. Williams 1995). Within this system, heterosexual men carry the most social power (R. Connell 1995). As the logic of homosocial reproduction suggests that people tend to associate with others most like themselves (Bird 1996), heterosexual men theoretically benefit from their relationships with one another in the workplace. A worker with any marked

TABLE 6.2 **Transmen and Homosocial Reproduction**

	Hetero cismen	Stealth transmen	Open transmen	Hetero ciswomen	Gay cismen	Lesbian ciswomen
Female				X		X
Homosexual					X	X
Transgender			X			

identity—woman, transgender, homosexual—has less access to these ho-mosocial networks as she or he is unlike heterosexual cisgender men in some way. This cultural logic can be represented graphically, as shown in table 6.2. Within this table, a simple device I am using to represent com-plex cultural schemas, individuals get an X for every identity that is not male, not cisgender, and not heterosexual. Following this cultural logic, stealth transmen move from being doubly marked as lesbians—and the furthest away from heterosexual men—to being unmarked as just guys at work. This transformation is theoretical, as not all stealth transmen transition from lesbians to heterosexual men. But people typically as-sume women with gender expressions marked as masculine are lesbians because of the historical conflation between homosexuality and gender nonconformity (Chauncey 1994; Garber 1997). And while not all stealth transmen are heterosexual, coworkers assume them to be unless they state otherwise. Stealth transmen, then, end up looking similar to het-erosexual, cisgender men—and different from open transmen, hetero-sexual women, gay men, and lesbians. And heterosexual open transmen may be incorporated into the homosocial networks of heterosexual cis-gender men on the basis of shared appearance and sexual identity. Illus-trating the importance of workplace context, openly gay transmen would be expected to have less social integration in such networks if they work in predominantly heterosexual workplaces, as would transmen of color in predominantly white organizations.

Within this cultural logic, coworkers can interpret transmen's transi-tions as an attempt to move up the gender and sexual hierarchy—an at-tempt to gain the "normalcy" of heterosexual maleness. While I have never encountered a transman who transitioned because he sought "male privilege"—a point with which other scholars also concur (Doz-ier 2005; H. Rubin 2003)—this interpretation of transmen's motivations for transitioning is evident in some feminist and lesbian writings (see G. Rubin 1992), an interpretation that holds individuals accountable for a structural system. Yet, while misguided, assumptions about normalization as a transition motive can be a powerful rationale for tolerance. A white transman who openly transitioned in a male-dominated blue-collar job illustrates this point in his before/after questionnaire response: "My transition went extremely smoothly. I was shocked at how smooth. No one even talks about it, and it had no effect on my pay. If anything, I have been better accepted at work because people don't see me as a dyke like before." Another white transman wrote, "I am a union laborer. When I started to transition, it was easier to go from job site to job site and be accepted." Gay transmen, in contrast, can face more resistance. In one presentation I gave about this research, an audience member directly asked me, "Why would transmen go through so much trouble just to be gay?" This question illustrates how gender transitions are easier to rationalize when people interpret them as a strategy for gaining normalcy. Becoming a *gay* man when you once lived as a heterosexual woman, in contrast, challenges heteronormative assumptions that heterosexuality is the desirable norm(al).

Under this same cultural logic, transwomen do not have an acceptable rationale for their transitions. From employers' and coworkers' viewpoint, transwomen have it all when they are working as men. Again, I represent this cultural assumption with a chart, shown in table 6.3. Transwomen begin their transitions being known at work as heterosexual, bisexual, or gay men. Regardless of this prior identity, a gender transition is a step down in regard to workplace power, as transwomen are purposefully shedding maleness—even gay men can have a gender advantage over women (Ward 2000; Newton 1993). While transwomen have diverse personal understandings of their gender and sexual identity, coworkers often read them through the lens of the long-standing cultural conflation of male femininity, homosexuality, and sexual deviance (Hennen 2008; Levine 2002). In legal cases and news stories, transwomen are conflated with gay men (see *Barnes v. City of Cincinnati* 2004; Brink

TABLE 6.3 **Transwomen and Homosocial Reproduction**

	Hetero cismen	Hetero ciswomen	Stealth transwomen	Gay cismen	Lesbian ciswomen	Open transwomen
Female	X	X			X	X
Homosexual				X	X	
Transgender						X

2002; *Cox v. Denny's, Inc.* 1999; *Tronetti v. TLC HealthNet Lakeshore Hospital* 2003) and/or pedophiles (*Boston Herald* 1994). Transwomen stand to lose homosocial networks with heterosexual men—a particularly strong loss for transwomen who worked in male-dominated careers, such as business management or construction. This loss was driven home for me during a transgender workplace panel in Texas. One of the participants transitioned in a professional job she held for many years as a man. Her colleagues—all men—could not make sense of her choice. One of them asked her, "Why would you want to be a second-class citizen?" Men can start to doubt transwomen's abilities, even when they worked with them for many years as men (Schilt and Connell 2007). Employers and coworkers can also read this transition as a sign of mental illness. In legal cases, it was not uncommon for employers to ask transwomen to submit to psychological testing. Among the transmen I interviewed— and in the news stories and legal cases—only one man reported being asked to submit to a similar request. And, after his initial session, he was deemed psychologically fit.

The cultural logic of homosocial reproduction that I have laid out theoretically is evident in workplace interactions. Many open transmen I interviewed reported top-down support from their employers— even when they expected some opposition or harassment. This support is not always effusive, but it is typically effective at setting the tone for the rest of the workplace. When this support is made visible, coworkers, particularly heterosexual men, often are willing to integrate transmen into their workplace interactions. Devin says, "I was always more afraid to tell men [about being transgender], but I have always gotten more of an enthusiastic response, which totally surprises me." Peter was nervous to tell the men he worked with. When he finally did, he was surprised by their reaction. "They were confused at first. But then one guy said, 'Well, that is fine with me.' This other guy told everyone that one of his family members was FTM. I think that really helped set a precedent for the other workers." Ethan asked one of the heterosexual men at work why he had fewer questions about Ethan's transition than the women. He responded, "It [your transition] doesn't make much of a difference. I met you as Ethan, and you're Ethan to me. You're a dude. You sit down to pee or whatever, but I don't really care." This support from men is not always offered, as the experience of a transman who transitioned on the police force in Oregon shows. He received little support from his superiors and was forced to move into the men's locker room before he felt comfortable with his physical appearance as a man. He was the target of harassment and had his locker vandalized—events that led him to bring charges against the police force (Bernstein 2000). In my interview study, Crispin also found little support from the men he worked with in a blue-collar job, a lack of support mirrored by his superiors.

Transmen had higher expectations for gay men, as they were theoretically part of the LGBT community. Yet these expectations were rarely met at work. Devin notes, "Gay men are the worst! The worst! They help less at it [treating you like a man]." He added, "The guy who coordinates the overnight trips at work is a gay guy. If a guy and a girl go on a trip, they get two rooms. If it is two guys, they get one room to cut costs. But he asked me, 'Do you want your own room?' I was kind of offended by that." Aaron and Christopher attributed much of their marginalization as "token trannies" to gay men. Christopher felt he was purposefully excluded from gay men's interactions at work. "They were just better at being gay. Like the stereotype of what gay men are supposed to act like? That is how they acted. They were part of this old gay boys' network." Aaron, who identified as queer, faced similar exclusion. "For my job, I am constantly talking about sex. And if my [gay supervisor] is there, and I am talking about sex to a gay man, he will add his two cents—like somehow my experience is not quite right." Transmen's higher expectations in these interactions may account for their greater criticism of gay men. However, such reactions from gay men—reactions documented by others (Califia 2002)—are not surprising under the cultural logic I have laid out, as gay men must make sense of transmen's change in gender vis-à-vis their own identity.

In my interviews, lesbian and heterosexual women also struggled with how to fit transmen into a gender system that disadvantages women. They often emphasized their knowledge that transmen were "still female" underneath their clothes. When transmen's employment histories are analyzed, barriers to an open transition typically came from women employers. Many transmen also recount women colleagues being more likely than men to question them at length about their motivations for modifying their bodies. Xavier was nervous to come out as transgender to his colleagues, a group of feminist heterosexual and lesbian women. While they were very supportive of his identity, they expressed concerns about hormones and surgery. "What brought up most issues for people, more than being on T, was the breast stuff [chest surgery]. . . . When I first told them, the reaction was a little mixed." Peter and Preston both faced policing reactions from women coworkers who asked invasive questions about their genitalia and worried whether they were "being honest" with women they were romantically interested in. "Being honest" for these women meant disclosing that Preston and Peter were not "really men." This boundary guarding from gay men, lesbians, and heterosexual women reflects the hierarchical cultural logic of the workplace. As people subject to sexism and/or homophobia, they can interpret transmen as getting an unfair advantage by moving closer to heterosexual cisgender men in appearance. Heterosexual men lose none of their social power by sharing with a transman—a lone case—while people with less social power see themselves as now at a disadvantage to someone without a "biological claim" to the power associated with maleness.

While some heterosexual men might be willing to incorporate a transman into their gendered workplace culture, they often lead the resistance against transwomen at work. The prevalence of this resistance suggests that transwomen present a unique challenge to men's sense of maleness and masculinity. The murder of Gwen Araujo, a stealth transwoman, by four men who had been sexually involved with her was defended in court as a logical reaction to an insult to masculinity (Bettcher 2007). This "trans panic" defense was so common in court cases with transgender victims, California passed the Gwen Araujo Justice for Victims Act in 2006 to limit the usage of this line of defense. A similar "panic" reaction can occur in the workplace in regard to transwomen, though violence appears to be more tightly regulated due to the organizational context (Schilt and Westbrook 2009). News stories and legal cases identify heterosexual men as the central perpetrators of these harassment campaigns across occupational contexts. This harassment of transwomen is excused as "natural" behavior for a man facing this situation. The article "His Sex Was Changed; Now She Wants Her Old Job" (Testerman and Malone 1990) describes a transwoman firefighter facing harassing comments from men she had worked with for many years prior to her transition. In response to her allegations, the captain of the firehouse replied, "Obviously there's going to be problems with acceptance of him by individuals on the job. . . . It's just basic human nature, he's going to have some problems" (ibid., 1B). This harassment comes even after employers make gestures toward inclusion. "City Hall Worker Steps into a Woman's Shoes" recounts an employer's acceptance of Camille Hopkins, a transwomen who openly transitioned in a job she had held as a man for fifteen years (Meyer 2002). Four years later, Hopkins made news again with the headline "Transsexual Reports Being Harassed" (Meyer 2006). Hopkins told reporters she brings a baseball bat and pepper spray to work in fear for her safety.

Gay men, lesbians, and heterosexual women are not always more welcoming to transwomen. Presented with transwomen, some gay men emphasize their maleness—and question what kind of person would purposefully give up being male-bodied (Rupp and Taylor 2004; Perkins 1983). Lesbians can engage in boundary guarding, separating transwomen from "real women" on the basis of so-called biological authenticity (G. Rubin 1992; Serano 2007; Stone 1991). Heterosexual women can include transwomen in "girl talk" at work (Schilt and Connell 2007), but they can also position transwomen as sexual threats in the workplace. It is opposition from heterosexual women in the workplace that typically creates problems with access to the women's bathroom. In *Goins v. West Group* (2001), women in the workplace complained that sharing a bathroom with a transwoman constituted a hostile work environment. These reactions illustrate how hierarchies work. Compared to transwomen, gay men, lesbians, and heterosexual women have more workplace power. Rather than benign neglect or making attempts at inclusion, they erect boundaries to keep this new group out of the "charmed circle" (G. Rubin 1984) and to keep their little piece of social power. Yet, illustrating the power of top-down support, employers can, in some cases, put an end to such harassment. Reflecting this power, a white transwoman who transitioned in a blue-collar job she had held as a man for over ten years wrote on her questionnaire, "My first month on the job after I came out was rough. Mean notes were taped in the ladies room I used . . . and my employer was threatened if I was not fired." She added, "After a month, things finally cooled down. My employer finally put down rules: respect everyone; do your work or get fired. Everything has been good for me since."

Why heterosexual men would begin harassment campaigns against transwomen is an interesting question. An exit from the top of this cultural hierarchy theoretically gives more resources to men, as there are fewer people with whom to share. However, it also reveals the precariousness of the power associated with maleness. Masculinity is predicated on the overreaction to femininity and the subordination of women. Some psychoanalytic theorists locate this "dread of women" as stemming from the division of labor in the family—as men are raised by women, they must do more work to individuate (Chodorow 1971). While this framework is useful for understanding socialization, the cultural devaluation of the feminine is an integral part of a heteronormative, hierarchical gender system that gives rewards based on positionality. This gender order creates and is created by cultural schemas about natural differences that become internalized in individual psyches. These schemas are also embedded in organizational structures and enacted in everyday, face-to-face interactions. Men have to be seen as innately more suited to leadership and authority in order for the system to work. One of their own kind, so to speak, leaving the category of "man" presents a problem. If transwomen can become women and keep their social power, it suggests that the power associated with maleness is arbitrary rather than immutable and innate. If power is arbitrary, it can be changed—a realization that becomes a warrant for reallocating reward and privilege at work and in society at large.

White, middle-class, heterosexual men benefit the most from the patriarchal dividend—the advantage men in general gain from the subordination of women (R. Connell 1995). To maintain that power, they resist attempts at redistribution (ibid.; Goode 1992). Yet the workplace incorporation of transmen and marginalization of transwomen by heterosexual men illustrates a key point about power: the power to exclude is also the power to include (Spelman 1988). In other words, heterosexual men can incorporate a transman as one of the guys at work—changing individual boundaries—and still maintain structural boundaries between men and women. This incorporation occurs on the institutional level, as heterosexual men helmed most of the workplaces that incorporated transmen in this study. This incorporation also occurs on the interactional level. Heterosexual men can transform transmen into "gender apprentices," which creates a superior/subordinate relationship that mirrors the cultural model of father/son relationships. Or the transition can be erased from public discussion, as it is rationalized away as the appropriate professional reaction to an individual case that is biologically anomalous. In both cases, transmen stand to benefit on an individual level from being incorporated as one of the guys, though they may not experience all the same workplace benefits as cisgender men. Structurally, the gender/sexual order of the workplace remains the same, as it does when transwomen are pushed out of the workplace. These transgender differences at work, then, are the result of the same structural and interactional mechanisms that maintain workplace gender inequality and heteronormativity more broadly.

The cultural devaluation of the feminine underlies this heteronormative gender system. Research on childhood and gender illustrates disparate reactions to so-called cross-gender behavior (Chodorow 1971; Kane
2006; Thorne 1993). Boys expressing an interest in culturally feminine
activities, such as playing with dolls, are labeled as sissies, while girls engaging in culturally masculine activities, such as sports, are called tomboys. While *tomboy* can be a derogatory, dismissive term, it also can
carry positive connotations (Thorne 1993) or at least signal benign neglect (Bem 1993). *Sissy*, however, is always a derogatory term used to
police boys, as "the label 'sissy' suggests that a boy has ventured too far
into the contaminating 'feminine,' while 'tomboys' are girls who claim
some of the positive qualities associated with the 'masculine'" (Thorne
1993, 111). The devaluation of the "sissy"—tied to anxieties about adult
male homosexuality—is institutionalized. Waves of "sissy panic" aimed
at young boys have been historically documented in United States politics (Kimmel 2006). Even among gay men, individuals who often are culturally stereotyped as feminine (Hennen 2008), men who behave "too
girly" or who dress in feminine drag are stigmatized (R. Connell 1995;
Rupp and Taylor 2004).

The cultural devaluation of characteristics and behaviors coded as
feminine that underlies this hierarchical, heteronormative gender system is clearly visible in the workplace. For both men and women, "feminine" qualities, such as nurturing and emotional support, consistently
are devalued in the workplace in favor of "masculine" qualities, such as
rationality and assertiveness (Valian 1998; C. L. Williams 1995; Padavic and Reskin 2002). Women can be held accountable for displaying behavior that does not fit with feminine gendered norms, as evidenced by
the *Hopkins v. Price Waterhouse* case. Ann Hopkins filed a sex discrimination suit after being denied a partnership at the accounting firm. Op-
ponents to her promotion charged that she "needed a course in charm
school" and should "walk more femininely, talk more femininely, dress
more femininely, and wear make-up and jewelry" (Rhode 1997, 161).
Hopkins ultimately won her case. However, "there is little indication . . .
that the Court would have found it to be sex discrimination if a prospec-
tive accounting partner had instead been told to remove her makeup and
jewelry and to go to assertiveness training class instead of charm school"
(Case 1995, 3). In *Hopkins*, the Court ruled that women have a right to
claim masculinity, as masculine traits carry greater benefits. The lack
of legal protections for men who are harassed on the basis of gender—

harassment that typically labels men as gay or feminine—legitimizes the
policing of men by other men (Talbot 2002).

The patterns identified in this book suggest that the gender system
should be conceived of as *heterosexist*, as power is allocated via positioning in gender and sexual hierarchies. The workplace experiences of
transmen and transwomen illuminate how this system works. Transmen
can benefit from the patriarchal dividend (C. Connell 1995) because they
can be culturally interpreted as attempting to shed two devalued identities: female and lesbian. In contrast, transwomen can be marginalized
for giving up two powerful identities: male and heterosexual. Viewed
from within this system, the harassment of transwomen is not the result
of a few "bad apples" but rather an outcome of institutionalized heteronormativity that gets its continued legitimacy from natural differences
schemas.

Why Can't a Man Be More Like a Woman?

Workplace gender transitions occur within the cultural logic of gendered
organizations. Within this gender order, power relations between men
and women shape norms for femininity and masculinity by defining what
is gender-appropriate in institutional locations and in individual interactions (R. Connell 1987; Lorber 2005; Risman 1998, 2004; West and Zimmerman 1987). The gender order is hierarchical, which means there is
consistently a higher value on masculinity than on femininity, on maleness than on femaleness (Bem 1993; R. Connell 1995; Schippers 2007),
even in some female-dominated workplaces (C. L. Williams 1995). These
gender relations are also heteronormative—heterosexual men receive
the most social power, and women and sexual minorities are in subordinate positions. The marginalization of women, then, is intimately tied
to the marginalization of transgender and homosexual people. The experiences of transgender people within the cultural logic of a heteronormative gender system illustrate the necessity of further theoretical and
empirical analyses of how heterosexism works institutionally and interactionally across different workplace contexts.

The patterns of differences between transmen and transwomen at
work also reflect the cultural logics that maintain the persistence of
workplace gender inequality more broadly. The workplace has a gendered division of labor. However, many workplaces are also facially in-

clusive of "diversity"—as evinced by the language corporations use to justify giving employment benefits to gays and lesbians, and transgender workers (Chang 2008; Raeburn 2004). These experiences show that commitment to diversity may be abandoned when it means a change in business as usual.

Highlighting the importance of contextuality, these differences I identify are specific to the workplace. And the strength of these differences varies across occupational settings. In other words, transmen and transwomen who work in low-wage service jobs may have more similar experiences than their professional or blue-collar counterparts. Looking outside of the workplace, the inclusion of transmen as men within the family—as illustrated by the controversy surrounding Thomas Beatie, the pregnant man (Reuters 2008)—still is precarious. Transmen can be husbands and fathers, but not birth parents and caretakers—as these roles violate gender norms for men. Further, within institutional settings, such as prisons and the military, which rely on a sharp separation of men and women, transmen and transwomen both stand to face negative experiences (Bryant and Schilt 2008; Edney 2004). And heterosexual men can react very differently to transmen outside of work, as the rape and murder of Brandon Teena, a female-bodied man, reflects (Schilt and Westbrook 2009). The flexibility of boundaries between men and women, then, varies by context, and by the logics of the underlying organizational system. It is the particular logic of the workplace that encourages everyone to adapt to masculine expectations and devalue femininity (Blair-Loy 2003; Case 1995) that shapes these transgender differences at work.

CHAPTER 7

Same as It Ever Was?

Inequality, Reproduction, and Transformation

In February 2009, the long-running feminist magazine *Ms.* featured newly elected American president Barack Obama on the cover—the first man to grace the cover in twelve years. The computer-generated Obama is tearing off his shirt, Superman-style, to reveal a T-shirt with the words "This is what a feminist looks like." This image encapsulated the hope that Obama's presidency would usher in a new era for gender equality—an optimism supported by Obama's signing the Lilly Ledbetter Fair Pay Act of 2009 into law a mere nine days after his inauguration. Yet Obama's appointment of Larry Summers as the director of the National Economic Council, and his consideration of Summers for treasury secretary, raised concerns. Many women's groups and feminist blogs voiced opposition to Summers's involvement in the Obama presidency in any capacity, particularly in an esteemed cabinet position. While Summers ultimately was not appointed to the cabinet, he continued to serve as Obama's "economic guru" (Walsh 2009). As Summers himself noted, it was good "to be back in power at a historic time" (ibid., 1).

The "return of Larry Summers" (Loenhardt 2008) to political life two years after his resignation from the presidency of Harvard signals the continued legitimacy of natural differences schemas as an explanation for unequal outcomes between men and women. These schemas exhibit a staying power, even as studies testing for gender differences in cognition or spatial ability indicate only small differences or yield inconclusive results (National Academy of Sciences 2007; Valian 1998). Experimental studies provide further counterevidence for biological explanations, as women applicants in the sciences are evaluated more negatively than men regardless of their qualifications (Brouns 2000; Budden et al. 2007; Carnes et al. 2005)—as they are in other fields such as music (Goldin and Rouse 2000) and business (Heilman et al. 2004). Yet, while Summers is trained as an economist, not a biologist, his supporters laud him for his willingness to speak these "unpopular truths" about innate gender differences. Reflecting on the controversy three years later in her *Washington Post* editorial "Was Summers Right?" Ruth Marcus (2008) concludes, "Summers was boneheaded to say what he said, in the way that he said it and considering the job that he held. But he probably had a legitimate point—and the continuing uproar says more about the triumph of political correctness than about Summers' supposed sexism" (ibid., 1).

The back-and-forth of these debates about gender, culture, and nature brings to mind the aphorism "The more things change, the more they stay the same." In many ways, this book can be read in a similar light. As men at work, some transmen benefit from the "patriarchal dividend" (R. Connell 1995, 79), the advantages that men in general gain from the subordination of women—particularly educated, white transmen who physically pass as men. These changes in workplace experiences these transmen describe are not reflective of a personal intention to gain privilege; rather, they reflect the outcome of changing social locations within a racialized gender system. As Sandra Harding notes, "The benefits of gender and race accrue regardless of the wishes of the individuals who bear them" (1986, 660). The willingness of many employers and coworkers to incorporate transmen as one of the guys shows how gender boundaries can shift on an individual level without a challenge to cultural schemas about natural gender differences. Rather, coworkers can position transmen as biological anomalies who should have been born male. Viewing a transman's transition as a medical solution to a private, biological anomaly provides justification for reshaping individual gender boundaries. This biological frame allows coworkers to repatriate transmen into the male side of the gender binary without challenging deeply held beliefs about the naturalness of this system. Transmen who are incorporated as one of the guys at work clearly benefit on an individual level when compared to transmen who are fired or marginalized. Yet structurally these responses do the same work: maintain the gender status quo.

This reproduction occurs at the organizational level, as employers give stealth transmen "men's jobs" and rehire open transmen as men. In open transitions, many employers give top-down dictates about regendering transmen through adherence to male pronouns and new names. Employers and coworkers go to great lengths to treat transmen as men, engaging them in a variety of homosocial and heterosocial gender rituals. While coworkers may not come to see open transmen as "really men," many of them are willing to be supportive when the transition is given workplace support. For some transmen, this incorporation signals success in aligning their personal and social gender identities. Transmen who seek to be visible as female-socialized men and/or transmen, in contrast, can be less satisfied with their workplace relationships—particularly if employers and coworkers want them to be 120 percent male. These responses show anxiety on the part of cisgender people about maintaining the seeming naturalness of the connection between gender identity, bodies, and biological sex.

The workplace experiences of stealth and open transmen underscore the social processes that account for the persistence of gender inequality. Yet it would be a misreading to take this book as simply a story about structural and cultural reproduction. As Marshall Sahlins notes, "The worldly circumstances of human action are under no inevitable obligation to conform to the categories by which certain people perceive them. In the event that they do not, the received categories are potentially revalued in practice, functionally redefined" (1981, 67). He adds, "One may question whether the continuity of a system ever occurs without its alteration, or alteration without continuity" (ibid.). Sahlins, of course, has time on his side—three hundred years—in his analysis of historical and structural transformation in Hawaii. The modern push for workplace gender equality—of which this study is the newest historical moment—is much younger. For all the legislative changes designed to close the workplace gender gap, women still continue to earn less than men while their workforce participation is at a high point, which can make change look very slow (Lipman 2009). Originally proposed in 1994 (Raeburn 2004), ENDA has not passed at the end of the 2000s—leaving LGBT workers without federal, and in many cases local, workplace protections. Yet, as Sahlins (1981) suggests, in looking for cultural and structural transformation, it is important to realize that the more things *appear* to stay the same, the more they *actually* change.

Some of these changes are readily apparent. The idea that transmen could openly transition and remain in the same jobs was questionable in the 1990s. Yet, in the 2000s, increasing numbers of transmen are doing just that. As this book shows, employers and coworkers can be overtly and covertly hostile to these attempts. But, in other cases, transmen do find workplace support. Some employers make clear that harassment is not an appropriate response—an action that increases the likelihood that transmen will find coworker support for their transitions. Some coworkers take on the role of pronoun police, reminding others to use male pronouns—an action that many transmen appreciate. Other co-workers write notes and e-mails of support and, in some cases, welcome transmen into the men's bathroom. Some ask for additional information about the transition process, so they can educate themselves. In some workplaces, transmen continue or develop friendships with coworkers, friendships that defy the expectation that being out as transgender always carries a discredited stigma. These supportive reactions from coworkers—people who typically have less personal investment in a transman colleague than his friends and family members—signal a change from merely a decade prior. Yet that some transgender and genderqueer people receive less visible support from employers and coworkers illustrates that more change is needed. Achieving workplace gender identity and gender expression protections should be a central goal for gender equality activism. In other words, the employment discrimination and harassment transgender and genderqueer people can face at work should not be relegated to being a "special rights" issue but rather viewed as part of the struggle for workplace equality.

Workplaces that support an open gender transition are never the same, even when they appear to be engaging in business as usual. Most human resources departments have never dealt with a transition request and often are not sure where to turn for the appropriate protocol. The resulting anxiety can lead to a decision to cement the transition policy in case it ever comes up again. In turn, businesses with official policies and/ or nondiscrimination policies attract more transgender workers, as these policies can be taken as a sign that a particular workplace will be supportive of an open transition or an openly transgender employee. Having these policies on the books does not ensure a smooth transition, but it does theoretically provide some recourse if a problem related to transition arises. It also signals that this workplace has at least some knowledge about transgender people. Transmen who are met with workplace support can become spokespeople for their workplaces, which can attract more transgender workers. Having more than one transgender employee in the same workplace exponentially increases the visibility of transgender lives—an important step in combating discrimination (Escoffier 1975). It also puts cisgender people into closer personal contact with transgender people, a form of education that was key to gaining domestic partner benefits for gays and lesbians in *Fortune* 500 companies (Raeburn 2004).

When transmen transition into social maleness, the category of "man" also undergoes transformation. While the feminist movement opened up new possibilities for being a woman (Echols 1989), hegemonic masculinity still exerts tight social control on men (R. Connell 1995; Kimmel 2004). The history of masculinity is fraught with crises that call for shoring up masculinity (Kimmel 2006), social movements to revive manhood (Messner 1997), and medical and social interventions to "fix" broken masculinity (Loe 2004). Femininity remains something women simply are, while masculinity is something men must constantly achieve (Chodorow 1971). A male body—supposedly a product of nature—is the battleground on which the struggle to achieve masculinity is waged. As Raewyn Connell notes, "True masculinity is almost always thought to proceed from men's bodies—to be inherent in a male body or to express something about a male body" (1995, 45). Yet, as this book shows, when transmen are socially gendered as male, whether they have XY chromosomes matters little. As female-socialized men, transmen bring the gains of the feminist movement—the idea that there are many different and acceptable ways to live a life—into maleness. While this inclusion will not spark an instant gender revolution, over time it can bring a more expansive definition of what it means to be a man in arenas such as the workplace and the family.

Becoming men at work can motivate some transmen to challenge gender inequality—inequality they often describe as being more visible from their outsider-within perspective. In situations in which transmen do point out unfair practices at work, changes that can improve the workplace outcomes of individual women can result. These challenges have the potential to work as cultural models for other men who see inequality but do not know how to disrupt it—an important step for changing structural inequality of all kinds (Picca and Feagin 2007). In order for gender equity at work to be achieved, men must take an active role in challenging the subordination of women (Acker 1990; P. Martin 2003; Rhode 1997; Valian 1998; C. L. Williams 1995). Inequality can seem difficult to change, particularly when it is attributed to biology and tradition. Yet the willingness of heterosexual men to redraw gender boundaries to include transmen shows the power some individuals have to reallocate rewards and privileges. Redrawing these boundaries will not change natural differences schemas overnight, but these schemas will never go back to exactly the way they were before. There will always be new possibilities for organizational and individual action that did not exist previously, even when it looks like business as usual.

In emphasizing change, I want to end by noting that this book should not be taken as the final word on transgender workplace experiences—experiences that are changing rapidly, though unevenly, across the country and around the world. My data provide a wide, historical lens that illustrates how transmen's and transwomen's workplace options in the States have grown since the early 1980s. With the increase in visibility of transgender lives—particularly transgender men—since the mid-2000s, I expect to see major changes in transgender workplace experiences in the decade of the 2010s. While my data do not focus on genderqueer people specifically, their workplace experiences also need elucidating. As more states and cities enact gender identity and gender expression protections, it will be possible to research how these protections impact workplace outcomes for transgender and genderqueer workers. My research also suggests that occupational context shapes workplace outcomes, particularly for open transmen, as does regional and national context. Future research should continue this project of documenting how variables such as occupation, gender, race, region, and national identity impact transgender workplace experiences. More historical and national comparative work is needed in these areas, as this type of methodological analysis aids in documenting changes in social and cultural processes.

Implications of This Study

This study has three major implications. First, this research highlights the importance of documenting the social processes that maintain and reproduce workplace inequality more broadly. Second, this book raises serious questions about the adoption of biological frames for challenging transgender inequality. Third, the data on the workplace experiences of transmen and transwomen contribute empirical weight to theoretical discussions of how gender is "done" and how it might be "undone."

The Social Processes of Workplace Inequality

Patterns of workplace discrimination often are the focus of sociological research that examines disparate workplace rewards for various minority groups—people of color, poor people, women, mothers, gay men and lesbians—vis-à-vis white, heterosexual men (Badgett 2003; Bertrand and Mullainathan 2004; Brouns 2000; Cole, Feild, and Giles 2004; Correll, Bernard, and Paik 2007; Elliott and Smith 2004). These studies tend to be large-scale quantitative analyses or experimental audit studies that manufacture employment decisions in lab settings. The statistical findings of these studies are necessary for documenting that the workplace is not a neutral location that rewards workers on the basis of human capital alone. Rather, the abilities and skills of workers are filtered through various cultural schemas that advantage whiteness, heterosexuality, and maleness (Ridgeway and Correll 2004; Valian 1998). Yet the mechanisms and social processes that produce these unequal outcomes—mechanisms that generally are more identifiable via qualitative methods—need to be a central part of this research on workplace discrimination (P. Martin 2003). Without the "common element of [inequality's] daily unfolding" (Fenstermaker, West, and Zimmerman 2002, 22), the cultural schemas that underlie these unequal outcomes remain hidden—which naturalizes inequality and makes change seem daunting.

Analyzing these social processes in the experiences of transgender workers shows that leveling the playing field for workers who fall outside the norms of white, middle-class, heterosexual maleness requires interplay among legal protections, enforced organizational policies, and individual actions. Legal protections provide some official recourse for individuals who have experienced discrimination on the basis of a protected status. But the protections these laws offer work in practice only when supported by organizations and individuals. Construction sites legally cannot exclude workers on the basis of gender or race. Yet, when the inclusion of these workers is not supported by an organization, the numbers of women and people of color remain only at the level of legally defined quotas (Paap 2006).

A tripartite of legal protections, enforced organizational policies, and interactional adherence to these policies is necessary for effectively challenging workplace inequality. Organizations set the tone for the particular workplace culture by defining what types of interactions are acceptable and unacceptable. In the case of transgender workers, employers can codify acceptance of diversity into nondiscrimination policies—regardless of whether a city or state law exists. These policies should include sexual identity, gender identity, and gender expression—as transgender people experience homophobia as well as sexism and transphobia. These policies could offer some protection to stealth transmen, as they could not be fired explicitly on the basis of their transgender status if they came out or were outed at work. As the experiences of transmen in this book show, these policies do not always work in practice; however, they are an important step in addressing workplace discrimination.

In open workplace transitions, employers can ease open transitions by setting top-down dictates about changing names and pronouns with transgender colleagues. Transgender people who receive top-down support from employers generally report less harassment and overt opposition from coworkers than those who do not—regardless of whether they live in a state with employment protections for gender identity—just as women who work in blue-collar workplaces that express zero tolerance for gender and sexual harassment experience less harassment (Paap 2006; Welsh 1999). Employers should also work with the transitioning employee to find a bathroom solution that is not burdensome to that employee. Coworkers can show support by adopting a new name and new pronouns and by being respectful of personal boundaries. In other words, while they might be very curious about the physical aspects of a gender transition, they should refrain from asking personal questions of their transgender colleague unless invited to do so. They can also disrupt harassment and marginalization when they see it. This disruption can be overt—challenging other coworkers—or it can be as simple as having lunch with transgender colleagues or including them in conversation. These types of supportive interactions can play a major role in easing the experience of transgender people, as they model for others that the transition is not a big deal.

Some transmen in this book report integration into their workplaces as men. Yet to see transmen as a group that does not experience employment discrimination would be a major misreading of this research. Individual transitions occur within a cultural system that places a higher value on whiteness, heterosexuality, and maleness. The end result of transitioning within this system is that transmen who are white, tall, and passable as men report more integration in general than transmen who are racial minorities, short, or visibly gender-variant. Transmen who are educated and who work in professional jobs are also more likely to report integration than transmen who do not have a college degree and/or who work in service jobs. Yet it is important to keep in mind that transmen can feel pressure to conform to normative behavioral and appearance standards for men in order to maintain employment—a long step away from freedom of gender expression. Additionally, any integration and/or economic gains stealth and open transmen experience are precarious. Their status at work relies on continued organizational and interactional support. This precariousness puts transmen in a shaky position that is far from privileged. While federal protection for gender identity and expression will not be a panacea for inequality, it is an important step toward alleviating the precariousness of being an unprotected class of workers.

Biology and Inequality

This study documents how natural differences schemas shape social structures, interactions, and individual outcomes. These schemas hinge on commonsense views of biology, as gender differences are framed by many as innate offshoots of the configuration of chromosomes, genitalia, and internal psyches that fall into stable arrangements for males and females. The research presented in this book is one of many studies that document how what appears as biological reality often is the outcome of social and cultural processes (Dozier 2005; Garfinkel 1967; Goffman 1977; Kessler and McKenna 1978; Kessler 1998; Lancaster 2003; Laqueur 1990; Lorber 2005; Valian 1998; C. L. Williams 1995). Yet that this study is still necessary despite all its predecessors demonstrates how resistant these cultural schemas are to change. I want to consider why these schemas are so resistant to change and explore the implications of invoking biological etiologies and natural differences as argument against inequality.

Biological essentialism is a compelling framework because it provides an easily understood etiology for complex outcomes (Lancaster 2003). If the workplace gender gap comes from biological sex differences, for example, changing it is beyond an individual's control (though many individuals fight "biology is destiny" in arenas such as aging, fertility, and disease) and beyond the control of an organization, such as a workplace.

Social constructionist perspectives, in contrast, require a probing look not just at history and social structure but also at personal and organizational investment in maintaining an unequal system. While social constructionism provides a strong argument for change, as it shows that the current order of things has shifted historically and cross-culturally, this perspective can easily be misread as being about choice. This reading presents people who fall outside of some kind of social norm as choosing to be different—a framework used to justify reparative therapy for homosexuality and transgenderism (Kennedy 2008). The heyday of queer theory and queer activism in the 1990s brought renewed emphasis on the social construction of gender and sexuality. Yet the 2000s have seen a return to biological and genetic explanations for gender and sexual difference in the popular press (see Angier 2007; Wade 2007) and within the field of natural and social sciences research (Epstein 2007). This circular debate suggests that there is no clear answer to this nature/nurture debate—particularly as we enter an age in which personal body projects involve antiaging fights, in vitro fertilization, and genetic disease monitoring (Lancaster 2003). And this (re)turn to biology is unsurprising: when inequality does not go away, the debates about the sources of this inequality remain salient.

There are undeniable biological differences between what are classified as male and female bodies. Yet, as Sherry Ortner notes, "Biological facts are not irrelevant . . . but these facts and differences only take on significance of superior/inferior within the framework of culturally defined value systems" (1971, 9). Adding complexity to the situation, biological essentialism has increasingly been used as a justification for the existence of homosexual and transgender people. This argument puts forth the idea of biological diversity: homosexuality is a natural (read not pathological) offshoot of the development of sexuality (Wade 2007), and transgenderism is a natural offshoot of the development of gender (Roughgarden 2004). Biological diversity could, in theory, challenge the cultural logics of a heteronormative system predicated on a male/female binary. This frame can be a compelling justification for tolerance. As public belief in homosexuality as innate has increased, so has support for gay civil rights (Sherrill and Yang 2000). And coworkers and employers can use this biology frame to justify transmen's open transitions—though this frame has less power for transwomen, reflecting that these frames are filtered through the cultural logic of a heteronormative gender system. Yet, as transmen's experiences at work show, biological frames for transgenderism can leave deeply held ideas about the naturalness for most people of a biologically derived binary of males and female untouched—which, in turn, contributes to the persistence of gender inequality.

The deployment of a biological frame as a justification for civil rights is a double-edged sword. This frame enters the cultural terrain with a particular yardstick—be that men, cisgender people, or heterosexuals—and tries to justify a difference from what becomes a norm(al). Groups that are different can win tolerance and public support for their right to exist vis-à-vis these other groups—because their existence cannot be helped. But being tolerated is not the same thing as being accepted on one's own terms. Highlighting this distinction, public support for gay employment rights has increased exponentially in the 2000s, but support for granting gays and lesbians access to legal marriage—a government-sanctioned heteronormative institution—has not (Herek 2002; Sherrill and Yang 2000). Relatedly, coworkers can support a transgender person's individual transition as a personal choice but balk at the idea of transgenderism as a legitimate political issue. Women have the legal right to work in a harassment-free workplace, but they still overwhelmingly work in occupations without child-care and family leave programs—reflecting the male yardstick that shapes workplace policies (Blair-Loy 2003). These examples highlight that tolerance for difference does not necessarily mean equality. Biological diversity arguments, while very successful at winning tolerance for individuals, may not be successful in challenging the dominant cultural schemas that justify structural inequality.

(Un)Doing Gender Inequality

In this book, I empirically document how cultural schemas about natural differences between men and women contribute to the persistence of workplace gender inequality. I follow in the theoretical tradition of symbolic interactionist and ethnomethodological theories of gender that highlight how masculinity and femininity are not natural offshoots of maleness and femaleness, respectively, but rather social products that shape and are shaped by interactional and institutional practices (Garfinkel 1967; Goffman 1977; Kessler and McKenna 1978; West and Zimmerman 1987, 2009). These schemas position men and women as polar opposites in skills, abilities, and emotional landscapes, though "from the standpoint of nature, men and women are closer to each other than is anything else—for instance, mountains, kangaroos and coconut palms" (G. Rubin 1975, 179). People are accountable to expectations of either masculinity or femininity, depending upon whether they are read as male or as female (West and Zimmerman 1987). As maleness and its associated characteristics receive a higher value than femaleness and femininity in the current gender system (Bem 1993; Schippers 2007), these seemingly innocuous schemas about difference naturalize inequality. While the content of the normative expectations of masculinity and femininity changes over time, the hierarchical relationship between maleness and femaleness remains consistent—raising, for me, serious questions about whether gender equality is possible within a system predicated on a male/female binary.

This body of theorizing on gender, particularly Candace West and Don Zimmerman's (1987) article "Doing Gender" and Candace West and Sarah Fenstermaker's (1995) "Doing Difference," has faced an array of critiques. Some critics argue that the focus on gender as an interactional achievement overemphasizes face-to-face interaction, giving social structures no "ongoing, relatively independent existence" (Winant 1995, 504; see also Andersen 2005; Collins 1995; Thorne 1995). These critiques often lump "doing gender" together with theories of gender performativity (J. Butler 1989), as these bodies of theory share an emphasis on the reproduction of gender and draw on people conceived of as making "gender trouble" (drag queens or transgender people) to illustrate theoretical points. Showing this conflation, Barrie Thorne ends a critique of the article "Doing Difference" (West and Fenstermaker 1995) with the statement: "Gender extends beyond daily cultural performance, and it will take much more than doing drag and mocking naturalized conceptions to transform it" (Thorne 1995, 499). Relatedly, critics argue that the emphasis on accountability to doing gender—the idea that expectations of masculinity and femininity are ubiquitous to social life (West and Zimmerman 1987)—renders social change impossible (Deutsch 2007; Thorne 1995). While masculinity and femininity can undergo radical changes, people's accountability to doing gender in everyday interactions can never lessen.

From these critiques has emerged a theoretical conception of "undoing gender" (Deutsch 2007; Risman 2009), a theoretical framework supported by empirical suggestions about how to "degender" the social world (Lorber 2005).[1] The idea of undoing gender moves the analytic focus from accountability to resistance. As Francine Deutsch explains, "It is time to put the spotlight squarely on the social processes that underlie resistance against conventional gender relations and on how successful change in the power dynamics and inequities between men and women can be accomplished" (2007, 107). Judith Lorber (2005) lays out concrete suggestions for how degendering might be possible, such as transforming gendered language (from *husband* and *wife* to *spouse*) and removing male and female classifications from legal documents. Building on these suggestions, Barbara Risman (2009) critiques the recent trend in gender scholarship toward describing resistant gendered practices and embodiments as "alternative" masculinities and femininities. This terminology cements the idea of traditional or hegemonic masculinity and femininity, the original to which these other identities are an alternative. This construction also maintains the male/masculine and female/feminine model, but with more options. Risman eloquently argues, "No one should have to identify as female to appreciate silky fabric and ruffles next to one's skin. No one should have to identify as male to be allowed to be tough and domineering" (ibid., 84). Highlighting the impact of feminist gender scholarship since the 1970s, she adds that this new need for specifying alternatives suggests that we are moving closer to a postgender society.

Finding ways to undo the institutionalization of a male/masculine and female/feminine binary is an important step toward greater gender equality. As the experiences of transmen in this book show, carrying a binding, legal gender creates employment and housing dilemmas that could easily be remedied by removing the "M" and the "F" from legal documents. Changing gendered language also opens new possibilities for which people can hold what identities. Yet language changes do not alter gender schemas overnight. We may now call all people who serve drinks on airplanes "flight attendants," but women still bear the brunt of the emotional labor in that particular job (Claire Williams 2003). Increasing numbers of married heterosexual couples use the term *partner* rather than *husband* or *wife*. Yet, at the end of the 2000s, gay men and lesbians still do not have a federal right to marry—showing a continued divide between partners who are state-recognized and partners who are not (J. Butler 2004). And, beyond theoretical arguments, it is questionable whether transcending gender is an empirical possibility. I raise this question not to discount the major changes that have occurred in gender possibilities since the middle of the twentieth century but rather to identify the need for unpacking what it would actually mean "on the ground" to transcend gender.

Where would transgender people fit in a postgender world? Presenting my research on transmen in the workplace at conferences, I have been admonished by feminist theorists that transgender people cannot, by their very nature, be part of a revolution invested in transcending gender. While younger generations of feminists (the oft-labeled "third wave" (Heywood and Drake 1997) have made strides toward embracing transgender perspectives (Schilt and Zobl 2008), much of academic gender theory has kept transgender people at arm's length by locating them within queer theory and LGBT studies rather than as part of a conversation about gender equality. This easy dismissal of transgender people as a whole relies on a particular construction of gender as an oppressive set of culturally constructed expectations that must be undone or abandoned. That some transgender people bring their bodies in line with a personal sense of gender identity—an identity that differs from how they were assigned at birth—positions them, under this frame of gender, as uncritically buying into a flawed system. Yet, as this book shows, some transgender people have an acute awareness of how gender inequality works because they have lived on both sides of the male/female binary— an awareness they put into practice by challenging unequal workplace practices or taking part in feminist activism (Serano 2007). And, as Catherine Connell (2006) argues, some transgender people "do transgender" at work in an effort to challenge expectations of masculinity and femininity for their coworkers. However, just as with cisgender men and women, not all transgender people are aware of gender inequality or have an investment in working to change it. True gender equality means granting transgender people the same rights as cisgender people to hold different views on gender relations.

The sociocultural frame of the transsexual–as–gender dupe has lost its dominance in gender theory in the 2000s, particularly as the diversity of gender identities and personal body projects housed under the term *transgender* or *genderqueer* has gained visibility (Valentine 2007). Yet an implication that transgender or genderqueer people who do not modify their bodies surgically and/or hormonally are a more progressive improvement over body modifiers haunts some gender scholarship (see Finn and Dell 1999; Halberstam 2005) and continues to surface at academic presentations on transgender research I attend. Rather than measuring transgender people on a doing/undoing gender continuum, a measurement that can create good genderqueers and bad transsexuals, I offer that a better goal would be to consider whether there is something inherently complicit about seeking an alignment between personal gender identities, social gender identities, and bodies.

Stealth transmen often describe pleasure at being accepted as one of the guys. This pleasure comes from finally gaining a social maleness that aligns with their personal, often long-standing, sense of being male. While transgender people may be more able than cisgender people to articulate this pleasure because it is a new achievement, this feeling of pleasure is shared by many cisgender people. Transmen's workplace experiences suggest that women find it pleasurable to talk about "female things," such as menstruation, with other women at work. This talk can be a form of boundary guarding that keeps men out (C. L. Williams 1995), but it can also be an expression of the pleasure of making socially visible what Judith Butler describes as a "felt sense of self" (1990, 109). Transmen's integration into "guy talk" at work also suggests that men find a similar pleasure in discussing experiences and feelings men are thought to share naturally. These interactions are ritualized (Goffman 1977). But even rote performances can be rewarding when the actors involved feel they are reflecting an innate truth about the order of the social world.

While people may experience expectations of masculinity and femininity as oppressive in some situations, having a feeling of coherence among bodies, personal genders, and social genders can be a major reward for doing gender the "right" way (J. Butler 1989). Showing this pleasure, even feminists have written volumes about the embodied sense of being female, such as the "profoundly physical pleasure of suckling a baby" (D. Smith 2009, 76). Yet feminist theory relegates transwomen to the position of appropriating, rather than embodying, femaleness (J. Butler 2004; Serano 2007). This distinction is unsurprising, as cisgender women write the bulk of feminist theory. From a cisgender yardstick, transgender experiences of gender are inauthentic. Sociology of gender supports this frame by holding on to "sex" as the biological distinctions between males and females (chromosomes, reproductive systems, genitalia), and "gender" as the cultural meaning put onto these differences. This explanation stabilizes a male/female binary as authentic and real—a conceptualization that does not hold up under empirical evidence (Fausto-Sterling 2000; Kessler 1998)—and reifies the biological essentialism feminist scholars have long disavowed (De Beauvoir 1953; Chodorow 1978;

Mitchell 1966; Hartmann 1979). This need to separate transgender people's experiences with gender from "natural" experiences suggests there is something meaningful to many feminist scholars about the feeling of innate sex/gender coherence. Perhaps the problem with doing gender as a theory is not the focus on accountability but the lack of focus on the pleasure that can come from experiencing this coherence. I acknowledge this pleasure not to normalize it but rather to illustrate why natural differences schemas have proved so intractable in the face of major societal changes in what men and women can do.

Reflecting these major changes, gender theorists today seem to stumble over the best way to represent men's and women's experiences without naturalizing a male/masculine and female/feminine model. Gender scholarship that crosses my desk for review often suffers from what I think of as the quotation mark problem. To avoid reifying gender, authors write about "men," "women," "reality," "biology," and "sex." Yet the idea that all of this change suggests a move toward transcending or undoing gender mistakes content and form. The content of masculinities and femininities has changed widely since just the 1950s. Yet the form of a male/female binary remains. As the experiences of transmen at work show, people can socially cross this binary; however, attempts to move beyond it (the queering of the binary) often result in penalties. These workplace experiences in this book raise, to me, serious questions of whether a binary as a form can ever be equal, even if the content of the binary undergoes radical change. Retaining sex but trying to transcend gender expresses a desire to "escape domination" while maintaining "fundamental social categories" (Delphy 1993, 1). Without a focus on undoing sex, the content of gender can change, but natural differences schemas deeply linked to biology and tradition will remain untouched, and inequality will continue as business as usual.

Methodological Appendix

This research began, as many projects do, somewhat serendipitously. During my graduate training, I initiated an ethnographic study at a non-profit organization. At the onset of my research, I was focusing on how the different branches of the organization dealt with situations that challenged each other's goals and strategies. To gain a deeper understanding of the work of each branch, I spent a year interning at the organization. A few weeks into my job, one of my coworkers with whom I had developed a good relationship informed me that one of our colleagues "used to be a woman." As this open workplace transition had occurred years before my arrival at the workplace, I became interested in how long this particular kind of "office gossip" circulated about transgender employees who transitioned and remained in the same jobs. Coworkers who had witnessed the transition also discussed with me the interactional difficulties they felt the situation had created for them, such as what they were supposed to say when someone called and asked for their transgender colleague by his former name. I left this project with a set of questions about how employers and coworkers make sense of an open workplace transition. I developed an interest in what happens specifically to trans-*men* in the workplace, as transitioning from women to men could be perceived as an attempt to "move up" the gender hierarchy—a type of status change understudied in sociology.

I began my research on transmen's workplace experiences with pre-liminary or "diagnostic" participant observation (Duneier 1999; Luker 1984) in the transgender community in California. My purpose was to gain a deeper understanding of the range of transgender workplace experiences as well as to develop a vocabulary that reflected transmen's experiences. A few months into my research, I was invited to attend a

monthly group meeting for transmen. The meeting was a social and educational venue rather than a therapeutic environment. As such, it was
open to significant others, friends, family, and allies (SOFFAs). At the
meetings, I identified myself as a researcher interested in studying the
workplace experiences of transgender men. Participating in these meetings was invaluable. I was able to hear many different perspectives from
transmen, their partners, and their family members. Once I began my interviews, I took my data analysis back and asked for feedback, an important step in any research project attempting to represent people's lived
experiences (Emerson and Pollner 1988). I attended these meetings between 2004 and 2006. I did similar participant observation in the transgender community in Texas between 2006 and 2008.

During this fieldwork, I participated in social groups and planning
meetings for transgender community activism and fund-raisers. I led
workshops on employment issues and did Transgender 101 sessions for
therapists, parents, and teachers. I also volunteered my research skills,
such as survey design and data analysis—an important way to both establish rapport and give back to the community of study (Small 2004).
As many of my respondents attended these events, I could follow up on
developments in their workplace experiences, which contributed to my
understanding of the flexibility of workplace strategies. I also attended
transgender conferences—conferences designed by and for transgender
people—whenever possible. Between 2003 and 2007, I attended ten such
conferences in California, Washington State, Texas, Illinois, and Pennsylvania. These conferences featured panel discussions and workshops
on employment experiences. Attending these conferences allowed me to
compare my interview data with the workplace experiences of transgender people outside of California and Texas. I also presented my research
at some of these conferences, getting valuable feedback on my findings.

Between January 2004 and February 2006, I conducted in-depth interviews with thirty-one transmen in California. For a regional comparison, I also conducted in-depth interviews with twenty-three transmen in Texas between 2007 and 2008. In both states, I selected a city
known for being politically liberal and a city known for being politically
conservative—cities I do not identify by name in the interest of maintaining anonymity for stealth transmen. Generating a random sample of transmen is not possible, as they are not evenly dispersed geographically and
there are no transgender-specific neighborhoods from which to sample. I
recruited interviewees from online discussion lists, support groups, and

personal contacts. Some of the men I interviewed were deeply integrated into transgender activist groups, while others were only peripherally involved in transgender networks, typically as a way to access transition-related resources. This recruitment strategy did leave out transmen who were "deep stealth," a term that signifies a lack of attachment to any transgender networks or social groups. I did get a range, however, of transmen who had transitioned recently as well as those who had transitioned more than ten years prior to our interview.

As I was interested in how transmen negotiated *working* as men and/or transmen, I limited the criteria of inclusion to people who had transitioned and remained in the same jobs, had found new jobs where they were known only as men, or who had found new jobs where they were known as transgender. Transmen did not have to be currently working to be included in the study. But I did require that they have once applied for a job and/or been hired as men, or have once told potential or current employers and/or coworkers that they preferred male pronouns and identified as men and/or transmen—regardless of whether they were successfully hired or retained after this announcement. Three men I interviewed were about to begin the process of an open transition, so I interviewed them before the announcement and again six months later to see how it had gone. I interviewed two additional transmen, one who was a home caregiver to a family member and one who transitioned on disability, to gain insight into the transition process when public employment is not a salient factor.

There were few demographic differences between respondents in Texas and California. Table A.1 shows transmen's first workplace strategy and their current strategy. As strategies are fluid, the same man could have experience being stealth and open across his career. Twenty-four transmen had been stealth at work at some point in their lives, twelve from each state. Thirty-six had openly transitioned or sought employment as openly transgender at some point in their lives, twenty in California and sixteen in Texas. The majority were white (86 percent), with relatively equal numbers of queer, bisexual, and gay men (49 percent) and heterosexual men (40 percent). Most queer, gay, and bisexual men, however, were not out at work at the time of our interview. The majority of transmen had a BA/BS degree (31 percent) or an advanced degree, such as an MA, a PhD, or a JD (26 percent) at the time of the interview. The rest had a high school education (19 percent) or an associate's degree (24 percent). The average age of California respondents at the time

TABLE A.1 **Workplace strategies for first job and current job** (*N* = 54)

	First job		Current job	
	Open (%)	Stealth (%)	Open (%)	Stealth (%)
Student	4	0	0	4
Retail/service	18	11	7	11
Semiprofessional	24	4	20	4
Blue-collar	11	0	4	5
Professional	18	6	24	13
Unemployed/retired	4	0	4	4
Total	79	21	59	41

Note: In tables A.1 and A.2, retail/service jobs include food service, clothing stores, and stores that sell goods and services, such as bookstores. Semiprofessional includes noncollege teaching careers and administrative assistant jobs. Blue-collar includes construction and factory jobs. Professional includes lawyers, professors, and therapists. Within the professional category, I also included graduate and advanced training for professional careers.

TABLE A.2 **Types of occupations, first job and current job** (*N* = 54)

	First job as men (%)	Current job (%)
Student	4	4
Retail/service	29	19
Semiprofessional	28	24
Blue-collar	11	9
Professional	24	37
Unemployed/retired	4	7
Total	100	100

of the interview was higher than that of the Texas respondents (thirty-five years versus twenty-five years). California transmen also had a wider range of years of transition—from the mid-1980s to the mid-2000s—while all of the transmen who openly transitioned in Texas did so in the early to mid-2000s. Table A.2 shows the types of occupations transmen began working in as men and the types of occupations they worked in at the time of the interviews. As they aged, many of them moved out of retail/service jobs and into professional careers—a move that typically reflected the transition from a high school or college temporary job into a career. For other transmen, this change reflected a career transition.

The majority of interviews were conducted in public settings, such as a coffee shop or restaurant. The rest were conducted at the homes of my respondents. Three transmen requested phone interviews. The in-person interviews ranged in length from an hour and a half to four hours (with two hours being the average), while the phone interviews were about forty-five minutes in length. The telephone format yielded much more concise responses than the in-person interviews. All respondents were provided with an informed consent sheet to sign that contained my contact information and details about the project. I use pseudonyms in the book to protect their anonymity.

Drawing on sociological research on transgender people (Bolin 1988; Garfinkel 1967; Kessler and McKenna 1978), and work and gender scholarship (Padavic and Reskin 2002; Reskin and Hartmann 1986; Reskin and Roos 1990; Valian 1998; C. L. Williams 1995), I had three central research questions going into the project: (1) Does occupational context aid or hinder the success of an open transition? (2) Are employers and coworkers willing to "do gender" with their transitioning colleague? (3) Do stealth and open transmen receive the benefits associated with being men in the workplace? I predicted the following outcomes: (1) Occupations that were heavily skewed toward one gender (such as blue-collar occupations and "women's professions") would provide the least hospitable locations for open transitions. (2) Open transmen would either still be treated as women or be marginalized as "gender others"—particularly by heterosexual men, who would guard the boundaries of who counts as a man. (3) Stealth transmen would see gains at work, while open transmen would see no difference or a negative difference in their workplace outcomes.

In the interviews, I used a semistructured interview schedule with an emphasis on workplace experiences. I adopted this approach because close-ended data collection methods have difficulty capturing complex events, such as workplace transitions. I also wanted transmen to tell me about their experiences rather than simply answer questions that reflected my theoretical hypotheses. While the flow of each interview varied, I asked all participants to discuss several key points: the decision to transition, decisions about body modifications, the transformation from being socially gendered as women to being socially gendered as men, employment history, decisions about being stealth or open, and any noticeable differences between working as women versus working as men. I began with the question "Walk me through your work history." After gaining a detailed work history, I asked, "What led up to your decision to transition?" and "Did you undergo any body modifications in this process?" After we discussed the transition process, I asked, "Do you notice any differences living as a man versus when you lived as a woman?" Finally, if this topic had not emerged already, I asked each participant what he thought of the idea of "male privilege." Each of these questions generated a great deal of discussion, which I probed for clarity.

All interviews were audio-recorded and transcribed. After I had amassed fifteen interviews, I initiated preliminary coding. Reading through the transcripts, I devised a coding schema for participants' experiences. I began to see reoccurring codes, which I developed into a master list of codes. When a new code emerged, I went back to older interviews and recoded the data. I paid particularly attention to accounting for negative cases. I created a set of memos that pulled together data fragments for particular codes. From these memos, I constructed my analysis. Transmen's responses to the question "Do you notice any differences working as a man versus working as a woman?" illustrate this coding and analysis process. The majority of transmen said "yes" to this question and elaborated on these differences. They often described these changes in positive or negative terms. Yet what they saw as positive varied: some transmen felt it was positive to receive more respect, while others viewed that change as negative because they felt it devalued women. In my analysis, I coded the content of the changes (or lack of changes) they described. It was through this coding that I identified the central analytic categories in chapter 3. Transmen's accounts of changes fell broadly into what I categorized as "gains," "losses," and "no changes." Within gains, they described increases in "respect," "authority," and "economic possibilities." Within losses, their experiences reflected differing returns from embodiments of masculinity, such as being a racial minority, being short, or not being passable as a man. Within no changes, the important code was occupational context. I provide this example to illustrate that my analysis was not driven by transmen's perspective of whether they had "good" or "bad" workplace experiences but rather by a detailed analysis of the patterns identified in their employment histories. And, as I demonstrate in this book, the interview data, combined with the additional forms of data collection I detail below, countered many of my initial hypotheses.

Before starting the interviews, I was unaware of how I would be received as a cisgender woman doing research on transgender men. While insider status does not necessarily guarantee rapport or ease at gaining access to a community (Merton 1972; Reissman 1987; Wolf 1996), when I met someone for an interview, it typically was the first time we had met—a situation from which it can be hard to establish rapport. In an effort to be transparent about my intentions, I made clear that I was happy to answer personal questions about myself. I was often asked why I was interested in this type of research and whether I had transgender people in my family. After several months of my participant observation in both states, I became more of a familiar figure, which eased the interview process enormously. By the end of my data collection, the person I was interviewing typically knew someone else who had interviewed with me. Overall, I do not feel that being a cisgender woman hindered my research. I was not expected to know about what it feels like to be transgender, so I was able to get a great deal of rich data on the topic. Additionally, I did not know what it was like to work as a man, so I could ask copious questions on the topic. While my respondents might have phrased their responses differently to a trans or cisgender man, particularly regarding what men talk about when they are in all-male groups—a topic they were often hesitant to discuss with me at first—I do not think that information would be more honest or authentic than the data I gathered (see K. Martin 1996; C. L. Williams and E. Joel Heikes 1993).

Workplace transitions are interactional events. Relying on interview data can be problematic, as it means a reliance on "a source of information about events not witnessed" (Becker and Geer 1957, 29). An ethnographic investigation of an open workplace transition would have provided rich data on the "saying and doing" of gender rather than on the "said and done" (P. Martin 2003). However, this methodological approach would have imposed a tremendous burden on potential respondents and their coworkers and would probably have produced compromised results due to constant research presence. As a way to generate a fuller picture of open transitions, I instead sought "knowledgeable informants" (Weiss 1994): coworkers of open transmen. Eight open transmen provided me with coworkers' contacts: four men and ten women. This group was predominantly heterosexual, with one gay man and one lesbian. The majority of these interviews were conducted over the phone, as requested by the coworkers. These interviews discussed the process of notification, the process of changing names and pronouns, reactions to the news, and how other coworkers responded to the news. These interviews lasted between thirty minutes and two and half hours. While the telephone format was limiting in my transmen interviews, I felt it was more useful in coworker interviews, as the relative anonymity seemed to be freeing. I do not indicate occupations of the coworkers to protect their anonymity.

To gain a wider perspective on transgender workplace experiences, I drew on two additional sources of data: a content analysis of news stories and legal cases about transgender employment, and questionnaire data. For the content analysis, I gathered news accounts and legal cases about transgender workers from the databases of LexisNexis and Westlaw. In May 2008, I did a LexisNexis search for "general news" in major U.S. papers for the last fifty years. This search limit included nationally read papers, such as the *New York Times* and the *Washington Post*, as well as major regional papers from all fifty states, such as the *Houston Post* and the *Times-Picayune*. I used a variety of keyword searches, such as "employment," "bias," "sued," and "fired," with "transgender" and "transsexual." To find early pieces written before the more politically correct coverage of LGBT issues, I searched under "sex change" as well as variations on terms such as "he-she," "she-he," and "she-male." On Westlaw, I used the terms "transsexual," "transgender," and "sex change." I sorted through all the cases and eliminated those that were not related to employment. Once I had a database of cases, I eliminated multiple newspaper stories about the same person and newspaper stories that overlapped with legal cases. Table A.3 shows the number of cases before and after that adjustment. I coded these stories and cases for the gender of the plaintiff and the type of occupation as well as for the framing of the workplace issue from both the plaintiff and the defendant. These cases provided a historical overview of the gender breakdown of transgender workplace complaints as well as additional evidence of how gender transitions have been framed by reporters, employers, and coworkers.

To gain a further gender comparison, I gathered questionnaire data on workplace experiences before and after transition from both transmen and transwomen. Responses came from three transgender conferences held between 2004 and 2005 in California, Washington State, and Texas. The questionnaire was also posted on transacademics.org. The

TABLE A.3 **Results of content analysis, real and adjusted**

	All cases		Adjusted cases	
	MTF	FTM	MTF	FTM
News	104	12	58	8
Legal	43	5	43	5
Total	147	17	101	13

questions were modeled after the 2002 Current Population Survey. Respondents were asked to report on their last job prior to transition, their first job after transition, and their current job. Respondents were also asked about their decisions about body modification. The majority of the respondents were white and college-educated, a bias that reflects the demographics of the conferences where the data were collected. Respondents worked predominantly in private-sector and government jobs. Twelve states were represented, predominantly from the South, the East Coast, and the West Coast. Transwomen in the questionnaire also transitioned on average about ten years later than transmen (forty-five versus thirty-five). The questionnaire yielded sixty-five total responses, with sixty-one being usable for qualitative content analysis (thirty-six from transmen and twenty-five from transwomen). Four were excluded because the respondents were working in the gender they were assigned at birth, or they were included in my interview study.[1]

In my content analysis of the questionnaire data, I was interested in patterns of workplace experiences, regardless of their statistical significance. I coded the questionnaires for type of occupations, the frequency of job change, whether jobs were left voluntarily, part-time versus full-time employment, and the adoption of open or stealth workplace strategies. I also coded any written comments on the questionnaire. Some of these comments were in response to the final question, "Is there anything else you would like to tell us about your workplace experience?" while other comments were written randomly on the questionnaire instrument. About one-third of transmen and transwomen elected to write comments on the questionnaire. This analysis revealed no difference in reports of being fired for being transgender. Three transmen and three transwomen recorded leaving a job involuntarily due to being transgender. Yet transmen were much more likely to describe themselves as "always" passing as men, while transwomen were more likely to report a range from passing as women "some of the time" to "never." The written comments also showed a gendered pattern in workplace experiences: transwomen wrote about being harassed or fired, while transmen wrote about how their employers and coworkers handled their transitions professionally.

A gender pattern also emerged in the statistical analysis of the questionnaire, which included forty-three usable responses (sixteen MTF and twenty-seven FTM). Questionnaires were unusable for this statistical analysis if the respondent had not answered every question, if the respondent was included in my interview study, or if the participant was still working in the gender he or she was assigned at birth. The statistical results were analyzed with Matthew Wiswall, an economist at New York University. While the response rate was small, the respondents were the "best-case scenario" in many ways. When compared to the general population of men and women, these respondents had on average more education and more human capital in terms of work experience. Yet transwomen lost on average nearly one-third of their salaries after transition, while transmen saw no change or a slight increase. Further methodological details about the statistical analysis of the questionnaire data can be found in Schilt and Wiswall 2008.

Notes

Introduction

1. Estimating the size of the transgender population is complicated. Most researchers count only individuals who have undergone genital surgery. Yet, as transmen have—both in the past and today—undergone genital surgery less frequently than transwomen, they are underestimated in these models. See De Cuypere et al. 2006, Meyerowitz 2002, and Olyslager and Conway 2007 for a larger discussion of estimation issues.

2. *Cis* is the Latin prefix for "on the same side as," while *trans* is the prefix for "across from."

Chapter One

1. Qualitative research provides a "thick description" (Geertz 1973) of research participants and their settings. My descriptions may seem thin in contrast. However, half of the men I interviewed are stealth or may choose to go stealth in the future. To preserve anonymity, I do not provide identifying information, such as exact birth years, city locations, occupational titles, or descriptions of appearances. I also use pseudonyms for all respondents.

2. *Essentialism* can have a negative connotation, as it is typically juxtaposed with the seemingly more progressive idea of "social constructionism" (see D'Emilio 1998). I use this term in its more general meaning—something essential or necessary.

3. Transsexual and gender-variant people have a long history of involvement in activism to combat discrimination against sexual and gender minorities (see Meyerowitz 2002 and Stryker 2008 for an expanded discussion).

4. Debates about this removal continue in the late 2000s (see Serano 2007).

5. An essentialist understanding of gender dominated 1990s autobiographies

(see Hewitt 1995; McCloskey 1999; Rees 1996; Thompson 1995). Genderqueer and transformative understandings of gender began to emerge in autobiographical writings in the 2000s (see Diamond 2004; Nestle, Howell, and Wilchins 2002).

6. The original rubric was *GLBT*. However, lesbian activists argued that this order put gay men first—a constant source of tension in gay and lesbian communities (Faderman and Timmons 2006; Newton 1993).

7. http://www.genderspectrum.org/about_us.htm (accessed April 1, 2008).

8. In 2006, a documentary about FTMs who had borne children, *Transparent* (Rosskam 2005), played the LGBT film festival circuits. The topic entered more mainstream discussion in 2008 when Thomas Beatie, an Ohio transman, wrote an essay about being a pregnant man for *The Advocate*. Beatie's story drew major media attention, and he appeared in *People* magazine as well as on *Oprah*.

Chapter Two

1. Sam and Robert began living as boys in adolescence. Wayne felt that because he looked so androgynous as a child, his peers and teachers did not treat him like "one of the girls." I highlight these experiences to show that not all transmen experience childhood in the same ways.

2. As decisions about and reactions to surgical and hormonal body modifications are the central focus of other works on transmen (see Devor 1997; H. Rubin 2003), I focus instead on the lesser documented interactional processes involved in achieving social maleness.

3. Du Bois uses *double consciousness* to explain how African-Americans struggle to blend their African-ness (their heritage) and their American-ness (their new cultural identity). Transmen face a similar task of synthesizing two identities seen as inherently separate, a synthesis that is not culturally validated.

Chapter Three

1. Sam and Robert had never been employed as women. While Cole and Clark were hired as women, clients typically viewed them as male. They all felt limited in their abilities to speak about gender differences at work. I mention this to illustrate that developing an outsider-within perspective varies, as transmen have different "before" life experiences.

2. Because some transmen held multiple jobs as both stealth and open, the same people could report gains and losses. And, because workplace interac-

tions are complex, transmen could see gains and losses in the same job. I highlight these points to account for why some transmen are discussed in both sections.

3. Sexual identity is another key issue that can impact workplace rewards. However, the transmen I interviewed who identified as gay, queer, bisexual, or pansexual were not out to coworkers about their identity or worked in LGBT organizations where queerness was the norm. Future research should explore how transmen who are out as gay and/or queer experience their "before and after" workplace experiences.

Chapter Four

1. These dates reflect the time period when this particular person began his physical transition.

2. Some stealth transmen do feel that they are closeted when they are not out as transgender at work. Henry identified as a transman and was a vocal activist outside of work. However, his was a professional workplace that he characterized as "conservative," and he had concerns about keeping his job if he came out as transgender. Yet not being able to talk about his activism with coworkers created personal discomfort. He decided to come out as transgender at work several months after our interview. His feeling of being in the closet was anomalous among stealth transmen in this study.

Chapter Five

1. Harassment is difficult to measure. When I directly asked my interviewees if they felt they experienced harassment related to being transgender, the majority said no. Yet these same people often recounted being asked invasive questions about their genitalia by their coworkers—interactions I would define as potentially harassing. Some transmen, in contrast, saw these questions as positive, since they could signal coworkers' attempts to educate themselves about the transition process. I mention this to show the difficulty of using "harassment" as a concept in workplace studies.

2. This request can be seen as a symbol of workplace support. However, it can also be a burden to transgender employees, as it opens them up to invasive questions from coworkers.

3. Incorporation happened in blue-collar jobs, too. But there were so few cases of transmen who openly transitioned in these jobs, I hesitate to describe this reaction as "typical."

Chapter Six

1. I hypothesize that transmen in this study faced less "border war" tension because they worked with fewer lesbians, even in LGBT-related organizations. Typically in these organizations, they worked with heterosexual women and gay men. This lack of lesbians may reflect "queer sexism" (Ward 2000) in the LGBT movement (Faderman and Timmons 2006; Newton 1993).

2. A gendered pattern also exists in media accounts of the murders of transgender people. Examining media accounts in major U.S. newspapers between 1990 and 2005, Laurel Westbrook identified 157 cases in which reporters specified the gender of the person accused of murdering a transgender person. Of these cases, 149 (95 percent) described a cisgender man or men killing a transwoman. The remaining 8 cases involved a cisgender woman killing a transwoman (2 percent), a cisgender man or men killing a transman (2 percent), and a transwoman killing another transwoman (1 percent) (Schilt and Westbrook 2009).

3. Only two transmen wrote about negative experiences. One describes his transition ending his employment because he was in an all-female band—something his fellow band members wanted to continue. Another transman wrote that going stealth had limited his employment history, as he could not include jobs he had held as a woman on his résumé.

4. Not all people who identify as transgender are interested in having an unequivocal social identity as men or women. Some genderqueer people also choose to blend elements of masculinity and femininity in their gender presentation. My argument here refers only to people who seek to change their social gender to unequivocally male or female.

5. These news stories predominantly focus on white, middle-class transwomen in professional and blue-collar jobs. Some research suggests that transwomen of color and working-class transwomen have different trajectories to transition (Valentine 2007). Research is greatly needed on racial differences in the transition experiences.

Chapter Seven

1. Judith Butler (2004) wrote about undoing gender in her book of the same title. However, her argument is much more in keeping with the theory of accountability in West and Zimmerman's original argument. For this reason, I do not include her work in the critique of "doing gender" theories.

Methodological Appendix

1. This overlap occurred in only two cases in California. I recognized the two people whom I had also interviewed when they returned their completed questionnaires to me. I marked their documents to be pulled later. None of the questionnaires received in the mail came from transmen, so there was no possibility of overlap from these cases.

References

Acker, Joan. 1990. "Hierarchies, jobs, bodies: A theory of gendered organizations." *Gender & Society* 4 (2): 139–58.

American Psychiatric Association. 2001. *Diagnostic and statistical manual of mental disorders IV.* Washington, DC: American Psychiatric Association.

Andersen, Margaret L. 2005. "Thinking about women: A quarter century's view." *Gender & Society* 19 (4): 437–55.

Angier, Natalie. 2007. "Birds do it, bees do it, people seek the keys to it." *New York Times*, April 10. http://www.nytimes.com/2007/04/10/science/10desi.html (accessed January 10, 2010).

Associated Press. 1979. No title, August 11, Domestic News, A3.

———. 1982. "Transsexual loses sex bias suit," March 31, Domestic News.

Badgett, M.V.L. 2003. *Money, myths, and change: The economic lives of lesbians and gay men.* Chicago: University of Chicago Press.

Barber, J. Matt. 2007. "A 'gay man' trapped in a woman's body and other nonsense." http://www.cwfa.org/articles/14405/CFI/family/index.htm (accessed January 20, 2010).

Barnes v. City of Cincinnati, Ohio. 2004. 401 F.3d 729.

Barres, Ben. 2006. "Does gender matter?" *Nature* 442: 133–36.

Becker, Howard, and Blanche Geer. 1957. "Participant observation and interviewing: A comparison." *Human Organization* 16 (3): 28–32.

Begley, Sharon. 2006. "He, once she, offers own view on science spat." *Wall Street Journal*, July 13, B1.

Bem, Sandra. 1993. *The lenses of gender: Transforming the debate about sexual inequality.* New Haven, CT: Yale University Press.

Benjamin, Harry. 1966. *The transsexual phenomenon.* New York: Warner Books.

Bernstein, Maxine. 2000. "Board denies disability claim, criticizes police." *Oregonian*, April 13, B2.

Bertrand, Marianne, and Sendhil Mullainathan. 2004. "Are Emily and Greg more employable than Lakisha and Jamal? A field experiment on labor market discrimination." *American Economic Review* 94 (4): 991–1013.

Bettcher, Talia. 2007. "Evil deceivers and make believers: On transphobic violence and the politics of illusion." *Hypatia* 22: 45–62.

Biddle, Jeff E., and Daniel S. Hamermesh. 1994. "Beauty and the labor market." *American Economic Review* 84 (5): 1174–94.

———. 1998. "Beauty, productivity, and discrimination: Lawyers' looks and lucre." *Journal of Labor Economics* 16 (1): 172–201.

Billings, Dwight, and Thomas Urban. 1982. "The socio-medical construction of transsexualism: An interpretation and critique." *Social Problems* 29: 266–82.

Bird, Sharon. 1996. "Welcome to the men's club: Homosociality and the maintenance of hegemonic masculinity." *Gender & Society* 10 (2): 120–32.

Blair-Loy, Mary. 2003. *Competing devotions: Career and family among women executives.* Cambridge, MA: Harvard University Press.

Blee, Kathryn. 2003. "Studying the enemy." In *Our studies, ourselves: Sociologists' lives and works,* ed. Barry Glassner and Rosanna Hertz, 13–23. Cambridge, UK: Oxford University Press.

Bolin, Anne. 1988. *In search of Eve: Transsexual rites of passage.* South Hadley, MA: Bergin & Garvey Publishers.

Bolton, Kenneth, and Joe Feagin. 2004. *Black in blue: African-American police officers and racism.* New York: Routledge.

Bornstein, Kate. 1994. *Gender outlaw: On men, women, and the rest of us.* New York: Routledge.

Boston Herald. 1994. "Conn. drops transsexual's bias suit." December 29, B2.

Bourdieu, Pierre. 1977. *Outline of a theory of practice.* Cambridge, UK: Cambridge University Press.

Brekhus, Wayne. 2003. *Peacocks, chameleons, centaurs: Gay suburbia and the grammar of social identity.* Chicago: University of Chicago Press.

Brink, Graham. 2002. "Fired transsexual teacher sues church." *St. Petersburg Times,* June 20, City and State, 3B.

Britton, Dana. 2003. *At work in the iron cage: The prison as gendered organization.* New York: New York University Press.

Broadus v. State Farm Insurance, Inc. 2000. WL 1585257.

Brouns, Margo. 2000. "The gendered nature of assessment procedures in scientific research funding: The Dutch case." *Higher Education in Europe* 25: 193–99.

Bryant, Karl, and Kristen Schilt. 2008. "Transgender people in the U.S. military." Research report published by the Palm Center. http://www.palmcenter .org (accessed January 18, 2010).

Buchanan, Wyatt. 2007. "San Francisco; More U.S. employers cover sex transition surgery; Large corporations follow city's lead in offering benefit." *San Francisco Chronicle,* January 31, B4.

Budden, A., T. Tregenza, L. Aarssen, J. Koricheva, R. Leimu, and C. Lorie. 2007. "Double blind review favors increased representation of female authors." *Trends in Ecology and Evolution* 23: 4–6.

Burana, Lily, Roxxie, and Linnea Due, eds. 1994. *Dagger: On butch women*. San Francisco: Cleis Press.

Burke, Phyllis. 1996. *Gender shock: Exploding the myths of male and female*. New York: Anchor Books.

Butler, D., and F. L. Geis. 1990. "Nonverbal affect responses to male and female leaders: Implications for leadership evaluation." *Journal of Personality and Social Psychology* 58: 48–59.

Butler, Judith. 1989. *Gender trouble: Feminism and the subversion of identity*. New York: Routledge.

———. 1990. "Gender trouble, feminist theory, and psychoanalytic discourse." In *Feminism/Postmodernism*, ed. Linda Nicholson, 324–51. New York: Routledge.

———. 1993. *Bodies that matter: On the discursive limits of "sex."* New York: Routledge.

———. 2004. *Undoing gender*. New York: Routledge.

Byrd, Barbara. 1999. "Women in carpentry apprenticeship: A case study." *Labor Studies Journal* 24 (3): 3–22.

Calasanti, Toni M., and Kathleen F. Slevin. 2001. *Gender, social inequalities, and aging*. Walnut Creek, CA: Alta Mira Press.

Califia, Patrick. 1997. *Sex changes: The politics of transgenderism*. San Francisco: Cleis Press.

———. 2002. *Speaking sex to power: The politics of queer sex*. San Francisco: Cleis Press.

Campos, Paul. 2000. "Should boss let man wear skirt with pride?" *Milwaukee Journal Sentinel*, May 19, News, 23A.

Carnes, M., S. Geller, E. Fine, J. Sheridan, and J. Handelsman. 2005. "NIH director's pioneer awards: Could the selection process be biased against women?" *Journal of Women's Health* 14 (8): 684–91.

Case, Mary Anne. 1995. "Disaggregating gender from sex and sexual orientation: The effeminate man in the law and feminist jurisprudence." *Yale Law Journal* 105: 1–105.

Chang, Althea. 2008. "Unusual perks: Goldman Sachs covers sex changes." http://money.cnn.com/2008/02/08/news/companies/gender.fortune/index.htm (accessed August 22, 2008).

Chauncey, George. 1994. *Gay New York*. New York: Basic Books.

Chodorow, Nancy. 1971. "Being and doing: A cross-cultural examination of the socialization of males and females." In *Women in sexist society: Studies in power and powerlessness*, ed. Vivian Gornick and Barbara K. Moran, 186–201. New York: Basic Books.

———. 1978. *The reproduction of mothering: Psychoanalysis and the sociology of gender.* Berkeley: University of California Press.

Cole, M. S., H. S. Feild, and W. F. Giles. 2004. "Interaction of recruiter and applicant gender in résumé evaluation: A field study." *Sex Roles* 51: 597–608.

Collins, Patricia Hill. 1986. "Learning from the outsider within: The sociological significance of Black feminist thought." *Social Problems* 33 (6): S14–S31.

———. 1990. *Black feminist thought.* New York: Routledge.

———. 1995. "Symposium: On West and Fenstermaker's 'Doing difference.'" *Gender & Society* 9 (4): 491–94.

Connell, Catherine. 2006. "This isn't who we hired: Transgender negotiations of gender in the workplace." Master's thesis, University of Texas–Austin.

Connell, R. W. 1987. *Gender & power.* Berkeley: University of California Press.

———. 1992. "A very straight gay: Masculinity, homosexual experience, and the dynamics of gender." *American Sociological Review* 57 (6): 735–51.

———. 1995. *Masculinities.* Berkeley: University of California Press.

Connell, R. W., and James Messerschmidt. 2005. "Hegemonic masculinity: Rethinking the concept." *Gender & Society* 19 (6): 829–59.

Correll, Shelley, Stephen Bernard, and In Paik. 2007. "Is there a motherhood penalty?" *American Journal of Sociology* 112 (5): 1297–1338.

Cox v. Denny's, Inc. 1999. Not reported in F. Supp. 2d. 1999 WL 1317785.

Cram, Bestor. 1996. *You don't know Dick: The courageous hearts of transsexual men.* Video. Available from University of California Extension Center for Media and Independent Learning, 2000 Center Street, Fourth Floor, Berkeley, CA 94704.

Crenshaw, Kimberle. 1989. "Demarginalizing the intersection of race and sex: A Black feminist critique of antidiscrimination doctrine, feminist theory, and antiracist politics." *University of Chicago Legal Forum* (1989): 139–67.

Crimp, Douglas. 1990. *AIDS demographics.* San Francisco: Bay Press.

Cromwell, Jason. 1999. *Transmen and FTMs: Identities, bodies, genders, and sexualities.* Chicago: University of Illinois Press.

Currah, Paisley, Richard M. Juang, and Shannon Minter. 2006. *Transgender rights.* Minneapolis: University of Minnesota Press.

Curry, Lynne. 2007. "Co-worker's sex change is upsetting." *Anchorage Daily News*, July 30, Money, F1.

Dalton, Susan, and Sarah Fenstermaker. 2002. "'Doing gender' differently: Institutional change in second-parent adoptions." In *Doing gender, doing difference*, ed. Sarah Fenstermaker and Candace West, 169–88. New York: Routledge.

Daly, Mary. 1978. *Gyn/ecology.* Boston: Beacon Press.

Davis, Kathy. 1995. *Reshaping the female body: The dilemma of cosmetic surgery.* New York: Routledge.

De Beauvoir, Simone. 1953. *The second sex.* New York: Bantam Books.

De Cuypere, Griet, et al. 2006. "Prevalence and demography of transsexualism in Belgium." *European Psychiatry* 10 (2): 1–5.

DeFao, Janine. 2005. "Top physician tells colleagues, patients at Kaiser that he is finally becoming a woman." *San Francisco Chronicle*, March 16, Bay Area, B1.

Delphy, Christine. 1993. "Rethinking sex and gender." *Women's Studies International Forum* 16 (1): 1–9.

D'Emilio, John. 1998. *Sexual politics, sexual communities: The making of a homosexual minority in the United States, 1940–1970.* Chicago: University of Chicago Press.

Deutsch, Francine. 2007. "Undoing gender." *Gender & Society* 21 (1): 106–27.

Deux, K., and J. C. Ullman. 1983. *Women of steel: Female blue-collar workers in the basic steel industry.* New York: Praeger.

Devor, Holly. 1989. *Gender blending: Confronting the limits of duality.* Bloomington: University of Indiana Press.

——. 1997. *FTM: Female-to-male transsexuals in society.* Bloomington: Indiana University Press.

Diamond, Morty, ed. 2004. *From the inside out: Radical gender transformation, FTM and beyond.* San Francisco: Manic D Press.

Doe v. United Consumer Financial Services. 2001. Not reported in F. Supp. 2d. WL 34350174.

Dozier, Raine. 2005. "Beards, breasts, and bodies: Doing sex in a gendered world." *Gender & Society* 19 (3): 297–316.

Du Bois, W.E.B. 1903. *The souls of black folk.* Chicago: A. C. McClurg & Co.

Duneier, Mitchell. 1999. *Sidewalk.* New York: Farrar, Straus, and Giroux.

Dvorak, Petula. 2005. "The right person for the job." *Washington Post*, June 2, Metro, B1.

Ebaugh, Helen Rose Fuchs. 1988. *Becoming an ex: The process of role exit.* Chicago: University of Chicago Press.

Echols, Alice. 1989. *Daring to be bad: Radical feminism in America, 1967–1975.* Minneapolis: University of Minnesota Press.

Edney, Richard. 2004. "To keep me safe from harm? Transgender prisoners and the experience of imprisonment." *Deakin Law Review* 9 (2): 327–38.

Eisenberg, Susan. 1998. *We'll call you if we need you: Experiences of women working construction.* Ithaca: Cornell University Press.

El-Bashir, Tarik. 1998. "Auto racing: Driver with sex change finds her career stalled." *New York Times*, May 17, section 8, 6.

Elliott, James R., and Ryan A. Smith. 2004. "Race, gender, and workplace power." *American Sociological Review* 69 (3): 365–86.

Emanuelle v. U.S. Tobacco, Inc. 1987. Not reported in F. Supp., 1987 WL 19165 0.

Emerson, Robert, and Melvin Pollner. 1988. "On the uses of members' responses to researchers' accounts." *Human Organization* 47 (3): 189–98.

Enriquez v. West Jersey Health Systems. 2001. 342 N.J. Super. 501, 777 A.2d 365.

Epstein, Steven. 2007. *Inclusion: The politics of difference in medical research.* Chicago: University of Chicago Press.

Escoffier, Jeffrey. 1975. "Stigmas, work environment, and economic discrimination against homosexuals." *Homosexual Counseling Journal* 2 (1): 8–17.

Espiritu, Yen. 1997. *Asian American women and men.* Thousand Oaks, CA: Sage.

Essed, Philomena. 1991. *Understanding everyday racism.* London: Sage.

Estate of Gardiner. 2002. 273 Kan. 191, 42 P.3d 120.

Faderman, Lillian, and Stuart Timmons. 2006. *Gay L.A.: A history of sexual outlaws, power politics, and lipstick lesbians.* New York: Basic Books.

Fausto-Sterling, Anne. 2000. *Sexing the body: Gender politics and the construction of sexuality.* New York: Basic Books.

Feinbloom, Deborah. 1976. *Transvestites and transsexuals.* New York: Delta Books.

Fenstermaker, Sarah, and Candace West, eds. 2002. *Doing gender, doing difference: Inequality, power, and institutional change.* New York: Routledge.

Fenstermaker, Sarah, Candace West, and Don Zimmerman. 2002. "Gender inequality: New conceptual terrain." In *Doing gender, doing difference*, ed. Sarah Fenstermaker and Candace West, 25–40. New York: Routledge.

Ferguson, Ann Arnett. 2000. *Bad boys: Public schools in the making of black masculinity.* Ann Arbor: University of Michigan Press.

Festinger, Leon. 1957. *Theory of cognitive dissonance.* Palo Alto, CA: Stanford University Press.

Festinger, Leon, Henry Riecken, and Stanley Schachter. 1956. *When prophecy fails: A social and psychological study of a modern group that predicted the destruction of the world.* New York: Harper Torch Books.

Fetner, Tina. 2008. *How the religious right shaped gay and lesbian activism.* Minneapolis: University of Minnesota Press.

Finke, Nikki. 1980. "Stole for operation to make him a woman but going to prison a man." Associated Press, March 11.

Finn, Mark, and Pippa Dell. 1999. "Practices of body management: Transgenderism and embodiment." *Journal of Community & Applied Social Psychology* 9: 463–76.

Foucault, Michel 1978. *The history of sexuality.* Vol. 1. New York: Pantheon Books.

Franck, Kurt. 1982. "Sex-change cop files suit." Associated Press, Domestic News. August 27.

Fung, Richard. 2004. "Looking for my penis: The eroticized Asian in gay video porn." In *Men's Lives*, 6th ed., ed. Michael S. Kimmel and Michael Messner, 543–52. Boston: Pearson.

Gamson, Joshua. 1996. "Must identity movements self-destruct?" In *Queer theory/sociology*, ed. Steven Seidman, 395–420. Cambridge, MA: Blackwell Publishers.

———. 1998. *Freaks talk back: Tabloid talk shows and sexual nonconformity.* Chicago: University of Chicago Press.

———. 2004. *The fabulous Sylvester: The legend, the music, and the seventies in San Francisco.* New York: Henry Holt.

Garber, Marjorie. 1997. *Vested interests: Cross-dressing and cultural anxiety.* New York: Routledge.

Garfinkel, Harold. 1967. *Studies in ethnomethodology.* Englewood Cliffs, NJ: Prentice-Hall.

Geertz, Clifford. 1973. *The interpretation of cultures: Selected essays.* New York: Basic Books.

Gerson, Judith, and Kathy Peiss. 1985. "Boundaries, negotiation, consciousness: Reconceptualizing gender relationships." *Social Problems* 32 (4): 317–31.

Giddens, Anthony. 1984. *The constitution of society.* Berkeley: University of California Press.

Glauber, Rebecca. 2008. "Race and gender in families and at work: The father-hood premium." *Gender & Society* 22 (1): 8–30.

Goffman, Erving. 1963a. *Behavior in public places: Notes on the social organization of gatherings.* New York: Free Press of Glencoe.

———. 1963b. *Stigma: Notes on the management of spoiled identity.* New York: Simon & Schuster.

———. 1977. "The arrangement between the sexes." *Theory and Society* 4 (3): 301–31.

Goins v. West Group. 2001. 635 N.W.2d 717.

Goldenberg, Suzanne. 2005. "Why women are poor at science, by Harvard president." *Guardian*, January 18. http://www.guardian.co.uk/science/2005/jan/18/educationsgendergap.genderissues (accessed August 22, 2008).

Goldin, Claudia, and Cecilia Rouse. 2000. "Orchestrating impartiality: The impact of 'blind' auditions on female musicians." *American Economic Review* 90 (4): 715–41.

Goode, William. 1992. "Why men resist." In *Rethinking the family*, ed. Barrie Thorne with Marilyn Yalom, 131–50. Boston: Northeastern University Press.

Gray, John. 1992. *Men are from Mars, women are from Venus.* New York: HarperCollins.

Green, Eli R. 2006. "Debating trans inclusion in the feminist movement: A trans-positive analysis." *Journal of Lesbian Studies* 10 (1): 231–48.

Green, Jamison. 2004. *Becoming a visible man.* Nashville: Vanderbilt University Press.

Green, Richard. 1987. *The "sissy boy" syndrome and the development of homosexuality.* New Haven, CT: Yale University Press.

Greenberg, Julie, and Marybeth Herald. 2005. "You can't take it with you: Constitutional consequences of interstate gender identity rulings." *Washington Law Review* 80: 815–85.

Griggs, Claudine. 1998. *S/he: Changing sex and changing clothes*. New York: Berg.

Gruber, J. E., and L. Bjorn. 1982. "Blue-collar blues: The sexual harassment of women auto-workers." *Work and Occupations* 9: 271–98.

Halberstam, Judith. 1998a. *Female masculinity*. Durham, NC: Duke University Press.

———. 1998b. "Transgender butch: Butch/FTM border wars and the masculine continuum." *GLQ: A Journal of Lesbian and Gay Studies* 4 (2): 287–310.

———. 2005. *In a queer time and place: Transgender bodies, subcultural lives*. New York: New York University Press.

Hale, Jacob. 1998. "Consuming the living, dis(re)membering the dead in the butch/FTM borderlands." *GLQ: A Journal of Lesbian and Gay Studies* 4 (2): 311–48.

Hall, Stephen. 2006. *Size matters: How height affects the health, happiness and the success of boys—and the men they become*. Houghton Mifflin Harcourt: New York.

Halle, David. 1984. *America's working man*. Chicago: University of Chicago Press.

Hamamoto, Darrell. 1994. *Monitored peril: Asian Americans and the politics of TV representation*. Minneapolis: University of Minnesota Press.

Harding, Sandra. 1986. "The instability of the analytic categories of feminist theory." *Signs* 11 (4): 645–64.

Hartmann, Heidi. 1979. "The unhappy marriage of Marxism and feminism." *Capital and Class* 8: 1–25.

Heath, Melanie. 2009. "The state of our union: Marriage promotion and the contested power of heterosexuality." *Gender & Society* 23 (1): 27–48.

Heilman, M. E., A. S. Wallen, D. Fuchs, and M. Tamkins. 2004. "Penalties for success: Reactions to women who succeed at male gender-typed tasks." *Journal of Applied Psychology* 89 (3): 416–27.

Hennen, Peter. 2008. *Fairies, bears, and leathermen: Men in community queering masculinity*. Chicago: University of Chicago Press.

Herek, Gregory. 2002. "Gender gaps in public opinion about lesbians and gay men." *Public Opinion Quarterly* 66 (1): 40–66.

Hewitt, Paul. 1995. *Self-made man: The diary of a man born in a woman's body*. London: Headline Books.

Heywood, Leslie, and Jennifer Drake. 1997. *Third wave agenda: Being and doing feminism*. Minneapolis: University of Minnesota Press.

Hochschild, Arlie Russell. 1990. *The second shift*. New York: Avon Books.

Holloway v. Arthur Andersen and Company. 1977. 566 F.2d 659.

Holt v. Northwest Pennsylvania Training Partnership Consortium, Inc. 1997. 694 A.2d 1134.

Israely, Jeff. 2008. "The Pope's Christmas condemnation of transsexuals." Time. com, December 23. http://www.time.com/time/world/article/0,8599,1868390, 00.html (accessed October 27, 2009).

Kando, Thomas. 1973. *Sex change: The achievement of gender identity among feminized transsexuals.* Springfield, IL: Charles C. Thomas Publisher.

Kane, Emily W. 2006. "'No way my boys are going to be like that!': Parents' responses to children's gender nonconformity." *Gender & Society* 20 (2): 149–76.

Kantaras v. Kantaras. 2004. 884 So. 2d 155.

Kanter, Rosabeth Moss. 1977. *Men and women of the corporation.* New York: Basic Books.

Kaplan, Elaine Bell. 1997. *Not our kind of girl: Unraveling the myths of black teenage motherhood.* Berkeley: University of California Press.

Kaveney, Roz. 1999. "Talking transgender politics." In *Reclaiming genders: Transsexual grammar at the fin de siècle,* ed. Kate More and Stephen Whittle, 146–58. London: Cassell.

Kennedy, John. 2008. "The transgender movement." *Christianity Today.* February. http://www.christianitytoday.com/ct/2008/february/25.54.html?start=5 (accessed April 12, 2008).

Kessler, Suzanne. 1998. *Lessons from the intersexed.* New Brunswick, NJ: Rutgers University Press.

Kessler, Suzanne, and Wendy McKenna. 1978. *Gender: An ethnomethodological approach.* Chicago: University of Chicago Press.

Kimmel, Michael. 2004. "Masculinity as homophobia: Fear, shame and silence in the construction of gender identity." In *Feminism and masculinities,* ed. Peter Murphy, 182–99. New York: Oxford University Press.

———. 2006. *Manhood in America: A cultural history.* 2nd ed. New York: Oxford University Press.

Kirk, Stuart, and Herb Kutchins. 1992. *The selling of DSM: The rhetoric of science in psychiatry.* New York: Aldine de Gruyter.

Kitzinger, Celia. 2005. "Heteronormativity in action: Reproducing the heterosexual nuclear family in after-hours medical calls." *Social Problems* 52 (4): 477–98.

LaFleur v. Bird-Johnson Company. 1994. 4 WL 878831 (Mass. Super.).

Lamont, Michele. 1992. *Money, morals, and manners: The culture of the French and American upper middle classes.* Chicago: University of Chicago Press.

Lancaster, Roger. 2003. *The trouble with nature: Sex and science in popular culture.* Berkeley: University of California Press.

Landen, Mikael, and Sune Innala. 2000. "Attitudes toward transsexualism in a Swedish national survey." *Archives of Sexual Behavior* 29 (4): 375–88.

Laqueur, Thomas. 1990. *Making sex: Body and gender from the Greeks to Freud.* Cambridge, MA: Harvard University Press.

Laub, Donald, and Norman Fisk. 1974. "A rehabilitation program for gender dysphoria syndrome and surgical sex change." *Plastic and Reconstructive Surgery* 53: 388–403.

Lees, Sue. 1993. *Sugar and spice: Sexuality and adolescent girls.* New York: Penguin Books.

Leidner, Robin. 1993. *Fast food, fast talk: Service work and the routinization of everyday life.* Berkeley: University of California Press.

Levine, Judith. 2002. *Harmful to minors: The perils of protecting children from sex.* Minneapolis: University of Minnesota Press.

Lie v. Sky Pub. Corp. 2002. Not reported in N.E. 2d, 2002 WL 31492397.

Lienert, Tania. 1998. "Women's self-starvation, cosmetic surgery, and transsexualism." *Feminism and Psychology* 8 (2): 245–50.

Lipman, Joanne. 2009. "The mismeasure of women." *New York Times*, October 23, Op-Ed., A21.

Littleton v. Prange. 1999. 9 S.W.3d 233.

Loe, Meika. 2004. *The rise of Viagra: How the little blue pill changed sex in America.* New York: New York University Press.

Loenhardt, David. 2008. "The return of Larry Summers." *New York Times*, November 25. http://www.nytimes.com/2008/11/26/business/economy/26leon hardt.html?em (accessed March 30, 2009).

Lopez v. River Oaks Imaging & Diagnostic Group, Inc. 2008. F. Supp. 2d, 2008 WL 902937.

Lorber, Judith. 1994. *Paradoxes of gender.* New Haven, CT: Yale University Press.

———. 2005. *Breaking the bowls: Degendering and feminist change.* New York: W. W. Norton & Company.

Lothstein, Leslie. 1983. *Female-to-male transsexualism: Historical, clinical and theoretical issues.* Boston: Routledge & Kegan Paul.

Luker, Kristin. 1984. *Abortion and the politics of motherhood.* Berkeley: University of California Press.

MacKenzie, Gordene. 1994. *Transgender nation.* Bowling Green, OH: Bowling Green University Press.

———. 1999. "50 billion galaxies of gender: Transgendering the millennium." In *Reclaiming genders: Transsexual grammar at the fin de siècle*, ed. Kate More and Stephen Whittle, 193–218. London: Cassell.

MacKinnon, Catherine. 1982. "Feminism, Marxism, method and the state: An agenda for theory." *Signs* 7 (13): 515–44.

———. 1987. *Feminism unmodified: Discourses on life and law.* Cambridge, MA: Harvard University Press.

MacRobbie, Angela. 1991. *Feminism and youth culture: From "Jackie" to "Just Seventeen."* Boston: Unwin Hyman.

Maffei v. Kolaeton Industry, Inc. 1995. 164 Misc.2d 547, 626 N.Y.S.2d 391.

Marcus, Ruth. 2008. "Was Summers right?" *Washington Post,* December 3. http://www.washingtonpost.com/wp-dyn/content/article/2008/12/02/AR2008 120202724.html (accessed March 30, 2009).

Martin, Karin. 1996. *Puberty, sexuality, and the self: Girls and boys at adolescence.* New York: Routledge.

Martin, Patricia Yancy. 2003. "Said and done" versus "saying and doing": Gendering practices, practicing gender at work. *Gender & Society* 17 (3): 342–66.

Martin, Susan. 1994. "'Outsiders-within' the station house: The impact of race and gender on black women police officers." *Social Problems* 41: 383–400.

Martino, Mario. 1977. *Emergence: A transsexual autobiography.* New York: Crown.

Mason-Draffen, Carrie. 2005. "Dismissed for a sex change?" *Newsday,* October 7, Business and Technology, A56.

McCloskey, Deirdre. 1999. *Crossing: A memoir.* Chicago: University of Chicago Press.

Merton, Robert. 1972. "Insiders and outsiders: A chapter in the sociology of knowledge." *American Journal of Sociology* 78 (1): 9–47.

Messner, Michael. 1992. *Power at play: Sports and the problem of masculinity.* Boston: Beacon Press.

——. 1997. *The politics of masculinities: Men in movements.* Thousand Oaks, CA: Sage.

——. 2000. "Barbie girls vs. sea monsters: Children constructing gender." *Gender & Society* 36 (1): 85–102.

Meyer, Brian. 2002. "City hall worker steps into a woman's shoes." *Buffalo News,* September 16, Local, B1.

——. 2006. "Transsexual reports being harassed." *Buffalo News,* August 29, Local, B1.

Meyerowitz, Joanne. 2002. *How sex changed: A history of transsexuality in the United States.* Cambridge, MA: Harvard University Press.

Miller, Laura. 1997. "Not just weapons of the weak: Gender harassment as a form of protest for army men." *Social Psychology Quarterly* 60 (1): 32–51.

Minter, Shannon Price. 2006. "Do transsexuals dream of gay rights? Getting real about transgender inclusion." In *Transgender rights,* ed. Paisley Currah, Richard Juang, and Shannon Price Minter, 141–70. Minneapolis: University of Minnesota Press.

Mitchell, Juliet. 1966. "Women: The longest revolution." *New Left Review* 1 (40): 1–27.

More, Kate, and Stephen Whittle, eds. 1999. *Reclaiming genders: Transsexual grammar at the fin de siècle.* London: Cassell.

Namaste, Ki. 1994. "The politics of inside/out: Queer theory, poststructuralism, and a sociological approach to sexuality." *Sociological Theory* 12: 220–31.

Namaste, Viviane. 2000. *Invisible lives: The erasure of transsexual and transgender people.* Chicago: University of Chicago Press.

Nataf, Zachary. 1996. *Lesbians talk transgender.* London: Scarlet.

National Academy of Sciences. 2007. *Beyond bias and barriers: Fulfilling the potential of women in academic science and engineering.* Washington, DC: National Academies Press.

Nestle, Joan, ed. 1992. *The persistent desire: A femme-butch reader.* Boston: Alyson Publications.

Nestle, Joan, Clare Howell, and Riki Wilchins, eds. 2002. *GenderQueer: Voices from beyond the sexual binary.* Los Angeles: Alyson Books.

Newton, Esther. 1993. *Cherry Grove, Fire Island: Sixty years in America's first gay and lesbian town.* Boston: Beacon Press.

New York Times. 1976. "Teacher who underwent sex change loses job for a second time." October 10, national news, n.p.

Nieves, Evelyn. 1998. "After sex change, teacher is barred from school." *New York Times*, September 27, sect. A, 12.

Nixon, Darren. 2009. "'I can't put a smiley face on': Working-class masculinity, emotional labor and service work in the new economy." *Gender, Work & Organization* 16 (3): 300–322.

Nye, Robert. 2005. "Locating masculinity: Some recent work on men." *Signs* 30 (3): 1937–52.

Oakley, Ann. 1972. *Sex, gender and society.* London: Temple Smith.

Olian, J. D., D. P. Schwab, and Y. Haberfeld. 1988. "The impact of applicant gender compared to qualifications on hiring recommendations: A meta-analysis of experimental studies." *Organizational Behavior and Human Decision Processes* 41: 180–95.

Oliver, Mary Beth. 2003. "African American men as 'criminal and dangerous': Implications of media portrayals of crime on the 'criminalization' of African American men." *Journal of African American Studies* 7 (2): 3–18.

Olyslager, Femke, and Lynn Conway. 2007. "On the calculation of the prevalence of transsexualism." http://ai.eecs.umich.edu/people/conway/TS/Prevalence/Reports/Prevalence%200f%20Transsexualism.pdf (accessed August 22, 2008).

Orenstein, Peggy. 1994. *Schoolgirls: Young women, self-esteem and the confidence gap.* New York: Anchor Books.

Ortner, Sherry B. 1971. "Is female to male as nature is to culture?" *Feminist Studies* 1 (2): 5–31.

Paap, Kris. 2006. *Working construction: Why white working-class men put themselves—and the labor movement—in harm's way.* Ithaca, NY: Cornell University Press.

Padavic, Irene, and Barbara Reskin. 2002. *Women and men at work*. 2nd ed. Thousand Oaks, CA: Pine Forge Press.

Pascoe, C. J. 2007. *Dude, you're a fag: Masculinity and sexuality in high school*. Berkeley: University of California Press.

Perkins, Roberta. 1983. *The "drag queen" scene: Transsexuals in King's Cross*. Sydney: George Allen & Unwin.

Petrie, Michelle, and Paul Roman. 2004. "Race and gender differences in workplace autonomy: A research note." *Sociological Inquiry* 74 (4): 590–603.

Phelan, Shane. 2001. *Sexual strangers: Gay men, lesbians, and the dilemmas of citizenship*. Philadelphia: Temple University Press.

Philadelphia Daily News. 2001. "San Francisco will pay for workers' sex changes." May 1, National News, 14.

Picca, Leslie, and Joe Feagin. 2007. *Two-faced racism: Whites in the backstage and front stage*. New York: Routledge.

Pierce, Jennifer. 1995. *Gender trials: Emotional lives in contemporary law firms*. Berkeley: University of California Press.

Preves, Sharon. 2003. *Intersex and identity: The contested self*. New Brunswick, NJ: Rutgers University Press.

Prokos, Anastasia, and Irene Padavic. 2002. "There oughtta be a law against bitches: Masculinity lessons in police academy training." *Gender, Work & Organization* 9 (4): 439–59.

Prosser, Jay. 1998. *Second skins: The body narratives of transsexuality*. New York: Columbia University Press.

Queen, Carol, and Lawrence Schimel, eds. 1997. *Pomosexuals: Challenging assumptions about gender and sexuality*. San Francisco: Cleis Press.

Raeburn, Nicole. 2004. *Changing corporate America from the inside out: Lesbian and gay workplace rights*. Minneapolis: University of Minnesota Press.

Ramachandran, Rana. 2005. "Sexism and science." *Frontline: India's National Magazine*. March 12. http://www.hinduonnet.com/fline/f12206/stories/2005 0325000908300.htm (accessed August 22, 2008).

Raymond, Janice. 1979. *The transsexual empire*. London: Women's Press.

Rees, Mark. 1996. *Dear sir or madam: The autobiography of a female-to-male transsexual*. London: Cassell.

Reissman, Catherine. 1987. "When gender is not enough: Women interviewing women." *Gender & Society* 1 (2): 172–207.

Rentos v. Oce-Office Systems. 1996. WL 737215 (S.D. N.Y.).

Reskin, Barbara, and Heidi Hartmann. 1986. *Women's work, men's work: Sex segregation on the job*. Washington, DC: National Academic Press.

Reskin, Barbara, and Patricia Roos. 1990. *Job queues, gender queues*. Philadelphia: Temple University Press.

Reuters. 2008. "Pregnant 'man' tells Oprah: 'It's a miracle.'" http://www.msnbc .msn.com/id/23942218/ (accessed August 29, 2008).

Rhode, Deborah L. 1997. *Speaking of sex: The denial of gender inequality*. Cambridge, MA: Harvard University Press.

Rich, Adrienne. 1977. *Of woman born*. New York: Newton.

——. 1980. "Lesbian existence and compulsory heterosexuality." *Signs* 5 (4): 631–60.

Ridgeway, Cecilia, and Shelly Correll. 2004. "Unpacking the gender system." *Gender & Society* 4 (18): 510–31.

Ridgeway, Cecilia, and Lynn Smith-Lovin. 1999. "The gender system and interaction." *Annual Review of Sociology* 25: 191–216.

Risman, Barbara. 1998. *Gender vertigo: American families in transition*. New Haven, CT: Yale University Press.

——. 2004. "Gender as a social structure: Theory wrestling with activism." *Gender & Society* 18 (4): 429–50.

——. 2009. "From doing to undoing: Gender as we know it." *Gender & Society* 23 (1): 81–85.

Rockquemore, Kerry Ann, and David Brunsma. 2008. *Beyond black: Biracial identity in America*. Lanham, MD: Rowman & Littlefield.

Rosskam, Jules. 2005. *Transparent*. Video. Available from http://www.frameline .org.

Roth, Louise Marie. 2006. *Selling women short: Gender and money on Wall Street*. Princeton, NJ: Princeton University Press.

Roughgarden, Joan. 2004. *Evolution's rainbow: Diversity, gender, and sexuality in nature and people*. Berkeley: University of California Press.

Rubin, Gayle. 1975. "The traffic in women: Notes on the political economy of sex." In *Toward an anthropology of women*, ed. Rayna Reiter, 157–210. New York: Monthly Review Press.

——. 1984. "Thinking sex: Notes for a radical theory of the politics of sexuality." In *Pleasure and danger: Exploring female sexuality*, ed. Carol S. Vance, 267–319. Boston: Routledge and Kegan Paul.

——. 1992. "Of catamites and kings: Reflections on butch, gender, and boundaries." In *The persistent desire*, ed. Joan Nestle, 466–82. Boston: Alyson Publications.

Rubin, Henry. 2003. *Self-made men: Identity and embodiment among transsexual men*. Nashville, TN: Vanderbilt University Press.

Rudacille, Deborah. 2005. *The riddle of gender: Science, activism, and transgender rights*. New York: Pantheon Books.

Rupp, Leila, and Verta Taylor. 2004. *Drag queens at the 801 Cabaret*. Chicago: University of Chicago Press.

Sahlins, Marshall. 1981. *Historical metaphors and mythical realities*. Ann Arbor: University of Michigan Press.

Sandstrom, Kent. 1990. "Confronting deadly disease: The drama of identity construction among gay men with AIDS." *Journal of Contemporary Ethnography* 19 (3): 271–94.

Schafer, Sarah. 2001. "More transsexuals start new life with old job." *Times-Picayune*, February 4, Living, 15.

Schiebinger, Londa. 1999. *Has feminism changed science?* Cambridge, MA: Harvard University Press.

Schilt, Kristen, and Catherine Connell. 2007. "Do workplace gender transitions make gender trouble?" *Gender, Work & Organization* 14 (6): 596–618.

Schilt, Kristen, and Laurel Westbrook. 2009. "Doing gender and beyond: Transgender people, 'gender normals,' and heteronormativity." *Gender & Society* 23 (4): 440–64.

Schilt, Kristen, and Matthew Wiswall. 2008. "Before and after: Gender transitions, human capital, and workplace experiences." *B.E. Journal of Economics and Policy* 8 (1): 1–26.

Schilt, Kristen, and Elke Zobl. 2008. "Connecting the dots: Riot grrrls, ladyfests, and the international grrrl zine network." In *Next wave cultures: Feminism, subcultures, and activism*, ed. Anita Harris, 171–192. New York: Routledge.

Schippers, Mimi. 2007. "Recovering the feminine other: Masculinity, femininity, and gender hegemony." *Theory and Society* 36 (1): 85–102.

Schudson, Michael. 1989. "How culture works: Perspectives from media studies on the efficacy of symbols." *Theory and Society* 18 (2): 153–80.

Scott, Joan. 1988. *Gender and the politics of history.* New York: Columbia University Press.

Seidman, Steven, ed. 1996. *Queer theory/sociology.* Cambridge, UK: Blackwell.

———. 2002. *Beyond the closet: The transformation of gay and lesbian life.* New York: Routledge.

Serano, Julia. 2007. *Whipping girl: A transsexual woman on sexism and the scapegoating of femininity.* Emeryville, CA: Seal Press.

Sewell, William. 1992. "A theory of structure: Agency, duality, and transformation." *American Journal of Sociology* 98 (1): 1–29.

Shapiro, Eve. 2007. "Drag kinging and the transformation of gender identities." *Gender & Society* 21 (2): 250–71.

Shaver, Katherine. 1995. "Deputy reveals recent sex change." *St. Petersburg Times*, September 22, 1B.

Sherrill, Kenneth, and Alan Yang. 2000. "From outlaws to in-laws: Anti-gay attitudes thaw." *Public Perspective* 11 (1): 20–23.

Simpson, Ruth. 2004. "Masculinity at work: The experiences of men in female-dominated occupations." *Work, Employment & Society* 18 (2): 349–68.

Sloat, Bill. 2001. "Demoted transsexual officer sues." *Plain Dealer*, April 1, Metro, 4B.

Small, Mario. 2004. *Villa Victoria: Transformation of social capital in a Boston barrio.* Chicago: University of Chicago Press.

Smith, Allyson. 2002. "CWA opposes men in dresses lobbying congressmen for 'gender' rights." May 22. http://www.cultureandfamily.org/articledisplay.asp?id=613&department=CFI&categoryid=cfreport (accessed January 10, 2010).

Smith, Dorothy. 2009. "Categories are not enough." *Gender & Society* 23 (1): 76–80.

Snow, David, and Leon Anderson. 1987. "Identity work among the homeless: The verbal construction and avowal of personal identities." *American Journal of Sociology* 92 (6): 1336–71.

Spelman, Elizabeth. 1988. *The inessential woman: Problems of exclusion in feminist thought.* Boston: Beacon Press.

Stein, Arlene, ed. 1993. *Sisters, sexperts, and queers: Beyond the lesbian nation.* New York: Plume.

———. 1997. *Sex and sensibility: Stories of a lesbian generation.* Berkeley: University of California Press.

Stoller, Robert. 1968. *Sex and gender: On the development of masculinity and femininity.* New York: Jason Aronson.

Stone, Sandy. 1991. "The empire strikes back: A post-transsexual manifesto." In *Body guards: The cultural politics of gender ambiguity,* ed. Julia Epstein and Kristina Straub, 280–304. New York: Routledge.

Stryker, Susan, ed. 1998. "The Transgender Issue." Special issue. *GLQ: A Journal of Lesbian and Gay Studies* 4 (2).

———. 2008. *Transgender history.* Seattle: Seal Press.

Stryker, Susan, and Jim Van Buskirk. 1996. *Gay by the bay: A history of queer culture in the San Francisco Bay area.* New York: Chronicle Books.

Stryker, Susan, and Stephen Whittle, eds. 2006. *The transgender studies reader.* New York: Routledge.

Summers, Lawrence. 2005. "Remarks at NBER conference on diversifying the science and engineering workforce." http://www.president.harvard.edu/speeches/2005/nber.html (accessed August 22, 2008).

Swidler, Ann. 1986. "Culture in action: Symbols and strategies." *American Sociological Review* 51 (5): 273–86.

Talbot, Margaret. 2002. "Men behaving badly: When men harass men, is it sexual harassment?" *New York Times Magazine,* October 13. http://www.nytimes.com/2002/10/13/magazine/men-behaving-badly.html?pagewanted=1 (accessed January 10, 2010).

Testerman, Jeff. 1990. "Tampa department offers to rehire transsexual firefighter." *St. Petersburg Times,* August 25, Florida, Tampa Bay, and State, 6B.

Testerman, Jeff, and Mary Jo Malone. 1990. "His sex was changed; now she wants her old job." *St. Petersburg Times,* August 11, Florida, Tampa Bay, and State, 1B.

Thompson, Raymond, with Kitty Sewall. 1995. *What took you so long? A girl's journey into manhood*. London: Penguin Books.

Thorne, Barrie. 1990. "Children and gender: Constructions of difference." In *Theoretical perspectives on sexual difference*, ed. Deborah Rhode, 100–113. New Haven, CT: Yale University Press.

———. 1993. *Gender play: Girls and boys in school*. Piscataway, NJ: Rutgers University Press.

———. 1995. "Symposium: On West and Fenstermaker's 'Doing difference.'" *Gender & Society* 9 (4): 498–501.

Tronetti v. TLC HealthNet Lakeshore Hospital. 2003. Not reported in F. Supp. 2d. WL 22757935.

Valentine, David. 2007. *Imagining transgender: An ethnography of a category*. Durham, NC: Duke University Press.

Valerio, Max Wolf. 2006. *The testosterone files: My hormonal and social transformation from female to male*. Seattle: Seal Press.

Valian, Virginia. 1998. *Why so slow? The advancement of women*. Cambridge, MA: MIT Press.

Vance, Carol. 1995. *Passing by: Gender and public harassment*. Berkeley: University of California Press.

Wade, Nicholas. 2007. "Pas de deux of sexuality is written in the genes." *New York Times*, April 10. http://www.nytimes.com/2007/04/10/health/10gene.html (accessed January 10, 2010).

Walsh, Kenneth T. 2009. "Larry Summers, Obama's designated thinker in a troubled economy." Posted March 24. http://www.usnews.com/mobile/articles_mobile/larry-summers-obamas-designated-thinker-in-a-troubled-economy/index.html (accessed March 30, 2009).

Ward, Jane. 2000. "Queer sexism: Rethinking gay men and masculinity." In *Guy masculinities*, ed. Peter Nardi, 152–75. Thousand Oaks, CA: Sage Publications.

Warren, Valryn. 2008. "Transgender people step out, risk ridicule, worse; Jobs, friends, families at risk, but transgender people take chance to understand themselves and be understood." *Dayton Daily News*, March 16, A17.

Weiss, Robert. 1994. *Learning from strangers: The art and method of qualitative interview studies*. New York: Free Press.

Welsh, Sandy. 1999. "Gender and sexual harassment." *Annual Review of Sociology* 25: 169–90.

West, Candace, and Sarah Fenstermaker. 1995. "Doing difference." *Gender & Society* 9 (1): 8–37.

West, Candace, and Don Zimmerman. 1987. "Doing gender." *Gender & Society* 1 (2): 125–51.

———. 2009. "Accounting for doing gender." *Gender & Society* 23 (1): 112–22.

Wilchins, Riki Anne. 1997. *Read my lips: Sexual subversion and the end of gender.* Ithaca, NY: Firebrand Books.

Williams, Christine L. 1995. *Still a man's world: Men who do "women's work."* Berkeley: University of California Press.

Williams, Christine L., and E. Joel Heikes. 1993. "The importance of researcher's gender in the in-depth interview: Evidence from two case studies of male nurses." *Gender & Society* 7 (2): 280–91.

Williams, Claire. 2003. "Sky service: The demands of emotional labor in the airline industry." *Gender, Work & Organization* 10 (5): 513–50.

Willis, Paul. 1977. *Learning to labor: How working class kids get working class jobs.* New York: Columbia University Press.

Winant, Howard. 1995. "Symposium: On West and Fenstermaker's 'Doing difference.'" *Gender & Society* 9 (4): 503–6.

Wingfield, Adia Harvey. 2009. "Racializing the glass escalator." *Gender & Society* 23 (1): 5–26.

Wolf, Diane. 1996. *Feminist dilemmas in fieldwork.* Boulder, CO: Westview Press.

Woods, James D., with Jay H. Lucas. 1993. *The corporate closet: The professional lives of gay men in America.* New York: Free Press.

Yeung, Bernice. 2001. "Better than nothing." *SF Weekly*, April 18, Columns, A2.

Yoder, Janice, and Patricia Aniakudo. 1997. "Outsider within the firehouse: Subordination and difference in the social interactions of African American women firefighters." *Gender & Society* 11 (3): 324–41.

Index

Agnes, 8
Araujo, Gwen, 154

Barres, Ben, 2, 132, 138
bathrooms, 55–56, 122; gender policing in, 56, 65, 154–55; interactional rules of, 62–65; and open workplace transitions, 133
Beatie, Thomas, 159, 188n
Bem, Sandra, 31
Benjamin, Harry, 22
biological diversity: as a frame for transgenderism, 20, 46; and support for transgender and gay rights, 20, 40, 46, 169–70
biological essentialism, 2–4, 7, 168–70, 174–75. *See also* gender difference; "natural difference" schemas
"body projects," 34, 44–46
butch, 27, 31–32, 118; and "border wars" with transmen, 32; conflation of transmen with, 118; feminist critique of, 27; transmen formerly identified as, 31–32
Butler, Judith, 8, 174, 190n

cisgender men: assumptions of female incompetence by, 73–75, 78–80, 95, 98, 101–2; and chivalry, 63, 100; and the fear of homosexuality, 58–59, 97, 100, 124–25, 127; and gender apprenticing of transmen, 124, 156; and gender pleasure, 174; and gender rituals, 95–96, 124–26; interactions between, 57–58, 61, 73–74, 95–97, 123–26, 157–58; inter-

actions with women by, 57–58; strategies for deflecting sexism, racism, and homophobia, 63, 100, 164. *See also* coworkers; gay men
cisgender people, 14, 187n; as "gender normals," 9; investment in the gender binary by, 9, 89, 123–25, 146–49, 161–62; overdoing gender by, 123–26, 162
cisgender women: assumptions of male incompetence by, 74; bathroom policing by, 56, 115, 155; and gender pleasure, 174; and gender rituals, 95–96, 123–24; interactions between, 60, 95–96; interactions with men by, 60, 74, 95–96, 123–26; policing transmen's sexuality, 104, 153–54. *See also* coworkers; lesbians
cognitive dissonance, 145–49
Connell, Raewyn, 164
coworkers: and bathrooms, 121–22, 154–55; belief in the gender binary by, 9, 123–25, 146–49, 161–62; changing pronouns by, 84, 114, 117–18, 121–22, 146–47, 167; confronting of stealth transmen by, 93, 102–3; gender differences in reactions to transmen by, 126–27; and gender rituals, 123–25; and gossip/rumors about transmen, 93, 102–4, 126, 177; opposing of open transmen by, 115, 121, 125, 145, 152–53; opposing of open transwomen by, 152, 154–55; "passing" as supportive by, 127, 147; preconceived notions about transgender people of, 82–83, 114; reactions